FLAK IN WORLD WAR II

Donald Nijboer

STACKPOLE
BOOKS

Guilford, Connecticut

STACKPOLE
BOOKS

Published by Stackpole Books
An imprint of The Rowman & Littlefield Publishing Group, Inc.
4501 Forbes Blvd., Ste. 200
Lanham, MD 20706

Distributed by NATIONAL BOOK NETWORK
800-462-6420

British Library Cataloguing in Publication Information available

Library of Congress Cataloging-in-Publication Data available

ISBN 978-0-8117-1992-6 (hardcover)
ISBN 978-0-8117-6592-3 (e-book)

∞™ The paper used in this publication meets the minimum requirements of American National Standard for Information Sciences—Permanence of Paper for Printed Library Materials, ANSI/NISO Z39.48-1992.

Printed in the United States of America

To Janet. It would be no fun without you. And to the memory of all the young men and women who manned the guns and lost their lives in a war that now seems so far away.

CONTENTS

FOREWORD

WHEN WE THINK OF DEFENDING OUR BORDERS FROM AERIAL ATTACK, OUR DEFAULT IS to imagine brave aviators taking to the skies to defend against the winged invader. But from the beginning of man's ascent into the aerial battleground, there were antiaircraft defenses. One of the earliest recorded instances of land-based artillery being modified to protect against aerial forces was in 1794 when two Austrian 17-pounder howitzers were trained at French reconnaissance balloons.

When Donald asked me to write this foreword, I tried to imagine just what I could say about antiaircraft defense. I realized that it is a key component in the history of aerial defense and has developed in step with ever-evolving aviation technologies and military strategies . . . But having now read the manuscript, I can confirm that this is a fascinating subject and a great read.

Donald has wisely juxtaposed the development of aerial defenses with the tactical and strategic developments in aerial warfare and technologies they were designed to counter. This formula provides the total picture and in doing so dispels many myths about the efficiency of antiaircraft weapons and tactics. History often records antiaircraft defenses as a costly solution to threat from above, requiring as they do great numbers of resources across a wide defensive perimeter.

But Donald proves time and again that they contributed greatly to the destruction of a high percentage of the aircraft brought down, damaged, or with loss of valuable trained crews. Time and again he cites the numbers for aircraft-to-aircraft combat losses against those brought about by the antiaircraft defenses.

There is no question in my mind that this is an important book on a fascinating subject. It is essential for any serious library on military aviation history, and I will be proud to add it to mine. In the vernacular, Donald has scored a direct hit.

Stephen Quick
Former Director General
Canada Aviation and Space Museum

INTRODUCTION

Antiaircraft may be annoying but should be ignored.
—CAPT. LAWRENCE S. KUTER, U.S. AIR CORPS TACTICAL SCHOOL

FLAK WAS AN ABBREVIATION FOR THE GERMAN WORD *FLIEGERABWEHRKANONEN*, OR ANTI-aircraft guns, and was used to describe antiaircraft fire by Allied aircrew.

The great aerial campaigns of World War II have always been framed as fighter vs. fighter, or fighter vs. bomber. But it was not just the fighter pilots doing the shooting; it was antiaircraft (AA) gunners as well. Much has been written about the thousands of air battles fought during the war, but the contribution of the antiaircraft defenses is rarely mentioned.

Long the neglected stepchild in studies of World War II air campaigns, both Allied and Axis antiaircraft defenses have been frequently ignored or dismissed by American, British, German, Soviet, and Japanese historians as ineffective and wasteful. Historical analyses of ground defenses have tended to dismiss the contribution of antiaircraft guns and their support arms as insignificant. Indeed, after the war the British Bombing Survey Unit (BBSU) disparaged the *Luftwaffe's* antiaircraft defenses by describing them as "plentiful" but not "very lethal." The figure of 16,000 rounds of German 88mm ammunition being required to shoot down a heavy bomber is often quoted to show just how wasteful and ineffective antiaircraft fire really was. But that number is misleading. While it fits well into the Allied narrative of how the strategic bombing campaign robbed the German army of valuable munitions, it was only partially true.

The hard numbers, however, tell a different story, and this book will shed a new light on the old myths and show just how effective flak really was.

To compare the effectiveness of an antiaircraft gun with that of a fighter aircraft was and is a false metric. The Germans were guilty of this and failed to see how effective their guns and searchlight defense were. During the war in Europe, German flak defenses accounted for more than half of the combat losses suffered by the United States Army Air Forces (USAAF). Only late in 1943 did the USAAF take German flak seriously: "it is probable that the importance of flak has been grossly underestimated." From report titled Eighth Air Force's Loss and Battle Damage subsection.

One also has to remember that antiaircraft gun defenses both on land and on the sea did not operate in isolation. It was a combination of fighters and antiaircraft guns that made for an effective defense. Fighters alone could not do the job. They needed the guns.

It also bears remembering that the first job of an antiaircraft gun defense is deterrence. Its job was to make a bomber fly higher and decrease its accuracy, break up incoming bomber formations, or cause them to turn back altogether. Destroying the aircraft was secondary. Antiaircraft fire also contributed with many hidden effects. Flak proved a huge benefit to fighter pilots assigned to attack incoming raids. Flak-damaged bombers were forced out of formation, making them easy prey for marauding fighters. Flak damaged tens of thousands of bombers. These bombers required repair, causing service rates to fall and thus reducing the number of bombers available for new operations. AA shrapnel also killed and wounded tens of thousands of aircrew, significantly reducing the overall efficiency and morale of numerous squadrons.

At the beginning of the war, flak guns were not as effective as both the Allies and Germans had hoped. But there were some exceptions. Dutch AA defenses were able to destroy a huge number of German Ju-52s during the invasion of Holland. Early British bombing raids on German naval targets resulted in heavy losses. The combination of flak and fighters proved devastating, forcing the Royal Air Force (RAF) to switch from daylight attacks to a night bombing campaign.

On the sea early encounters between aircraft and capital ships showed just how vulnerable warships were to divebombing and torpedo attack. Here the evolution of the ships' antiaircraft defenses resulted in more and better guns, improved radar and fire-control systems. Fortunately for the Americans these advancements would be in place and ready for the devastating kamikaze attacks in 1944 and 1945.

The crucial role antiaircraft guns played in several key World War II battles—such as the defense of the port of Antwerp, Belgium—has been forgotten or ignored. Antwerp's defense was given solely to American and British antiaircraft guns, a decision critical to the Allies' success. There were no fighter squadrons assigned to help fend off the Germans. From October 1944 until March 1945, thousands of V-1 flying bombs were launched at Antwerp. There the gunners stood their ground with great success.

This book will expose many of the remaining myths surrounding the effectiveness of the antiaircraft gun during World War II. Many of the most well-known air battles will be reexamined and the contributions made by the AA forces revealed for the first time.

CHAPTER ONE

World War I—The Guns Turn Skyward 1914–1919

ON AUGUST 4, 1914, THE GREAT WAR BEGAN. AS GERMAN TROOPS SURGED THROUGH Belgium, the treaty-bound countries of France, Britain, Italy, Austria, and Russia were forced to wage all-out war. World War I was a war of industrial extremes. The machine gun and massed artillery would dominate the landscape, turning the field of battle into a sea of mud, trenches, disease, mass slaughter, and finally stalemate. At the beginning the flying machine was only eleven years separated from the Wright Brothers' first flight. As the great powers mobilized more than six million men for ground combat, fewer than 2,000 pilots and 1,000 aircraft were ready for war. These early aircraft were fragile, spectacularly slow, wood-and-canvas open cockpit machines. Army commanders on both sides thought the newfangled air machines would be of little use in the upcoming conflict and any role they played would be minor. That quickly changed. Early experiments in 1910 showed the best role for the airplane was reconnaissance. This morphed into the dual role of reconnaissance/artillery spotting, which would be the prime mission for aircraft on both sides in the early months of the war. These early missions would soon become indispensable, and both sides shot at anything in the air using rifles and machine guns.

Unfortunately, aircraft recognition by ground troops was nonexistent. The first British pilot and observer killed during the war were shot down by friendly rifle fire.

When Germany entered the war, its army was the only one that fielded purpose-built antiaircraft guns. German air defenses consisted of six motorized guns and twelve horse-drawn 77mm guns. This small but impressive force had very little to do. Early enemy aircraft were content to simply observe. There were instances of pilots tossing grenades or petrol bombs, but these caused little or no damage. In the opening days of the conflict, the six motorized units were attached to various army corps while the horse-drawn guns were placed at key bridges along the Rhine and zeppelin hangars in Germany. On the Allied side, both British and French antiaircraft defenses were thin and inefficient.

The antiaircraft (AA) gun was not new or a reaction to the emergence of the appearance of aircraft over the battlefield. As soon as the first reconnaissance balloons appeared, guns were soon trained to the sky. The first, reportedly, were a pair of Austrian 17-pounder howitzers aimed at French reconnaissance balloons in June 1794.

The first purpose-built antiaircraft gun dates back to the Franco-Prussian War of 1870–1871. To escape the besieged city of Paris, the Communards used the simple but effective hot-air balloon. Unable to stop the flights with simple rifle or artillery fire (Prussian siege guns could not be brought to bear), the German army urgently requested a gun that could effectively shoot down the French balloons. The Krupp armament works responded, producing five guns of a completely new design. The 37mm anti-balloon gun (*Ballonabwehrkanone*, or BAK) looked like an oversized rifle mounted on a mobile cart. During the siege some sixty-six balloons left Paris with all but one being shot down by the Germans.

At the turn of the century two new technologies—the airship and airplane—led many military leaders to see the potential of both the lighter-than-air and heavier-than-air aircraft for the purpose of reconnaissance and artillery spotting. The Germans invested heavily in dirigibles and later rigid airships. Count Ferdinand Zeppelin led the charge, assuring the military that an airship could provide eyes on the enemy "in any weather, by day and by night." Zeppelin's marketing campaign proved successful to both the military and private investors. Between 1910 and 1914 the zeppelin fleet achieved a commercial success by transporting approximately 34,000 people throughout Germany. It also raised eyebrows in England and France. The zeppelin had a darker side. Not only could they carry people, but they could also carry bombs. The fear of a surprise attack from the air on London and Paris was now a very real prospect. While the Germans were creating a new threat, they were also busily designing and building the world's first antiaircraft guns.

During the Berlin Auto-Exhibition of 1906, Rheinische Metallwaren–und Maschinenfabrik (later Rheinmetall) displayed their motorized 50mm anti-airship gun. In 1909 Krupp produced a new 65mm gun mounted on slewable legs giving it a 360-degree field of traverse. Interest in these guns was limited with very few orders being made by other European military forces.

Prior to the outbreak of World War I, it became clear that not only airships and zeppelins posed a threat, but the new heavier-than-air aircraft was an unknown quantity and one that had a greater potential for growth. Aircraft used in the Italian campaign in Libya in 1911–1912 and the Balkan War of 1912 showed their emerging versatility and potential. In France aviation experiments involving the bombing of point targets showed good results. The subject of air defense now became a new and burgeoning interest. In 1907 the Germans conducted several tests using standard army weapons against aerial targets. Conventional artillery pieces were fired at a balloon towed by a motorboat with very poor results. In a second evaluation standard infantry rifles and machine guns were used. A 50-foot-long balloon tethered at approximately 4,000 feet was peppered with 4,800 rounds of rifle fire followed by 2,700 rounds from several Maxim machine guns.

The first antiaircraft mounts for light machine guns were often crude affairs with no specialized gun sights. Here a pair of Australian soldiers mount their Lewis machine gun onto a tree stump ready for firing. The Mk 1 .303 caliber gun had a rate of fire of between 500 and 600 rounds per minute with an effective range of 880 yards. AUTHOR'S COLLECTION

After close examination the balloon showed only seventy-six punctures and was still airworthy. Slightly more than 1 percent of all the bullets fired impacted the balloon.

In 1913 Britain's first antiaircraft gun was tested. Mounted on the Needles Old Battery parade ground on the Isle of Wight, the Vickers-Maxim 1-pounder pom-pom was tested against a destroyer-towed kite in the English Channel. According to the local press it was a "great success."

From 1910 to 1914 the other major European powers turned their energies to the question of a purpose-built antiaircraft gun. The British company Vickers produced a 3-pounder quick-firing gun mounted on a Daimler car chassis; France took their excellent 75mm Mle 1897 field gun and produced a high-angle mounting on the back of a De Dion-Bouton car chassis. The British Admiralty, fearing their naval bases would be prime targets, developed a 3-inch 20-cwt high-angle gun. In the United States they developed a 3-inch split-rail gun that would serve as a dual-purpose field/AA gun. Italy's principal weapon was the 75mm 75/27 1906/15. The gun was in fact a Krupp design modified into a high-angle gun. In Germany Krupp produced the 77mm Bak L/27 gun, either mounted on a truck or towed by a team of horses.

By 1914 there were two schools of thought regarding the best antiaircraft method. Some backed the light rapid-firing gun like the 1-pounder pom-pom. Firing as much hot metal as possible in a short time increased the chances of hitting your target. Others insisted on a single well-aimed shot from a larger gun to be the best solution. The second option was rife with problems. As many hunters know, hitting a duck with a rifle bullet is next to impossible. The best the early guns could achieve was to get a shell close to their intended target. After that it was up to the shell to do the damage by exploding close to the target. At the beginning of the war, the standard projectile for light artillery was the shrapnel shell. These shells were equipped with a powder train fuse or igniferous time fuse. By rotating the upper part of the shell, the timing of the fuse was set. When fired the shock of the firing ignited the powder ring, and when the burn reached the fuse setting, the shell exploded.

The powder train fuse was not very precise. Above 15,000 feet the train fuses in early AA shells did not perform very well. Lack of oxygen and the projectiles' spin caused many duds or premature explosions. For the early pilots antiaircraft fire at the beginning of the war posed no real threat. It was so inaccurate pilots had little difficulty avoiding the small buffs of exploding shrapnel. Most aircrew reacted to the early attempts at AA fire with amusement. One pilot gave it the nickname "Archie," a name that survived until the end of the war. Antiaircraft fire was also known as "ack-ack" from the World War I phonetic alphabet. Although many fliers had little to fear, persistent AA fire during reconnaissance missions was a great source of anxiety. One Royal Flying Corps (RFC) diarist noted, "I noticed people's nerves are not as strong as they used to be and I am sure Archie is responsible."

The shrapnel shell was also shown to be ineffective against aircraft, balloons, and airships. The bullet-sized holes created were too small to do any serious damage, but the biggest drawback was that after the shell had exploded, the empty shell portion, which weighed 6 or 7 pounds, fell to earth. For the troops underneath a hunk of metal dropping from several thousand feet was a lethal weapon. The decision was soon made to use high explosive shells instead mated to the new mechanical (clockwork) time fuse. Powder fuse accuracy was about 2 percent of the total time of running, while the mechanical fuse cut this to about half of 1 percent. This meant a shell moving at 2,000 feet per second, fitted with a powder fuse, might explode anywhere on its flight from 400 feet short to 400 feet past its target. The mechanical fuse cut this to just 100 feet on each side. This produced a shell of greater accuracy and destructive power. Any aircraft or airship caught near an exploding high-explosive shell would be showered with both large and small fragments of razor-sharp shrapnel. The chances of severe damage or death were greatly increased and for the troops on the ground the chances of being hit by falling shrapnel was greatly reduced.

Throughout the First World War the limitations of the antiaircraft gun remained technological. Detecting approaching enemy aircraft was just the first step (this would remain a major problem throughout the war). Assessing its range, height, and direction only added to the mathematical equation. Tracking a target or squadron of aircraft in formation in a three-dimensional space and coordinating the fire of a single gun or battery was a formidable challenge. Gun crews needed specialized training and experience. A typical crew for the British 3-inch 20-cwt gun required ten men with six assigned to the fire-control problem alone. It was labor intensive and required men who were not only strong, but also highly intelligent. After two years of war, there was still no practical method of predicting an aircraft's future position in the sky. This technological limitation led to the wasteful "barrier fire" method. Gun crews created a wall of shells positioned between the attacking aircraft and its target. Aircraft were either forced to fly higher, break off the attack, or fly through the bursting flak. In 1916 the introduction of optical range finders gave gunners both elevation and azimuth for an incoming target, but many problems remained. The introduction of mechanically timed fuse ammunition and the marriage of optical range finders allowed gun crews to aim shells directly in front of an approaching aircraft or close to it. While a great improvement, timed fuses had to be set manually. That meant by the time a fuse was set, the shell loaded and fired, the intended target had moved. A typical World War I fighter like the Fokker Dr.I had a top speed of 103 mph. At an altitude of 9,000 feet, a shell fired with a muzzle velocity of 2,250 feet per second would require four seconds to reach it. In that time, however, the Fokker would have traveled 604 feet.

A French model 1897 Mle 75mm antiaircraft gun mounted on a De Dion-Bouton truck chassis. Like Germany and Britain, France quickly adopted the concept of mobility, putting antiaircraft guns on trucks. AUTHOR'S COLLECTION

By 1917 flak equipment, guns, training, and tactics greatly improved its effectiveness, especially at lower altitudes. Fighters assigned to strafing and ground attack missions found the low-level airspace to be extremely deadly. Machine-gun and rifle fire along with fire from guns like the German Maxim Flak M14 37mm auto cannon proved to be highly effective. Many pilots like RFC flight commander Arthur Gould Lee found trench strafing and bombing to be a dangerous and thankless task. "The greatest disadvantage of trench strafing was the danger to oneself and one's plane, especially when diving really low. A good machine-gunner could score a hit at 2,000 feet, and at 300 feet an aeroplane diving straight into his barrels was a gift. When there was one machine gun, there were always others near, as well as scores, or hundreds of rifles. You did not need to make many dives on such targets to run out of luck.

"An important factor in our antipathy to trench strafing was the intense nervous strain. Unless you were made of steel and completely impervious to fear, you had to summon all your will-power to dive into a nest of guns, with hundreds of carefully aimed bullets coming up at you. Your brain and senses were numbed, your spirit shrank from so inevitable and futile an end, for it would be a miracle if you weren't hit, and you couldn't rely on miracles indefinitely.

"To me, and to every fighter pilot with whom I discussed this subject, then and later in 1918, low-flying attacks were, with few exceptions, a wasteful employment of highly trained pilots and expensive aeroplanes."

At the outbreak of war, the number of purpose-built antiaircraft guns on all sides was extremely low. Existing field guns adapted for antiaircraft use by simply putting them at a higher angle on a raised turntable proved completely unsuited to the task. The Germans were quick to utilize captured artillery pieces in the air defense role. In 1915 alone approximately 1,000 captured French, British, Russian, and Belgian artillery pieces were turned into air defense guns. As the war progressed, new purpose-built guns took to the field. Guns like the British 13-pounder 9-cwt Mk I eventually proved to be the backbone of the British field AA defense system. The Germans would field their 88mm Kw-Flak gun, forerunner to the World War II 88mm Flak 18, 36, 37, and 41.

By the end of the war, the Germans had assembled the greatest number of antiaircraft guns with 2,770. They also introduced the first rudimentary fire directors (*Kommandogerate*) in 1917 and 1918. These directors transferred some of the burden for computing targeting solutions from individuals using optical range finders and fire-control tables to a mechanical computer. Just sixty of these fire directors reached front-line service, but the results were impressive. When matched with guns like the 88mm Kw-Flak and time-fused shells, the number of Allied aircraft shot down over Germany in the last year of the war went up (748 between January 1 and October 1918). And the number of shells required to shoot down an aircraft dropped dramatically. In 1914 German gunners would expend 11,500 artillery shells per aircraft destroyed. In 1918 that shrank to just 5,040. The Allies also improved. Similarly, French rounds per aircraft shot down decreased from

Three soldiers of the American Expeditionary Force take a relaxed pose with their M1914 Hotchkiss antiaircraft machine gun. Gas operated and air cooled, the Hotchkiss had a rate of fire of between 450 and 600 rounds per minute. NARA

Early in the war both the Germans and Allies adopted existing field guns, using them as antiaircraft pieces. The Germans used captured and older artillery pieces to fill the gap before more purpose-built guns could reach the front. This older artillery piece was extensively modified to permit high-angle fire. U.S. NAVAL HISTORICAL CENTER

11,000 in 1916 to 7,000 in 1918, and British rounds per claim dropped from 8,000 in 1917 to 4,440 in 1918.

The story of the antiaircraft gun in the First World War is often overshadowed by rapid advancement in aircraft technology and the rise of the fighter ace. By 1918 the single-engine fighter was reaching speeds of more than 130 mph, and bombers like the Handley Page Type O/400 heavy bomber were capable of delivering 6,000 pounds of bombs. But for all the advancement in aerodynamics and aircraft development, they were all still vulnerable to flak. As aircraft flew higher and faster, flak was a constant. While originally conceived to actually shoot down individual aircraft, it was obvious that hitting an aircraft traveling at 100 mph at 10,000 feet was next to impossible. It soon became apparent that shooting down an aircraft was not necessary for AA to succeed. Simply breaking up a bomber formation, forcing it to turn back, or forcing it to fly higher with decreased accuracy was a victory for the AA gunners and a failure for the attacking force. For Arthur Gould Lee, AA fire was a great deterrent: "If the enemy was already firing at you, you tended to release the bombs much too high, and yet anything short of a direct hit was a waste of effort."

German gunners use a captured French St. Etienne Mle 1907 machine gun. The St. Etienne was a gas-operated, air-cooled machine gun in 8mm Lebel that was widely used in the early years of the First World War. Rate of fire was adjustable between 80 and 650 rounds per minute. NARA

While the number of aircraft shot down by AA fire was low, its other effects were never measured. Damaged aircraft that made it back to base but would never fly again were not counted as shot down. The number of aircraft damaged by flak only to be shot down by a fighter is also unknown. Many bombs undoubtedly missed their targets due to accurate AA fire, but this was never measured. The psychological and mental stress of aerial combat was only amplified by constant exposure to flak taking a toll on the efficiency, reliability, determination, and mental stability of aircrews on both sides.

In just four years of war, German antiaircraft fire accounted for a total of 1,588 Allied aircraft shot down. In comparison the French would tally 500, the British 300 throughout the empire, U.S. gunners 58, and the Italians 129.

CHAPTER TWO

Between the Wars—Theory and Practice Collide

AT THE END OF WORLD WAR I, MANY SAW THE EMERGENCE OF THE FIGHTER AS THE best instrument for air defense. AA gunnery had proven itself to be more of a dark art rather than a science, and for many it was seen as a failure. The wisest judgment, however, was not to view fighters and AA gunnery in isolation, but to recognize the value of both. What had been missed was how effective low-level antiaircraft fire from both machine guns and automatic cannons like the Maxim 37mm gun really was (it would remain so into World War II and well into the Vietnam War). Fighters and purpose-built aircraft assigned to the ground attack role suffered heavy casualties. It was not unusual for a fighter squadron to suffer a 30 percent casualty rate after just a few days of ground attack missions. In response the Germans developed the world's first all-metal ground attack aircraft. The Junkers J.I was an extremely advanced design with a single-unit steel armored "bathtub" that extended from the nose to the rear crew position. The armor was 0.20 inch (5mm) thick and weighed 1,040 pounds (470 kilograms). This gave ample protection for the crew, engine, and fuel tanks. Where the antiaircraft guns fell short was in defending against the higher-flying zeppelins and large twin-engine and four-engine bombers like the German four-engine Zeppelin-Staaken R.VI strategic bomber.

During the Great War the bomber was primarily a tactical weapon and best used in support of ground troops. The German zeppelin raids that began hitting England in January 1915 were followed by the more effective Gotha bomber raids beginning in May 1917. While these attacks were "strategic" in nature, they did not achieve their objectives. By 1918 fifty bombing raids on British towns had killed or injured around 2,000 people.

On April 1, 1918, the Royal Air Force (RAF) was created. Born out of the German Gotha raids on London, the RAF was the world's first independent air force. Given the task of bombing Germany, the new RAF was now seen as an instrument of attack, not defense. During the last few months of the war, RAF bombers began attacking targets in Germany with limited success.

For some time the future potential of the fighter held sway and brought about a sharp divergence in the technical development between the fighter and AA gunnery equipment and research. For the next twenty years gun advocates watched AA gunnery languishing in the shadow of the "fighter first" air defense. The next two decades also saw the struggle between those who saw the bomber, and its theoretical power, as either a "strategic" bomber or an instrument of tactical support for the army.

For Germany World War I was a disaster. The Treaty of Versailles of 1919 dramatically reduced the size and offensive capability of the entire German armed forces. Article 160 of the treaty slashed the size of the German army to just 100,000 men. The treaty also restricted German antiaircraft artillery to just seven batteries of obsolete 77mm truck-mounted guns. In addition, the *Reichswehr's* seven infantry regiments were restricted to one battery of twenty-four guns each. Ammunition was also targeted with just 1,500 rounds allowed per gun. These tight restrictions did not prevent attempts by retired and active-duty military officers to examine the lesson learned from the First World War.

As restrictive as the Treaty of Versailles was for Germany, the other major powers including Britain, the United States, and France faced their own reductions. With the war over, military budgets were slashed, leaving Britain with just a single AA gun brigade and single searchlight battalion in 1919. The war also provided a vast surplus of every type of weapon. This meant all development in new aircraft, ships, guns, and tanks all but stopped for a good ten years.

The rapid development of military aircraft in the Great War presented military planners with a number of new methods of attack. Capital ships at sea were now vulnerable to torpedo bombers; ground troops were subject to bombing and ground attacks; while cities like London and the industrial areas of the Ruhr were subject to attacks by large bombers and zeppelins. All these targets needed protection. While the fighter had proven to be the most effective way to shoot down enemy aircraft, it could not be everywhere at all times. It was the AA gun that would provide the deterrence needed to hinder any attack, especially at low altitudes where AA fire was most effective.

In response to the Treaty of Versailles, Germany's new small army established an air technical office responsible for collecting and studying aeronautical information. They also developed means and ways in which to hide their activities and circumvent the treaty. The German army also closely watched antiaircraft developments in other countries. Throughout the 1920s the Intelligence Section of the *Truppenamt* (T-3) gathered a wealth of knowledge pertaining to training, doctrine, and technological developments in foreign air forces. The victors, however, returned to peacetime activities like teaching or developing air doctrine. During the 1920s and well into the Second World War, the British QF 3-inch antiaircraft gun of World War I remained standard equipment in both the British army and navy. In the United States the M3 3-inch gun was adapted as standard equipment. For low-level protection the Browning .30-caliber and .50-caliber machine guns were pressed into service. The French continued with their trusted 75mm gun, producing

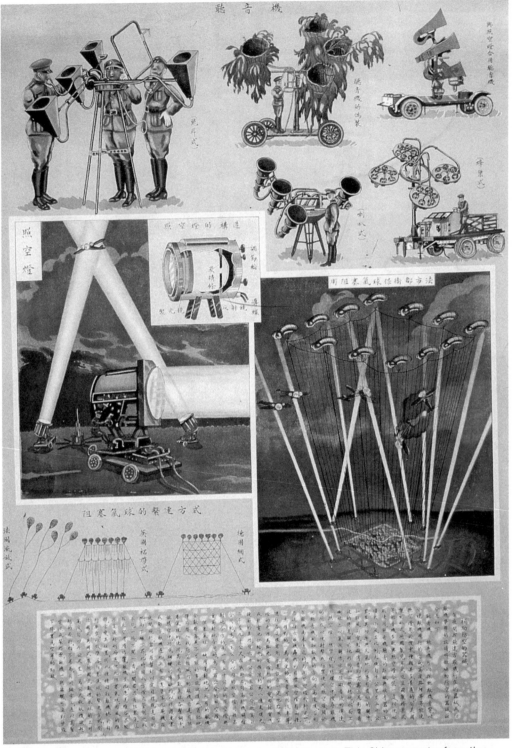

Early detection methods for AA guns depended on sound detectors. This Chinese poster from the 1930s depicts several different detectors and the use of searchlights and barrage balloons in air defense. Sound detectors were not very efficient and suffered from "sonic lag"; by the time the engine noise of an approaching aircraft reached a sound detector, the distance it had traveled would put it farther ahead. Wind and atmospheric conditions further complicated pinpointing the aircraft's location and computing a firing solution. Despite their problems the Germans still had 5,500 sound detectors in service in 1944. AUTHOR'S COLLECTION

The U.S. M3 3-inch antiaircraft gun was derived from the 3-inch 1917 AA gun, which entered service at the end of World War I. By the mid-1930s the M3 was considered obsolete, but in 1941 many were still in service in the Philippines and here in defense of the Panama Canal. NARA

models 1897 and 1928 antiaircraft mounts for both the army and navy. Not until 1938 did the French address the low-level regime with adoption of the Hotchkiss 25mm cannon.

Japanese development of antiaircraft guns and doctrine lagged badly behind the western powers. Largely insulated by oceans and focused on controlling Korea, Japan did not consider the full importance of a modern tactical air defense system (both fighters and AA guns). The Imperial Japanese Navy also suffered with a poor selection of antiaircraft weapons and fire-control systems. During the 1920s and up until the beginning of the war in the Pacific, Japan's Type 11 75mm antiaircraft gun was standard.

In the Soviet Union the German-Russian cooperation on aircraft design and testing in the early 1920s produced great benefits. This secret effort allowed Germany to circumvent the Versailles treaty's prohibition on designing and testing new weapons, while the Russians gained vital information. This partnership led to the Russian 76.2mm model 1931 and later to the superb 85mm M1939 gun. Unlike the western powers Russian doctrine placed a heavy stress on low- and medium-range automatic weapons. This included the liberal use of machine guns of both 7.62mm and 12.7mm. Medium-range weapons were primarily of the 37mm size, which included designs from Sweden, France, and Britain.

In Italy two new heavy guns would be produced, but in limited numbers. The first was the Cannone da 75/46 c.a. Modello 34 75mm gun, followed by the Cannone da 90/53 90mm gun. Both were excellent weapons, but Italy's inability to produce guns in quantity would become a major problem later during the Second World War. By 1942 just 226 75mm guns were delivered. For low-level work the Italians used both the reliable Scotti and Breda 20mm guns.

The Italian Cannone da 90/53 was first produced in 1939. An excellent weapon, the 90/53 compared favorably to any of its contemporaries. After the Italian surrender in 1943, the German valued the 90/53 so highly many were sent to Germany for the defense of the Reich and designated as the 90mm Flak 4(i). NARA

First introduced in 1934, the Italian Breda M/35 20mm cannon was an effective light AA gun. Seen here with Finnish troops, the Breda 20mm was fully automatic, but its rate of fire was adjustable with a practical rate of 150 rounds per minute. SA-KUVA

The rise of Adolf Hitler and his Nationalist German Workers' Party (NSDAP) in 1933 opened the door for the Reichswehr's plan for expansion and rearmament. Upon appointment as chancellor, Hitler declared the armed forces as "the most important institution in the State." Hitler strongly believed in a strong military, which included a strong defense of the Homeland against aerial attack. Hitler was also keenly aware of how vulnerable Germany would be to any future air attack and warned "with the present situation of German borders, there is only a very small area of a few kilometers which could not be visited by enemy aircraft within the first hour." For Hitler a strong ground-based air defense system in many ways became an obsession. In the years between 1933 and 1939, the German air defenses underwent a rapid expansion and would ultimately become the most extensive and powerful ground-based defensive system ever devised. Hitler's rise to power forced a new European arms race. As the Germans forged ahead, the Allies were forced to react.

Leading the race would be the famous German 88m flak gun. Developed in great secrecy by a team of technicians from Krupp, the new 88mm Flak 18 (*Flugabwehrkanone 18*) entered service in 1933, a full year before Hitler openly declared Germany was rearming. By 1935 the Reich's air defense system had fifteen heavy flak battalions and three light flak battalions. These battalions were well equipped. The heavy flak battalion included three batteries of four 88mm Flak 18 guns and two 20mm Flak 30 guns each, one battery of six 37mm Flak 18 guns, one battery of nine 150cm searchlights and six sound detectors, and one replacement battery. The light battalion consisted of three batteries of twelve 20mm and one battery of six 37mm guns. By the fall of 1936 the Luftwaffe air defense forces doubled in size to twenty-nine mixed (heavy and light flak guns) and eight light flak battalions.

Just as Germany began to rearm, the evolution of the combat aircraft took the next big step. In June 1933 the world's first all-metal bomber entered service with the U.S. Army Air Corps (USAAC). In terms of aerodynamics and design, the Martin B-10 was a huge leap forward. In a single stroke the new monoplane twin-engine bomber made all the world's fabric-covered biplane bombers and fighters obsolete. The B-10 was a streamlined monocoque construction equipped with retractable landing gear, a fully

Germany's rearmament in 1934 led to the rapid expansion of the Luftwaffe and its Flak arm. Arguably the most famous piece of German artillery during the Second World War was the 88mm Flak 18, which entered service in 1933. Early Flak field works tended to be simple earthen berms as shown here in 1939. A well-trained crew could fire up to fifteen rounds per minute. NARA

enclosed cockpit, internal bomb bay, full engine cowlings, variable pitch propellers, and a rotating front gun turret. Powered by two Wright-Cyclone R-1820 engines developing 775 horsepower each, the B-10 had a top speed of 213 mph (almost double the speed of Britain's last biplane bomber, the Handley Page Heyford, which entered service in 1933). This huge increase in speed meant antiaircraft defenses now had to deal with a high-flying, fast bomber. The time to detect, track, and engage this new target was now greatly reduced. The existing antiaircraft guns of the day were rendered obsolete. New early detection devices, the ability to track and aim accurately, and guns with higher velocities and range were now needed.

In July 1936 the Spanish Civil War erupted. Hitler decided to support Franco and his Nationalist rebellion. This gave the Luftwaffe a chance to test its new weapons, doctrine, and tactics on an actual battlefield. In late July 1936 one of the first German ships sailed from Hamburg with a cargo of twenty 20mm flak guns. By October 1936 the Condor Legion had been established with some 5,000 "volunteers," one hundred aircraft (which included the new monoplane Heinkel He-111 and Dornier Do-17 bombers along with the Junkers Ju-87 divebomber), and one flak section of eight gun batteries. One battery was designated as a training unit for the Nationalist forces with the rest, five 88mm batteries and two 20mm and 37mm batteries, assigned to air defense. In the first few months of the war, aerial targets were few and far between. Over a period of 277 days, the flak guns were active in 377 engagements, but only thirty-one were directed at aircraft. The remainder were directed at ground targets.

By 1938 the Republican air force had gained in strength. The infusion of Russian Polikarpov I-15, I-16 fighters and the all-metal monoplane Tupolev SB "*Katuska*" bomber greatly enhanced the Republican forces. When the war ended in 1939, the Luftwaffe flak "volunteers" of the Condor Legion were credited with fifty-nine aircraft shot down. That represented 15 percent of the legion's total of 386 Republican aircraft shot down by fighters. Considering the small size of the flak force, it was an impressive number. The new experience gained in Spain provided the Luftwaffe with a wealth of expertise and knowledge. The failure of flak at night was a result of the lack of searchlights and timely detection. But the Flak arm had also proven itself as a jack-of-all-trades capable of performing a variety of missions as both artillery in support of ground forces and air defense. This experience would soon be put to good use on the battlefields of Europe.

Well before the Spanish war began, Britain clearly knew the coming war with Germany would be fought with France as an ally and with the invasion of Holland and Belgium as a very real possibility. Not only could the Luftwaffe launch bombers from Germany, but with new bases in the Low Countries, the number and scale of air attacks would only increase in size and intensity. To meet the new threat, the Air Defenses of Great Britain (ADGB) had been busy. Since its formation in 1924, ADGB had studied the guns, fighters, and searchlights designed to defend the UK in detail. The rising speeds and altitudes of new aircraft made the existing 1913 vintage 3-inch 20-cwt gun all but obsolete. By 1933 trials had begun on a new set of guns that would modernize Britain's high-altitude antiaircraft defenses. In 1933 a specification for a new heavy antiaircraft gun was issued. In 1936 Vickers-Armstrong produced the 3.7-inch gun prototype with trials beginning in 1937. The gun was a great success, exceeding specifications and capable of firing a 28-pound shell to a maximum height of 41,000 feet at a rate of ten rounds per minute. This figure was misleading. Trial guns fired fuse-less solid rounds straight up. But guns in action had to fire explosive time-fused shells. In 1938 the maximum fuse-operating time was twenty-five seconds. With a gun at its normal elevation of 80 degrees, this reduced its effective ceiling to 28,000 feet. This would be later increased to 32,000 feet with the introduction of better fire control and new fuses.

This was followed by the more powerful Ordnance QF 4.5-inch Mk II, an adaptation of the 4.5-inch naval gun. The Admiralty needed a weapon specifically to defend ports and pointed to their existing commitment to their 4.5-inch gun. The War Office agreed and in 1936 the 4.5-inch gun was given the green light. The QF 4.5-inch Mk II was a

The QF 3.7-inch heavy antiaircraft gun was the most widely used AA gun by both Britain and its Commonwealth allies. It would see action on every front except the Eastern. Roughly the equivalent of the German 88m Flak 18 and American M1 90mm, the 3.7 (94mm) fired a 28-pound shell with an effective ceiling of 28,000 feet. Both the Germans and Japanese also used captured examples. Here Canadian troops train on the west coast of Canada. DEPARTMENT OF NATIONAL DEFENCE

American gunners man a British Stroud No. 1 Mk IV height-finder, Iceland 1942. Heavy antiaircraft batteries usually deployed in half-batteries of four guns. Each battery had its own height-finder and predictor. AUTHOR'S COLLECTION

powerful gun capable of hurling a 54-pound shell well over 25,000 feet. Unlike the 3.7-inch, the 4.5 would always be a static weapon. Married to these new guns were the Vickers Predictor AA No. 1, and the 15-foot-long Barr & Stroud height-finder and a smaller separate range finder. The Vickers Predictor was the world's first working Predictor.

During the First World War many simple aids to improve gun aiming and fuse settings were devised and tried, but with little success. It became clear that for an antiaircraft defense to be successful it needed a computing mechanism of considerable mathematical and mechanical complexity that was rapid and automated to a certain degree. In the 1920s several instruments were developed, but it was not until the introduction of the Vickers Predictor in 1927 that the problem was solved. The Americans followed with their Sperry T-6 Predictor and the Germans with their *Kommandogerat* P 27 fire director in 1930.

In essence the Predictor was an analog computer. When fed with the position, speed, height, range, and course of an aircraft together with data such as wind speed and direction, plus the battery's position, it could calculate the information needed to put an exploding shell in the path of an incoming bomber. This data was transmitted electrically to the guns, where dials showed the bearing, elevation, and fuse setting.

The British also, along with a number of other Allied nations, adapted the Swedish Bofors 40mm automatic cannon for low- and medium-altitude work. The Bofors has been called the greatest antiaircraft gun of World War II and for good reason. The first prototype was completed in November 1931 with production beginning in 1933. Firing a 2-pound high explosive contact fused shell at a velocity of 2,960 feet per second, at a rate of 120 rounds per minute, the Bofors was a deadly weapon up to 3,000 yards. Production in the UK began in 1937, but at the beginning of World War II, just 253 were available for action.

The invention of radar greatly improved antiaircraft defenses. Though they have often been credited with the invention of radar, the British were not alone in their quest. As early as 1933, the German navy was conducting initial tests with the new technology. This was followed by British experimental work, which began in 1935. The key to any effective defensive system against bomber attack was early detection. New high-flying bombers like the British Vickers Wellington, American Boeing B-17, and German Heinkel He-111 bombers could approach a target well beyond visual and sound range. Unless sighted early, intercepting fighters would be all but useless. Standing patrols of fighters over vital targets were extremely inefficient and required large numbers for any chance of success. Radar gave AA gunners time to prepare, giving them height and direction: information vital for any effective defense.

For AA gunners the coming war would prove to be an immense challenge. Aerial threats would come in at low, medium, and high altitude and include four-engine strategic bombers (Boeing B-17, Avro Lancaster, Boeing B-29), light bombers (de Havilland Mosquito, Douglas A-20), medium bombers (Mitchell B-25, Mitsubishi G4M, Junkers Ju-88), divebombers (Junkers Ju-87, Blackburn Skua, Tupolev Tu-2), ground attack (Ilyushin Il-2 Shturmovik, Henschel Hs-129), and fighter-bombers (Supermarine Spitfire, Focke Wulf Fw-190, Republic P-47). They would also face two new and terrifying weapons: the German V-1 flying bomb (the world's first cruise missile) and the Japanese kamikaze suicide attacks.

At the outbreak of war on September 1, 1939, the antiaircraft forces of the major European powers stood as follows:

- Germany: 2,628 88mm and 105mm guns, 6,700 20mm and 37mm guns, 1,692 150cm searchlights, and 2,052 60cm searchlights. This total also included three railroad flak battalions as well as seven naval flak battalions.

- United Kingdom: 1,296 heavy flak guns (4.5-inch, 3.7-inch, and 3-inch), an assortment of some 1,200 light guns (40mm Bofors, 2-pounders, 20mm guns with the majority being rifle-caliber Lewis machine guns), 2,500 searchlights.

- France: A diverse collection of 1,261 artillery pieces and some 1,800 machine guns.

"The primary mission of anti-aircraft artillery automatic weapons is to attack all enemy aircraft within range, particularly low-flying airplanes, to destroy them, to cause them to abandon their missions, or to decrease the efficiency of their operations." Designed for just that role, the American M1A2 37mm gun entered production in 1940 and would see service on every American front during the war. NARA TRAINING MANUAL 1944

- United States: The antiaircraft forces of the U.S. Army trailed those of the British and Germans and consisted mostly of 3-inch guns and machine guns. It was not until 1940 that the production of new 37mm M1 and 90mm M1 guns began.

Just as the all-metal monoplane bomber revolution had dramatically changed the AA air defense equation in the 1930s, the advent of the world's first carrier-borne divebombers and torpedo bombers also created a whole new set of problems for ship-borne AA guns.

During the Great Depression both the United States and United Kingdom suffered from tight military budgets. Desired antiaircraft upgrades were put aside with many ships equipped with guns from the First World War. As an example, the first new British battleship, HMS *Rodney* launched in 1922, was equipped with six QF 4.7 Mk VIII antiaircraft guns and eight 2-pounder automatic guns. This would remain as standard armament right up to the beginning of World War II.

The experience of World War I gave the navies of the world a new perspective on airpower. Both the British and Germans used torpedo bombers in combat. The British considered the reconnaissance zeppelins to be a major threat in the North Sea and aircraft proved their worth in anti-submarine operations. From 1931 to 1933 the Royal Navy's Anti-Aircraft Committee reviewed the situation and cited the rise of ship-based aircraft in the U.S. and Japanese navies as a growing threat.

The first purpose-designed and -built aircraft carrier to be laid down was the British HMS *Hermes* in 1918. This was followed by the Japanese carrier *Hosho* the following year. The *Hermes* was capable of carrying twenty aircraft and was armed with just four 4-inch antiaircraft guns. The *Hosho* carried fifteen aircraft and was armed with just two 80mm antiaircraft guns. By themselves these two carriers did little to alter the battleship-centric thinking of the world's major navies. Their small complement of aircraft offered the fleet good reconnaissance but little else. What they did provide was the chance to experiment and test new aircraft and flight deck techniques.

When the carrier USS *Saratoga* was introduced in 1928, its sheer size and capability set in motion a slow evolution from the primacy of the battleship to the carrier as the most powerful ships afloat. The *Saratoga* was a big ship at 888 feet long and 106 feet wide, capable of carrying between seventy and ninety aircraft. At the time of her launch, her main armament consisted of four double mounts of 8-inch/.55-caliber guns and twelve single 5-inch Mk 10/.25-caliber antiaircraft guns and eight .50-caliber machine guns. The 8-inch guns represented a thought process rooted in the past. It was believed the *Saratoga* would not require an escort and could engage surface ships head on. It was a flawed doctrine, but it was not until January 1942 that these guns were removed and replaced by four twin 5-inch/.38-caliber dual-purpose gun mounts.

In 1936 the *Saratoga*'s air group consisted of eighteen Grumman F2F-1 and 18 Boeing F4B fighters, with nine F2Fs in reserve. For strike operations her air group was equipped with twenty Vought SBU Corsair divebombers with ten spares and eighteen Great Lakes BG torpedo bombers and nine spares. With the *Saratoga* and her sister ship the USS *Lexington*, the U.S. Navy possessed a potent aerial strike force. At the time these two carriers were the fastest available and each carried more aircraft than any other carrier in the world.

Early studies by the U.S. Naval War College showed that very large numbers of aircraft would be required to gain any tactical advantage. After one of the U.S. Navy's annual Fleet Problems (fleet exercise in the late 1930s) in the Pacific, the main complaint of the battleship officers was the carriers had basically fought amongst themselves, depriving them of vital air cover. And because the carriers could operate well away from the battle line, leaving the battleships and themselves to their own devices, the need for more anti-aircraft guns became clear.

The Japanese, on the other hand, had little faith in antiaircraft gun defenses. They believed in high-speed maneuvering to avoid torpedoes and bombs and standing fighter patrols over shipboard guns. They were also firm in their belief that the best defense was to destroy the enemy carriers first before they could strike. It was a flawed doctrine and one for which they would pay dearly. The Japanese carrier *Soryu*, launched in December 1935, carried twelve 127mm Type 89 dual-purpose guns in six twin mounts. These were controlled by two Type 94 fire-control directors. Light antiaircraft defense was provided by just twenty-eight 25mm Hotchkiss Type 96 AA guns in fourteen twin mounts.

The British approach to carrier antiaircraft defense was much different than their American and Japanese counterparts. British carriers, by their design, carried fewer aircraft. The *Ark Royal*, while just as large as the USS *Saratoga*, carried sixty-six aircraft. Its antiaircraft defenses were, however, more robust. The British realized the real threat to their carriers would be from both carrier aircraft and ground-based bombers. Her main armament consisted of sixteen QF 4.5-inch dual-purpose guns in eight double turrets controlled by four directors using the High Angle Control System. Six eight-barreled 2-pounder pom pom guns and eight four-barreled Vickers .50-caliber machine guns provided low- and medium-altitude protection.

The Royal Navy faced a two-ocean problem. As Germany rearmed, it seemed that any future war would be fought against both the new *Kriegsmarine*/Luftwaffe and the Japanese Imperial Fleet. Shore-based bombers were now a real threat and neutralizing them by air attack alone would be impossible. Japanese carriers with their larger complement of aircraft were also a major threat. The British, unlike the Japanese and Americans, did not equip their carriers with specially designed fighter aircraft. Due to budget restrictions and because the Royal Air Force controlled the Navy's aircraft procurement, the Fleet Air Arm opted for multi-role aircraft like the Fairey Swordfish (torpedo bomber, level bomber, reconnaissance, anti-submarine) and the Blackburn Skua divebomber/fighter. In many ways it was a wise choice. During the 1930s it was obvious that observers on surface ships could not spot approaching aircraft early enough to launch interceptors. Within about five years and as bomber speeds increased, interception seemed impossible. Fighters would be useless. Under those circumstances the Royal Navy adapted the armored flight deck (actually armored hangar) and increased gun defenses. Facing an incoming attack all aircraft would be put below into the armored hangar. The combined guns of the fleet and aircraft carrier would be the sole defense. In the end the Royal Navy was unwilling to completely rely on guns alone and was forced to acquire small numbers of modified land-based fighters like the Gloster Gladiator biplane fighter and later the Hawker Hurricane.

For the American and Japanese navies, fighters remained an important part of the carrier group. The Japanese introduced the Mitsubishi A5M "Claude," the world's first all-metal naval monoplane fighter, in 1937 and the Americans followed with the Brewster F2A Buffalo in 1938. Ironically, just as the British fell behind in naval fighter development, radar was invented. As it was refined, radar could now give the carrier group sufficient warning time and the ability to vector fighters to the right spot for an interception. In the coming war naval fighters matched with radar would prove highly effective in defense of the fleet.

The rise of naval airpower in the 1930s proved a great challenge to naval antiaircraft defenses. By 1937 American carriers now fielded a potent strike package consisting of Grumman F3F fighters, Curtiss SBC-4 divebombers, and the first monoplane torpedo bomber, the Douglas TBD-1 Devastator. Ships would now have to fight off simultaneous attacks from both divebombers and torpedo planes. The advancement in naval aircraft was not matched by development of new AA guns. U.S. NAVAL HISTORICAL CENTER

As Germany rearmed, the Kriegsmarine concentrated on capital ship construction. It did, however, embark on the construction of two carriers with the first being laid down in 1936. The new *Graf Zeppelin* was designed to carry forty-two fighters and dive-bombers and a healthy antiaircraft gun defense consisting of twelve 105mm SK C/33 guns, twenty-two 37mm SK C/30 guns, and twenty-eight 20mm guns. These three guns would be the Kriegsmarine's primary antiaircraft armament on all of its heavy surface ships during the Second World War.

For the shipboard gunners the coming war would prove an immense challenge. Hitting an airborne target from a moving platform presented its own set of problems, but it was the number of weapons and tactics used against ships that would set the stage for some of the greatest antiaircraft battles of the war.

The first form of attack that had proven itself capable of sinking a moving ship at sea was the airborne torpedo. Proven during the First World War, the torpedo was a powerful weapon capable of sinking a battleship with a single hit. For a torpedo bomber to be successful, it had to approach its target at a height of between 80 and 100 feet with an airspeed of no more than 120 mph and a range of 2,000 yards. Against individual ships a single torpedo bomber stood little chance of success. Evasive action was often enough to survive. Between the two world wars, tacticians developed the group attack method. Aircraft attacking in groups from different directions would not only divide the antiaircraft defenses but cancel out any maneuvering.

In the early 1930s divebombing would emerge as the most important development in anti-shipping warfare. Divebombers could, while in their dive, adjust their sights over a moving target. They also had the element of surprise. Without radar detection divebombers could suddenly appear over the target unseen. Once in their dive fire-control systems designed to deal with level bombing could not cope. A divebomber was also a difficult target. Diving from 12,000 feet a single bomber would complete its dive in twenty seconds at a speed of around 300 knots. This gave gunners barely enough time to acquire a target and begin firing. And with numerous bombers following in trail, the defenses would be overwhelmed. The most effective tactic was a simultaneous attack by both divebombers and torpedo bombers. Gun defenses would be split and overwhelmed and no amount of maneuvering would suffice.

Level bombing from altitude proved entirely ineffective during World War II. A single bomber like a B-17 had almost no chance of hitting a maneuvering ship. A group of bombers had a better chance, but not much. The failure of level bombing led to other methods including skip bombing. Tested before the war, skip bombing was not that much different from torpedo bombing. It required an aircraft to approach at a low level, release its ordnance at extremely short range, and skip the bomb like a rock into the target ship. With the bomb gone the bomber pulled up, often flying over the ship at masthead height.

Strafing attacks by fighters or light bombers could not sink a ship, but they could render them inoperable. RAF Coastal Command attacks by Mosquitoes and Beaufighters on German coastal convoys would prove devastating by the end of World War II. A single strafing pass by a Beaufighter or Mosquito—armed with four 20mm cannons—on a flak ship or armed merchant vessel could shatter the upper decks rendering them inoperable.

The Germans would introduce the war's first guided weapons during World War II. Capable of being launched out of antiaircraft range, both the Henschel Hs-293 and Fritz X FX 1400 were radio-controlled glide bombs, guided to their target by a controller in the launch aircraft. Guidance was straightforward. After launch the controller, using a radio control link, focused on the burning flare in its tail, adjusting the missile's track. The Hs-293 was deployed against merchant ships and escort vessels while the FX 1400 was used against armored ships.

As World War II dawned, neither side realized that the most effective guided weapon of the war would be the Japanese kamikaze. These human guided weapons were much more difficult to counter compared to the German guided glide bombs. Kamikazes would be used in large numbers and guidance could not be jammed. Naval gunners would be horrified by the new tactics. Antiaircraft fire would no longer be a way to deter your enemy or cause him to drop his bombs or torpedo early. Now the aircraft had to be destroyed outright. It was a frightening proposition. Ships in danger areas had to be on constant alert. Attacks would occur with little warning, and while the ships' antiaircraft guns were able to engage, they had to be accurate and have enough weight to destroy the incoming aircraft. A hit from a 5-inch gun would obliterate its target. Multiple hits by weapons like the 20mm and 40mm guns would often cause great damage, but the kamikaze would continue to its target oblivious to the carnage. Mass attacks often saturated every level of fleet defense, from fighter direction and control down to gunfire control. Fortunately for the Americans their ships were equipped with some of the best shipboard antiaircraft guns and fire-control systems. As the war progressed, the Americans continued to add more antiaircraft guns to all their ships. By 1945 the Essex class carrier was heavily armed with twelve 5-inch/38 guns—eight in twin mounts fore and aft of the island and four single mounts along the port side. Medium-range protection was provided by up to eighteen 40mm quadruple mounts. This was backed up by between forty-six and fifty-eight 20mm guns.

In the coming war antiaircraft gunners would have no shortage of targets. As the war intensified, their importance and effectiveness only grew. Indeed Germany's air defense at its peak consisted of an incredible 6,387 heavy and 9,333 light flak guns and 5,360 searchlights. Often dismissed as ineffective and a waste of valuable material and personnel, antiaircraft defenses on both sides would make the skies above the battlefield a living hell for those who dared to fly above them.

CHAPTER THREE

The AA Battle over Europe 1939–1940

The true criterion of the efficiency of the AA defense guns is not the number of aircraft destroyed, but rather what more could the enemy have accomplished in the absence of AA artillery.

—TEXTBOOK OF ANTI-AIRCRAFT GUNNERY

ON SEPTEMBER 1, 1939, GERMANY INVADED POLAND, SETTING IN MOTION MAN'S MOST destructive war. The German attack on Poland did not catch the Poles unaware. As early as 1935, Poland began a Six Year (rearmament) Plan that included the addition of modern antiaircraft guns including some 300 40mm Bofors guns. In addition to foreign-bought weapons, the Poles designed and built forty-four 75mm antiaircraft guns. At the beginning of hostilities the Polish army had one regiment and eight detachments of heavy antiaircraft artillery and more than 300 light guns and 170 machine guns. The Poles did not have radar, leaving detection and command and control weak. The British and Germans had radar at the beginning of the war. German intelligence regarded Polish AA defenses insufficient in numbers, with poor aiming capabilities. The Poles' most critical weakness was communications, especially the AA forces. With no dedicated communication system, the AA gunners and air force commanders depended on army communication from local ground units with only ten radio stations to support aerial operations. Any disruption in the network quickly affected the delivery of timely messages, especially air raid warnings.

Having effectively dispersed its air force on several satellite fields, the Poles presented the Luftwaffe with a serious problem. Unable to destroy the Polish air arm in the first few days, the Luftwaffe suffered heavy losses to both fighters and AA fire.

The Polish air force continued to resist, albeit with diminishing numbers and effectiveness. Finally on October 6th the last major ground force surrendered at Kock.

Although victorious, the Luftwaffe's performance during the invasion of Poland did not match Nazi propaganda at the time. In the first two weeks of September, Luftwaffe losses numbered 285 aircraft destroyed, 19 percent of their force. Despite the weakness of the Polish air defense system, the Germans encountered significant AA fire and fighter air-to-air combat. Polish fighter pilots were credited with 126 kills, leaving the AA gunners with 159, plus another 279 German aircraft seriously damaged.

As Poland fought for its life, France and Britain, both treaty bound, declared war on Germany. For the prewar airpower theorists, who had scoffed at antiaircraft guns, the invasion of Poland had proven them wrong. Before the conflict began German flak doctrine stressed the importance of providing protection for the ground forces. This combined with the Luftwaffe's dedication to ground attack and battlefield interdiction made the German army a formidable fighting force.

During operations in Poland, Luftwaffe antiaircraft units were attached to each of the numbered German armies, the highest organizational echelon of the German army. Structurally this resulted in a poor performance by the Flak arm. Because of the rapidity of the campaign and because the flak units were initially held to the rear, few units reached the front lines or areas where they were needed most.

One aspect of the air war that is often brushed aside was the losses due to "friendly fire" (this would be a problem throughout the war), both air-to-air and AA fire. The Luftwaffe admitted the loss of sixty-seven Bf-109s with many being written off after being damaged by their own forces. The losses to friendly fire were legion during the campaign. Polish sources estimate their own AA forces shot down twice as many Polish aircraft as was claimed by the Luftwaffe.

During the campaign Germany's twenty mixed flak battalions and nine light flak battalions accounted for thirty-nine Polish aircraft shot down. The number may seem small, but when put beside the operational strength of the Polish air force at approximately 500, it was a significant number.

Just as the Polish campaign came to an end, the *Sitzkrieg*, or phony war, began. Both German and Allied forces eyed each other over the Dutch, Belgian, and French borders with very little ground or air activity. The small RAF bombing raids on German targets, however, proved prophetic.

On September 4, 1939, the Royal Air Force launched it first daylight bombing raid against Germany. Fourteen Wellingtons and fifteen Blenheims took off headed for warships in Brunsbüttel and Wilhelmshaven. The ten Blenheims (five others failed to find their target) carried out a low-level attack on the pocket battleship *Admiral Scheer* and the cruiser *Emden* in Wilhelmshaven harbor. The *Scheer* was hit with three bombs but all failed to explode and the *Emden* was damaged when a Blenheim crashed onto it. Both shore- and ship-based AA guns shot down five Blenheims. It was an auspicious start with half of the force brought down by flak. Two Wellingtons would also be lost, shot down by fighters over Brunsbüttel.

The German MG34 machine gun's high rate of fire made it ideal for light antiaircraft defense. This towed mount is equipped with two weapons, giving the gunner an unprecedented rate of fire of 1,800 rounds per minute. AUTHOR'S COLLECTION

This Bf-109 from the 9th Staffel JG 2 was shot down near Le Harre, France, by French AA fire during the Sitzkrieg, or phony war—September 1, 1939, to May 9, 1940. Flak damage to the spinner is clearly visible. NATIONAL MUSEUM OF THE USAF

Through October to the beginning of December, RAF bombers conducted North Sea sweeps in search of German ships. It was a dismal failure. After sixty-one sorties no ships were spotted and no bombs dropped.

On the morning of December 3rd, twenty-four Wellingtons attacked ships in and around Helgoland. The bombers suffered from both heavy flak and fighter attack. Two were damaged by flak with all aircraft returning to Britain. On December 14th twelve Wellingtons set out on an armed patrol looking for ships in the Schillig Roads. Poor weather forced the formation down to as low as 200 feet. Shortly after, German fighters and flak shot down five bombers. Not surprisingly the RAF was reluctant to concede that five of the bombers had been shot down by fighters. Officially it was hoped the losses were all due to flak. The RAF's belief in the self-defending bomber had been greatly shaken. Continued losses like this directly threatened the RAF's doctrine of daylight strategic bombing.

On December 18th the RAF tried again. Twenty-four Wellingtons were dispatched with strict orders not to attack at less than 10,000 feet to avoid the worst effects of flak. Even at this early stage of the war, flak guns were proving very effective at low and medium altitudes, and for the first time in the war a formation of aircraft was spotted by radar. Located on the island of Wangerope, an experimental Freya radar station was able to direct German fighters onto the incoming formation. Heavy flak guns were the first, however, to open the battle. Accurate fire forced the formation to open up, giving the German fighters better opportunities for attack. Twelve Wellingtons were shot down (the majority to fighters) for the loss of two German fighters.

The German Freya radar was a general search radar with a range of 74 miles (120 kilometers), but it could not provide the altitude of an incoming target. At the beginning of the war, the Germans had only eight Freya radar systems in operation. They soon quickly showed their worth by spotting the early British bombing attacks on naval targets. NARA

Ironically the British were reluctant to concede the achievements made by German fighters and officially hoped, again, the losses were due to flak. The Germans missed the fact that with sufficient warning, flak guns operating in cooperation with fighters increased the effectiveness of both. They needed to stop judging the effectiveness of the guns by counting how many aircraft were shot down and instead begin examining and including secondary effects. Flak-damaged bombers often fell out of formation and formations themselves could be broken up by accurate AA fire, creating opportunities for the fighters. What was also abundantly clear was how effective low- and medium-level flak really was.

These December missions deeply shook the RAF's faith in daylight bombing and forced a change in tactics. The validity of the self-defending bomber formation and the belief that "the bomber would always get through" had been proven false. The prewar "prophets" of airpower and their confidence in the bomber as a decisive weapon had been severely tested. What the strategic bomber proponents forgot was that for every good offense there was an equally good defense.

Now the RAF had to change tack and they had two choices: develop a long-range escort fighter or use the cover of darkness. Putting more gas into the Spitfire was briefly considered with the Mk IIA long-range version. Sixty Spitfire IIA Long Range were built with a 40-gallon fixed tank fitted under the port wing. These Spitfires were used as bomber escorts through 1941 with limited success. The only option left was night-bombing. On the night of May 10th/11th, RAF Bomber Command attacked Germany proper with thirty-six Wellingtons and nine Whitleys raiding an airfield and bridges across the Rhine.

The invasion of the Low Countries and France between May 10 and June 22, 1940, would expose the flak forces on both sides to a myriad of targets and tactical situations. Unfortunately for the Allies the Germans were well equipped and prepared. The Polish campaign provided the flak forces with their baptism of fire and a wealth of experience. Twenty-four mixed flak battalions and eleven light flak battalions (700 88mm, 180 37mm, and 800 20mm guns) were earmarked for action in the West.

To meet the coming offensive, the French fielded more than 900 75mm guns of various capabilities, many of 1918 vintage with old-style sights and fire control. They also had forty-two license-built 40mm Bofors guns, but with only 68,000 shells. The British would contribute three antiaircraft brigades equipped with 120 QF 3-inch antiaircraft guns, forty-eight QF 3.7-inch guns, more than a hundred 40mm Bofors guns, and .303-caliber Lewis machine guns for low-level defense. Each brigade had approximately thirty-eight heavy guns and thirty-nine .303-caliber Lewis machine guns. The Dutch were better equipped with about 275 modern antiaircraft guns, including 150 20mm Oerlikons, eighty-one 75mm Vickers Skoda guns, forty-two 40mm Bofors weapons, and 452 machine guns for low-level defense. The Belgium army would contribute twelve Vickers 3.7-inch guns, 132 75mm guns, and 110 40mm Bofors.

The second most numerous heavy gun in the Luftwaffe inventory was the 105mm Flak 38 and 39 gun. Resembling a scaled-up version of the 88 Flak 18 series, it was only marginally better than the 88. In action the 105mm gun required a crew consisting of a commander and nine men. NARA

The Dutch were well aware of Hitler's intentions and expected to be attacked. Even though Holland was a very small country, it would experience invasion from the air. It was a truly revolutionary concept and history's first. The attack would open with medium bombers and Ju-87 Stuka divebombing attacks. Airborne troops would be dropped onto four primary airfields: the main base at Waalhaven near Rotterdam, and three others near the Hague. The Germans needed Waalhaven intact in order to fly in a whole division. At the same time commando forces would attempt to seize all the key bridges, giving ground forces a good chance of linking up with the airborne forces.

The Dutch had studied Germany's actions in Poland carefully, noting the use of airborne forces. While surprised by the scale of the attack, German tactics and timing had been accounted for. On the morning of May 10, 1940, the Dutch air defense system was on full alert.

The Luftwaffe committed 430 Junkers Ju-52 transports to the invasion. The Germans planned to capture several Dutch airfields by putting 4,000 paratroops on the ground on the first day. It did not all go according to plan. Accurate light and medium antiaircraft fire shredded the slow-moving Ju-52s. During the short violent air war that developed,

Morane 406
Jagdeinsitzer

Aircraft recognition was more an art than science. Both Allied and Axis AA gunners and aircrews were not very good at it. To help improve their abilities, tens of thousands of aircraft recognition booklets and posters were produced to enhance their skills. This early German aircraft recognition-training poster shows the various angles of the French Morane-Saulnier M.S.-406 fighter. NARA

Dutch gunners man their Vickers 1931 75mm antiaircraft guns prior to the invasion of Holland. The Vickers gun proved a reliable weapon and at the time of invasion the Dutch would field eighty-one guns. After the battle the Germans seized ninety stored guns and pressed them into service as the 75mm Flak M 35(h). AUTHOR'S COLLECTION

the Dutch air force was essentially wiped out with 88 of its 140 aircraft destroyed. Even with the withering antiaircraft fire, enough paratroopers landed on several Dutch airfields to signal the second wave of Ju-52s. These were the follow-on troops, but once on the ground the Ju-52s found it difficult if not impossible to take off again. The soft mushy fields provided Dutch artillery and flak gunners a rich target environment. Of the 430 Ju-52s committed to the attack, 200 were destroyed. In total the Luftwaffe would lose 525 aircraft (both permanent and temporary during the operation) over Holland with the Dutch air force claiming between 30 and 40. The battle for the Netherlands was one of the bloodiest of the war with 2,032 Dutch soldiers, airmen, and sailors killed. More than 2,000 Germans were killed. While the Dutch defenders had fought very well, they were simply overwhelmed. Air base gun defenses were too few and spread too thin among the numerous airfields they had to cover.

While the German airborne invasion had been a success, it came at a heavy price. Any plans to use airborne troops for an invasion of England had to be scrapped.

Light and medium antiaircraft fire proved highly effective against low-flying transports. Any future airborne operations would require these weapons to be neutralized or avoided. Unfortunately for both the Germans and Allies, all future airborne operations would suffer from accurate and sustained light and medium antiaircraft fire.

After what could be considered the first great antiaircraft battle of the war, the Germans turned their attention to the Belgian, British, and French armies. The Allies would

The battle for Holland would prove a graveyard for the German Ju-52 transport force. During the battle for Velkenburg airfield, the Germans lost close to fifty Ju-52s to AA fire, fighters, and artillery attacks. AUTHOR'S COLLECTION

not be able to repeat the success the Dutch gunners had achieved, but they would inflict heavy losses on the Luftwaffe.

The Belgians mobilized 600,000 men with 300 aircraft, a formidable defensive force. Fully aware they would most likely be overwhelmed from the air, the Belgian airfields and vital points were protected by modern antiaircraft guns and machine guns. As with the attack on Holland, the Germans had no choice but to use airborne troops, but here, the Belgians would not have the same success as the Dutch gunners. To defeat Belgium the Germans had to eliminate the fort at Eben-Emael. Again they went to their airborne troops, but this time they would be delivered by glider. Gliders provided a far more accurate way to deliver small groups of infantry. Launched far from their target, they could approach silently without the telltale drone of a transport aircraft. The airborne attack was one of the most successful of the war. Just seventy-seven combat engineers landed on Eban-Emael, and after just twenty-eight hours neutralized the fort. No gliders or transports were claimed by Belgian antiaircraft gunners. From that point forward the Belgians fought a defensive battle with little chance of success.

With the battle fully joined, it was time for the British and French to add their weight to the onslaught. The French were ready to commit 510 single-engine fighters, 805 bombers, and more than 400 observation/reconnaissance aircraft. In terms of antiaircraft defenses, the French commander realized his forces were woefully equipped. The French army placed the majority of their antiaircraft guns with the army near Belgium and behind the Maginot Line for home defense. They had no tactical radar, but there were six British radar sites along the Franco-Belgian border from Calais to Le Cateau. The radars were severely limited in their range and did not work as well over land as over water. The flow of information from the radars to French air force and RAF fighters proved inadequate. Sadly the French and British had to rely on sound detectors and forward observers for early warning detection.

The Luftwaffe's plan to attack all the airfields they could find at the outset of the campaign paid big dividends. On the first day of the attack, the French were unwilling to make any cross-border raids. This quickly changed, but the priority was given to the German armored columns pouring across the border. RAF raids struck some bases but were complete failures. As a result, the Germans diverted no fighters or AA guns from their home bases. All told, 210 Allied aircraft were destroyed on the ground on the first day.

German air attacks were relentless through the entire campaign. In the early going British and French airfields were a priority with at least seventy-five successfully attacked. Allied AA gunners were hard pressed to defend the fields. In one example Dornier Do-17s from the 2nd *Kampfgruppe* executed a perfect low-level attack. Skimming just above the rooftops, the Do-17s achieved complete surprise. Neither the AA gunners nor Hurricane pilots on the base saw the incoming bombers. Once over the field the twelve Do-17s dropped a string of 100-pound bombs along a line of Blenheim bombers waiting for takeoff. The Germans made three bombing and strafing runs before breaking for home. Antiaircraft fire was minimal with just one Lewis machine gun engaging the enemy. In a single stroke half of the RAF's bomber striking force in France was put out of action. The continued attacks on British and French airfields proved devastating. Without early warning Allied AA gunners were at a severe disadvantage resulting in frustration and poor results. At least seventy-five airfields were attacked, and by May 10th the RAF's Advanced Air Striking Force (AASF) had lost 63 aircraft from its original strength of 135. The Allies did try and hit back, but with disastrous results.

German ground troops were well equipped and protected by Luftwaffe Flak units along with their own light machine guns. On May 10th the RAF mounted an attack on the *Panzer* columns in Luxemburg. The plane of choice was the slow Fairey Battle light bomber, an aircraft completely unsuited to the task (maximum speed was just 257 mph with four 250-pound bombs). Flying in very low—about 250 feet—Battles dropped their bombs. Lacking any light or medium flak guns, the Panzer troops put up intense machine gun and rifle fire. Three Battles were quickly shot down. Later that day a second mission met with similar results. Of the thirty-two Fairey Battles sent out that day, thirteen were shot down with the rest being damaged. The effectiveness of infantry rifles and machine guns was a great surprise to the Allies. The German MG34 machine gun was an excellent weapon for AA defense with rate of fire of up to 900 rounds per minute. The British Bren Gun in comparison could fire 700 rounds per minute.

The first line of AA defense for every army during World War II was the light machine gun. To increase the rate of fire, many were produced in twin mounts and in some cases quadruple configurations. Here a Finnish crew man their twin 7.62mm M/31 VKT antiaircraft machine gun in Vuosalmi, December of 1939. SA-KUVA

Just four days into the battle, the swift German armored advance had left the Allied ground forces in complete disarray. By May 13th General Heinz Guderian's three Panzer divisions reached the banks of the Meuse River at Sedan. That night German engineers began to span the river. At the same time Luftwaffe Flak units were digging in. The next morning Guderian had 150 armored vehicles on the far side. In a desperate attempt to destroy the pontoon bridges, the Allies launched an all-out attack. Previous losses due to low-level attacks forced the Allied bombers to come in at medium height and head to their target in a shallow dive. The attack was a shambles. Sixty-three Battles and five twin-engine Blenheim bombers fought through a storm of fighter attacks and concentrated flak. Forty were shot down. The French fared no better. Fighting over their own territory, the French could muster only twelve antiquated Amiot 143 bombers. Two were shot down with no results.

By the end of May 25th, the situation for the Allies was desperate. Unable to stop the German armored pincers, the British, Belgian, and French armies were now engaged in a fighting retreat. After reaching the Channel coast, the German forces swung north, separating the British Expeditionary Force (BEF), the French 1st Army, and Belgian army from the majority of the French army south of the German penetration. German forces were now set to capture the Channel ports, cutting off the Allies' last line of retreat. By May 26th the Allied armies were bottled up in a corridor about 60 miles deep and 15 to 25 miles wide with their backs to the Channel. With two German armies flanking them, the order to evacuate through the port town of Dunkirk was given. Trapped inside the pocket were the 1st, 4th, 6th, and 85th Anti-Aircraft Regiments Royal Artillery along with the 1st, 51st, 53rd, and 58th Light Anti-Aircraft Regiments Royal Artillery. The French added their own AA guns with approximately 144 75mm guns, forty-five 25mm guns, and one battery of four 90mm guns from the French navy. Unfortunately for the beleaguered AA troops, ammunition was in short supply and was soon exhausted.

Instead of squeezing the pocket with a direct attack, Hitler ordered his Panzers to halt. Hitler's Directive No. 13 of May 24th put the responsibility of destroying the French and British armies directly into the hands of the Luftwaffe. The "next goal of operations is the annihilation of the French, British, and Belgian forces. . . . During this operation the task of the Luftwaffe is to break all enemy resistance in the encircled parts and to prevent the escape of the British forces across the Channel." It was a tall order.

The British and French committed a huge number of warships to the task—one cruiser, the HMS *Calcutta*, and fifty-three destroyers (forty-one British, twelve French). There is no doubt the antiaircraft defenses of these ships had severe limitations. Most were of World War I vintage, but some had improved AA defenses. The HMS *Calcutta* was refitted in 1938 with eight QF 4-inch dual-purpose guns in four twin mounts, one quadruple 2-pounder pom-pom gun, and two quadruple Vickers .50-caliber machine guns. The most vulnerable ships were the destroyers. Most relied on World War I vintage 4.7-inch guns for air defense. Unable to elevate above 40 degrees, they were vulnerable to divebombing attacks. The majority of ships, however, possessed close-range weapons including at least two 2-pound pom-pom guns, one quadruple Vickers .50-caliber machine gun, and one or two twin Lewis .303-caliber machine guns.

Prior to the war there was no doubt the antiaircraft defenses of British warships were limited. Most senior naval commanders were initially satisfied and believed the protection provided was even more important than fighter defense. Not everyone agreed. Lt. Com. J. A. J. "Alec" Dennis described his ship's AA defense as "pathetic." As a junior officer on the

The one British naval AA gun that provided some protection against the Stuka Ju-87 divebomber was the Vickers .50-caliber quad machine gun. The destroyers fighting off of Dunkirk were normally armed with two quad mounts each. Effective range was 800 yards. A total of 137 Luftwaffe aircraft were shot down during the Dunkirk operation. Of that total Royal Navy gunners were credited with thirty-five. AUTHOR'S COLLECTION

HMS *Griffin*, he watched in disbelief as a radio-controlled Queen Bee target drone flew straight and level through the fleet's barrage emerging unscathed during a 1939 exercise.

Dunkirk would prove a graveyard for British and French destroyers. Presenting themselves as stationary targets (while loading troops), they were extremely vulnerable to divebombing attacks by the Luftwaffe's best ship-destroyer, the Junkers Ju-87 Stuka. Between May 4th and June 6th, they were repeatedly attacked by both divebombers and medium-level Ju-88s, He-111s, and Do-17s. For the loss of six British and three French destroyers, the ship's AA gunners managed to shoot down four Ju-87s and two Ju-88s with many more damaged. All told the Allies would lose 240 vessels with another forty-five badly damaged. The British army left behind 63,879 motor transports, 2,794 artillery pieces including most of its QF 3-inch guns, and 101 precious 40mm Bofors (seventy-two were also lost during operations in Norway). In return Operation Dynamo evacuated 308,888 troops.

With the Dunkirk battle over, the Germans still had to fight the rest of the French army. On June 3rd the Luftwaffe launched Operation Paula. Seeking to end all resistance, a series of attacks were mounted against thirteen air bases and aircraft production plants in the Paris area. The French responded with sixty fighter aircraft and the heaviest concentration of antiaircraft fire of the war. Twenty-six German planes were shot down. All of the French air bases were put out of action, but within forty-eight hours they were fully operational again. Ground operations resumed on June 5th with German forces striking the French on the Somme. Far from the *Blitzkrieg* success in the early weeks of the campaign, the German advance this time was slow and bloody. The rejuvenated French army fought for another three weeks only to finally surrender on June 25th.

The Allies' inability to protect its own airfields with fighters and flak proved fatal. Without an effective early warning system and enough guns, the battle to save their airfields was a disaster. Most of the Advance Air Striking Force's (AASF) Blenheims were destroyed on the ground. The Fairey Battles fared no better with most shot down by AA fire and fighters. Only at the beginning of June did the air defenses improve, but by then it was far too late. The Germans proved the best way to achieve air superiority was to destroy your opponent's air force on the ground and not in the air.

For their part Luftwaffe flak forces proved themselves highly effective in the operations against the Low Countries and France. Twenty-four mixed flak battalions and eleven light flak battalions took part in the war in the West. What set the Luftwaffe's flak units apart from those of the Allies was the role they played in assisting the army by engaging ground targets. Their versatility and fluid command structure gave the Germans a distinct advantage over the Allies. Flak units played a key role in the elimination of French positions in the Ardennes and along the Maginot Line. Heinz Guderian had high praise: "Eighteen days of hard fighting lie behind us. Flak Regiment 102 including the light flak battalions performed inestimable services for the army corps and contributed in an outstanding manner to [the corps'] success." The same could not be said for the Allied flak forces. By the end of the campaign the Luftwaffe Flak Corps tallied 503 aircraft, 152 tanks, 151 bunkers, 13 forts, and more than 20 warships and naval transports.

The Germans' startling success in France brought home the clear realization in Britain and the United States that their tactical gun AA defenses were inadequate. The QF 3-inch gun showed its age and ineffectiveness. There were some bright spots, however. The 40mm Bofors gun proved highly effective. After the fall of France, both countries began producing a large variety of armored, mobile antiaircraft weapons including .50-caliber machine guns, and 20mm, 37mm, and 40mm cannons.

CHAPTER FOUR

The Battle of Britain—
AA Command's Forgotten Contribution

We know that England is the hardest nut to be cracked in this war. Our experience at the front has shown us that final victory against England can only be attained by the systematic cooperation of all arms of the service and ruthless application of the elementary principle of concentrating all one's strength and effort at the vital strategic point. Even if the air arm is the most important weapon in total war, it cannot by itself ensure the decisive, final and total victory.

—Werner Baumbach

Shortly after the declaration of war on Germany, Britain's AA Command swung into action firing on targets over Sheerness and Thameshaven. The guns were accurate, but unfortunately the gunners' aircraft recognition skills were lacking, resulting in one Bristol Blenheim from 64 Squadron being shot down.

Britain's prewar air defense plans focused on a German "knock-out blow" on London. British intelligence estimated a Luftwaffe bombing force of 1,600 modern bombers could deliver 700 tons of bombs per day. It was a frightening prospect, but at the outbreak of war the Luftwaffe possessed just 1,180 twin-engine bombers (approximately 800 He-111s and 380 Do-17s). Of those, about 1,000 were serviceable. Flying from their German bases to London also meant a 760-mile round-trip, meaning neither bomber type could carry a full load of bombs. There was also no fighter escort available. Albeit a portion of the flight could be covered by the long-range Me 110 fighter.

Fortunately for the British, Hitler had no intention of bombing London or any other British city. On September 3, 1939, AA Command had just 622 heavy antiaircraft guns serviceable and ready to fire. Of the new 40mm Bofors guns, just seventy-two were available, the majority distributed among twenty radar stations. Airfields were defended chiefly by Lewis machine guns and a smattering of 3-inch guns and 20mm Hispano guns.

As weak as the AA gun defenses were, they were not designed to operate in isolation. At the beginning of the war, Britain possessed the most sophisticated air defense system in the world. During the 1930s the RAF built a chain of radar stations along the east coast of England and Scotland, known as Chain Home stations. These were the eyes of the system capable of detecting aircraft approaching at medium or high altitude more than 100 miles away. These radars all fed Fighter Command Headquarters at Bentley Priory, Stanmore, and the group and sector stations. A web of landlines formed a highly effective "nervous system," which allowed for the rapid flow of information. When an enemy formation was detected, its heading, altitude, and estimated strength was passed along to the Filter Center at Fighter Command Headquarters. The Fighter Command Center also received information from the Navy, RAF Coastal Command, and Bomber Command along with civil, air, and sea agencies. AA Command liaison officers were also present, ready to alert gun crews in the target areas. While radar was a key element in the British defense, it was not without its limitations. Chain Home radars could not track aircraft flying over land. Tracking raiders once they passed the coast fell to the Observer Corps. Hundreds of ground observer posts dotted the countryside. These human observers would report height, direction, and number of enemy aircraft directly into the system, giving the Fighter Command Filter Room a clear picture of what was happening behind the radars. One often overlooked aspect of early detection was signals intelligence. Radar by itself could not resolve the number of aircraft and type and could not see past 120 miles. Before Luftwaffe bombers took off, they had to be made ready. Radios were turned on and tested, giving British high frequencies listening stations a heads up. This intelligence gave the British up to a two-hour warning and detailed information on aircraft numbers, type, and routes.

One of the most important tools developed by the RAF was the Identification Friend or Foe unit installed in all fighter aircraft. This device responded to radar signals by transmitting a "beep tone" that identified the aircraft as friendly on a radar screen. It was a huge advantage, but not always reliable. It would in the end cut down on the number of friendly fire incidents both in the air and from the ground.

The contribution made by AA Command during the battle of Britain is often overshadowed by the heroics of the young pilots from RAF Fighter Command. The AA guns were often dismissed in the hundreds of books written about the battle. While Fighter Command shot down the lion's share of Luftwaffe aircraft, the guns did their fair share and contributed greatly in many unmeasured and hidden ways. Formations broken up and bombers damaged by flak were easy prey for fighters. Many fighter pilots increased their scores by hunting for flak-damaged bombers. Flak also had other hidden effects. Aircrew were killed and wounded. Heavily damaged aircraft were taken out of service for repair. Others received unseen damage. Nicked fuel and hydraulic lines or flying control cables

The static version of the British QF 3.7-inch antiaircraft gun was the Mk II. Along with the mobile version it was the mainstay of AA Command during the battle of Britain. The Germans, who captured a number during the battle of France, appreciated the guns' effectiveness so much they pressed them into service as the 94mm Flak Vickers M.39(e). They also went to the trouble of manufacturing their own ammunition for it. CHRIS GOSS

would fail at a later time causing accidents or aborts. There was also the mental and psychological toll on aircrew forced to fly through heavy flak on a daily basis. But the most important role of the AA gun was the prevention of accurate bombing. Once they did that everything else was a secondary bonus.

The British were far better prepared for the coming battle than the Luftwaffe was. In terms of AA defense the British were undergunned and hard pressed to provide enough barrels for every site they deemed important. They also had to provide high-, medium-, and low-level protection. The high-altitude threat fell to the Vickers 3.7-inch Mark I gun (the most numerous deployed) and a smaller number of QF 4.5-inch antiaircraft guns. The 3.7-inch gun fired a 28-pound shell at a maximum rate of about ten rounds per minute to an effective height of 25,000 feet. The exploding time-fused shell had a lethal radius of about 45 feet. The more powerful 4.5-inch gun fired a 55-pound shell to an effective height of 26,000 feet. This round had a lethal radius of 60 feet. In addition there were 270

FLAK IN WORLD WAR II

of the lower performance QF 3-inch guns left over from World War I with an effective ceiling of just 14,000 feet.

All heavy antiaircraft guns were usually deployed in half batteries of four. It was not uncommon, however, to have sites with two, six, or later eight guns. Each set of four guns had its own Stroud No. 1 Mark IV height-finder and a Vickers Armstrong Predictor No. 1 Mark III. The 3.7-inch gun was an excellent weapon capable of engaging a bomber at a slant range of 17,000 feet from the gun. When fired a shell took ten seconds to reach the incoming aircraft. During those ten seconds a bomber traveling at 180 mph flew exactly half a mile. To cause serious damage, the gunners needed to aim their guns and fuse the shells to explode at a point in space exactly 880 yards in front of the bomber's observed position.

The combination height-finder and predictor produced the necessary fire-control solution. All heavy AA guns worked this way. Information from the height-finder was fed into the predictor establishing the aircraft's previous flight path. The predictor then calculated where the aircraft and shells would meet. The predictor's information came out in the form of azimuth and elevation settings for the guns and time-of-flight fuse settings for the shells. This information was passed directly to the guns where the crews tracked the target's predictor position, set the fused shells, and fired.

Bomber formations and individual aircraft did not always cooperate by flying straight and level while in the target area. Upsetting the gunner's aim was as simple as changing altitude or weaving on approach. But "jinking" during the bomb run greatly reduced accuracy, causing bombs to impact well clear of the target.

To meet the Luftwaffe's high-altitude threat, AA Command had 359 4.5-inch guns, 666 3.7-inch guns, and 226 3-inch guns ready for battle. The first job of AA guns was to make bombers fly higher and reduce their accuracy. During the summer of 1940, Luftwaffe bombers flying through gun-defended areas usually flew above 15,000 feet. As a rule of thumb, each 5,000-foot increase in altitude halved the accuracy of heavy antiaircraft fire. At the same time bombing errors from 15,000 feet were about twice as great as those dropped from 5,000 feet. It was a battle for height and precision. Accurate hot metal going up prevented accurate cold explosive steel from coming down.

When engaging enemy formations heavy AA gun batteries had three methods of fire: continuously pointed fire, predicted concentration fire, or box barrage.

Continuously pointed fire was the most hazardous type of AA fire. Each battery tracked the formation leader at a predicted distance in the sky in front of it. Firing at a maximum rate, the guns would place their shells directly in front of the incoming formation for as long as the target aircraft remained in range or until it crossed the bomb release line.

Predicted concentration fire—used when darkness or cloud cover obscured the target—was far less effective than continuously pointed fire. Batteries would fire short barrages at points in the sky through which it was predicted the target formation would pass.

Designed in the 1920s, the Vickers No. 1 Mk III Predictor was vital for accurate AA fire. As an electro-mechanical computer, its function was to take height and range data from an optical range finder and compute a firing solution for the guns—elevation, direction, and fuse settings for the shells. All this information was electrically transferred to the guns where the gun layers moved the gun to match the pointers on the dial. CHRIS GOSS

Box barrage was the most wasteful and least effective. Used when darkness or cloud cover prevented the use of the predictor, gunners simply filled a box of sky, hopefully, in front of the bombers' supposed target.

The air battles over France and the Low Countries had proven light and medium flak to be extremely effective. To meet the anticipated low-level Luftwaffe raiders, AA Command had 3,538 light and medium antiaircraft guns in seven types. The majority of the

This poor but rare photo shows an He-111 of I./KG I encountering flak over the Thames Estuary on August 18, 1940. Flak bursts can be seen directly in front and below the aircraft and off to the right side. CHRIS GOSS

guns consisted of 3,028 Lewis machine guns followed by just 227 40mm Bofors guns, 132 3-inch guns prepared for low-altitude work, 114 2-pounders of one kind or another, and thirty-seven Hispano-Suiza 20mm guns. This mixed bag of guns was carefully invested. The Bofors guns went to most vital targets. Each radar station had three static guns, while the eleven aircraft factories were given guns proportional to their size and vulnerability—generally four or so. Industrial and other military targets like the Royal Ordnance Factory at Nottingham received a few Bofors while the remaining guns were shared among the more vital RAF airfields. Prewar planning estimated each field needed a minimum of sixteen Bofors and eight heavy AA guns. Few RAF installations ever acquired so many. The airfields of No. 10 and 11 Group based around London and west of the capital were the most vulnerable and each received a mixed bag of weapons.

In preparation for Operation Sealion (the invasion of Britain), the Luftwaffe had to achieve air superiority by destroying the RAF in the air and on the ground. Assigned to the task were 2,600 aircraft of which 760 were Bf-109 single-seat fighters and 220 twin-engine Me-110 fighters. The bomber force was a mix of He-111, Ju-88, and Do-17 medium bombers, and Ju-87 Stuka divebombers. Hermann Göring, the Luftwaffe commander, was overly confident, believing the task would be completed by September 15. On August 1, 1940, he issued a vague order that was shockingly short of detail and tac-

Three Hispano Suiza 20mm guns in a single mount to increase firepower. Just thirty-seven 20mm Hispanos were available during the battle with many assigned to airfield defense. CHRIS GOSS

tical understanding. "From Reichsmarschall Göring to all of Air Fleets 2,3,5. Operation Eagle. Within a short period of time you will wipe the British Air Force from the sky. Heil Hitler." *Adlertag*—"Eagle Day"—was set for August 13, 1940.

Knocking out the British airfields and radar stations proved far more difficult than previously experienced in France. The British now had the advantage of excellent early warning. Fighters were scrambled in time and the AA guns made ready. To achieve their goals the Luftwaffe used three different bombing methods: high-level bombing, dive-bombing, and low-level attacks by twin-engine bombers and Me-110s.

In the ensuing days both RAF sector stations and airfields were attacked by every means possible. The fighter stations of 11 Group were hit thirty times. On August 18th Kenley airfield was subject to a low-level attack by nine Dornier Do-17s of the 9th Staffel of *Kampfgeschwader* 76. This was followed by a high-level attack by roughly fifty Do-17s escorted by Bf-109s. Low-level attacks during the battle of France had proven highly successful for the Luftwaffe. KG 76 specialized in low-altitude attacks, and each aircraft was armed with a 20mm Oerlikon cannon in the nose for strafing.

Flying 60 feet above the English Channel, nine Dorniers flew undetected by British radar. Near Beachy Head the bombers crossed the coast and headed inland. Even though they had avoided radar detection, the Dorniers had not passed unnoticed. Here the Observer Corps proved their worth. Post K3 at Beachy Head reported the raiders' strength and heading. The information was quickly passed up the chain, and as the bombers continued inland, other posts reported their progress. To meet the raiders twelve Hurricanes of No. 111 Squadron were scrambled from Croydon and ordered to patrol over Kenley at 3,000 feet while No. 62 Squadron was scrambled to meet the high threat.

After a forty-minute flight the Dorniers arrived just south of Kenley. Thanks to the efficient plotting by the Observer Corps, Kenley's ground defenses were ready. They met the raiders with a mixed bag of antiaircraft guns—four 40mm Bofors guns, two obsolete 3-inch guns, and about twenty Lewis .303-caliber machine guns. The airfield was not only protected by guns, but by the new Parachute and Cable System (PAC). This unconventional

For low-level protection of airfields, heavy antiaircraft gun sites, and radar stations, the British were forced to rely on the .303-caliber Lewis machine gun. Nearly 86 percent of all the light antiaircraft guns available during the battle of Britain were Lewis guns. The gun would appear in single and two and four-gun mounts. AUTHOR'S COLLECTION

"secret weapon had yet to be tested in action and was introduced to help cover for the shortage of guns. Launched vertically into the path of low-flying enemy aircraft, the PAC consisted of a small rocket trailing a steel cable. The rockets were grouped in batteries of nine and shot vertically 300 to 400 feet into the air. Launched simultaneously they created a web of steel cables across the path of a low-flying aircraft. Reaching the top of its climb, a small parachute opened automatically. When an aircraft struck the cable, the shock of the impact opened a second drag chute attached at the bottom end of the cable. Any aircraft caught by the cable would experience a rapid deceleration, stall, and crash to the ground.

Skimming the treetops the Dorniers found their targets and began their runs. At first surprise seemed complete, but the AA gunners were ready.

Sweeping across the field the guns began firing. As tracers flashed past his bomber, *Unteroffizier* Guenther Unger pushed his aircraft even lower. Seconds later Lewis machine gun rounds ripped into his right engine bringing the engine to a smoking stop. Struggling to hold the Dornier straight, Unger's navigator hit the bomb release button.

Following the lead aircraft was Unteroffizier Schumacher. He watched in fascination as the bombs began to fall. "Hell was let loose. Three hangars collapsed like matchwood. Explosion followed explosion, flames leapt into the sky. It seemed as if my aircraft was grabbed by some giant."

Machine-gun rounds quickly found the range. Smashing into the instrument panel and left engine, Schumacher's bomber began to lose power.

A Dornier Do-17 of KG 76 seen here low over Sussex on its way to bomb Kenley airfield on August 18, 1940. This photo was taken from the cockpit of another Do-17, and the aircraft's shadow can be seen on the ground indicating the aircraft was at an altitude of about 70 feet. CHRIS GOSS

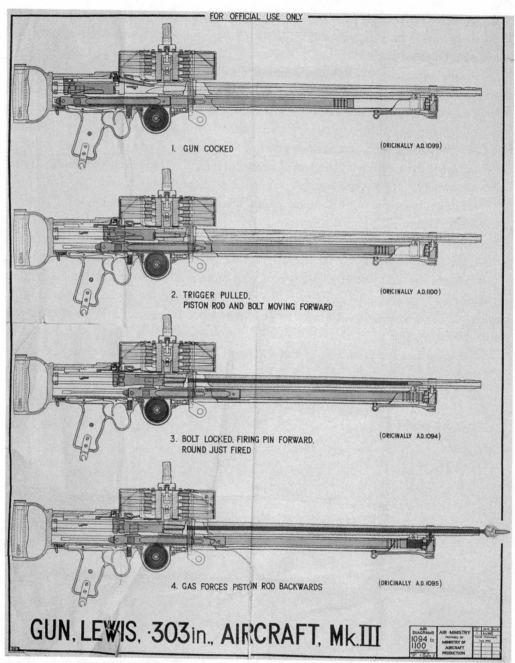

1. GUN COCKED

(ORIGINALLY A.D. 1099)

2. TRIGGER PULLED,
   PISTON ROD AND BOLT MOVING FORWARD

(ORIGINALLY A.D. 1100)

3. BOLT LOCKED, FIRING PIN FORWARD,
   ROUND JUST FIRED

(ORIGINALLY A.D. 1094)

4. GAS FORCES PISTON ROD BACKWARDS

(ORIGINALLY A.D. 1095)

GUN, LEWIS, ·303in., AIRCRAFT, Mk.III

AIR DIAGRAMS 1094 to 1100	AIR MINISTRY PREPARED BY MINISTRY OF AIRCRAFT PRODUCTION

The inner workings of the Lewis light machine gun. Gas operated, the Lewis had a rate of fire between 500 and 600 rounds per minute. Effective range was 700 yards. AUTHOR'S COLLECTION

Another Dornier was also hit with machine-gun fire, killing the pilot. Slumped over the controls, *Oberfeldwebel* Wilhelm frantically leaned over his dead pilot and grabbed the controls, saving the aircraft from crashing into the ground.

With bombs gone the Dorniers made good their escape. Hugging the ground they now faced the line of nine parachute-and-cable launchers. Three Do-17s were perfectly placed. Nine rockets suddenly soared vertically into the air. Surprise was complete. *Feldwebel* Wilhelm Raab, flying one of the Dorniers, had never seen anything like it: "Suddenly red-glowing balls rose up from the ground in front of me. Each one trailed a line of smoke about 1 meter thick behind it, with intervals of 10 to15 meters between each. I had experienced machine-gun and flak fire often enough but this was something entirely new." Here Raab's piloting skill and instincts took over. Needing room to maneuver, Raab jerked the Do-17 from the deck. Dropping the right wing, he aimed his bomber for the gap between two adjacent smoke trails. Suddenly a hefty tug caused his machine to yaw but straighten out. A cable had struck his wing. Fortunately it was close to the tip and never took hold. Speeding past the smoke trails, Raab went even lower as he headed for home.

One Dornier would fall to the cables. Already damaged and on fire, it struck a hanging cable. The combined drag from the two parachutes sent the bomber out of control crashing into the ground just outside the airfield boundary.

Seven Dorniers survived the guns and cables only to be attacked by the Hurricanes of No. 111 Squadron. After repeated attacks the Dorniers made the coast and headed for home. The survivors were in sorry shape. Two Do-17s ditched in the English Channel. Two more crash-landed in France, and two made normal landings but with wounded or dead crewmen. Only one Dornier returned without major damage or a seriously wounded crewman.

Minutes later twenty-seven Dorniers delivered a high-altitude attack delivering twenty 110-pound bombs each. As the smoke cleared, three out of Kenley's four hangars and several other buildings were destroyed. Four Hurricanes and one Blenheim were destroyed on the ground. The airfield was put out of action but only for a short time. Repair teams put out the fires and filled the bomb craters in the grass runway. Within two hours of the bombing, the airfield began limited operations. The next day it was fully operational.

In total the 9th Staffel would suffer nine killed, three wounded, and five taken prisoner. It was a disastrous result. Never again would it operate in the low-level attack role against Britain. But the result should not have been surprising. The Kenley attack was another example of how costly low-level attacks could be. What was even more surprising was how effective Kenley's weak AA defenses were. With just four modern 40mm Bofors and twenty World War I Lewis machine guns, they managed to destroy four Do-17s and damage all the rest.

One of the Do-17s shot down during the ill-fated raid on the Kenley airfield. Without the element of surprise, low-level attacks were extremely vulnerable to light and medium AA fire. It was a lesson that would be repeated throughout the war. CHRIS GOSS

Raids against well-defended targets with ample warning suffered heavy losses. Low-level flak was extremely effective and would be throughout the war. It was a hard lesson to learn and unfortunately both sides would continue the tactic with heavy losses.

August 18th was the gunners' best day during the battle of Britain. Thirty aircraft were destroyed, with a surprising number shot down by Lewis guns at searchlight sites. The Lewis gunners' "hosepipe" fire was deadlier than anyone had anticipated, credited with ten aircraft shot down.

The Luftwaffe's August offensive failed to knock out British radar stations and airfields. But it was close. The pounding the forward airfield and sector stations received was beginning to have the desired effect. One overoptimistic intelligence report had Fighter Command's strength of serviceable fighters at just one hundred. On August 15th Göring, frustrated by the lack of success against the radar stations, ordered the raids to be discontinued "in view of the fact that not one of those attacked has so far been put out of action." Albert Kesselring of Luftflotte 2 favored a massive sustained assault on London. "We have no chance of destroying the English fighters on the ground. We must force their last reserves of Spitfires and Hurricanes into the air." It was a costly mistake. Strategic errors and intelligence failures led to a change in objective. London was now the primary target.

OBSERVATION OF TRACERS

Diagrams showing outline of enemy Long-Range Bomber (viz. Heinkel He, IIIK Mk. Va.), used to attack shipping in the North Sea.

DIAGRAM (A)—PLANE CROSSING GUN'S POSITION

Appearance of TRACERS at or near Target:—

(A) in front;
(B) high;
(C) behind;
(D) low.

Leave no **curve** behind, and their trajectory is seen to be shorter and straighter.

* N.B.—The pronounced **curve** of Tracers **missing** (shown in DIAGRAMS (A) and (B) by red lines), is an optical illusion, caused by the high speed of the Target moving across the Line of Sight.

The effect on the eye may be compared with the continuous streak caused by passing a level row of lights at night, as seen from the window of an express train.

DIAGRAM (B)—PLANE APPROACHING DIAGONALLY

At the beginning of the war, the iron sights on most light machines were of little use. To improve the gunners' aim, soldiers were taught to use tracer fire. Tracer bullets had a pyrotechnic charge located at the base of the projectile. The charge was ignited during firing and could be easily seen. Usually every fifth bullet was a tracer round. This training drawing clearly shows what represents a hit and a near miss when aiming with tracer fire. AUTHOR'S COLLECTION

By August 1940 the capital had forty-eight static 4.5-inch guns, thirty-two static 3.7-inch guns, six mobile 3.7-inch guns, and six antiquated 3-inch guns for a total of ninety-two. That was just one-third of the heavy antiaircraft guns considered adequate for its defense. In September that number would increase to 199.

On the afternoon of September 7th, the Luftwaffe finally turned to London. As the 348 bombers and 317 escort fighters formed up over the Channel, British radar plotted their course, but for the most part they were taken by surprise. Fighter Command controllers had expected the massive formation to split up and head for individual separate targets. Instead it flew straight for London, targeting the East End and the docks. At 1654 batteries across the capital received word, "many hostiles in SE coming in." Minutes later they appeared. It was a towering formation. The bombers (He-111s, Do-17s, Ju-88s) approached in small "vics" of three aircraft, combining into arrowhead formations of ten to fifty machines. Above was the escort—Me-110s and Bf-109s. Starting from 16,000 feet, the whole armada stood more than a mile high.

As the formations approached, the gunners prepared, knowing their 4.5- and 3.7-inch guns were well within range. At 1701 the first victim was claimed by the gunners on the Hackney Marsh. Minutes later a Ju-88 was damaged by the 4.5s at Chadwell Heath. It was a clear fine day, giving the batteries all over east London a chance to fire. One by one they opened up and over the next hour eighteen batteries engaged. At the beginning of the attack, the gunners had a clear field of fire. Most of No. 11 Group's fighters were late in arriving. Expecting the raids to fall on the sector airfields, all squadrons were ordered in position to await the assault.

The raid came in three waves with the last hostile aircraft leaving around six o'clock. The damage was extensive with huge fires blazing at Thameshaven, in the dock areas near Tower Bridge, at the Woolwich Arsenal, and farther down the river among the oil depots and factories. The London and Thames & Medway gunners were credited with nineteen aircraft destroyed for the expenditure of a little over 1,000 rounds of heavy antiaircraft ammunition. These estimates were overly optimistic. The number of bombers damaged and later finished off by fighters is unknown.

The fires started that late afternoon provided an aiming point for London's first heavy night raid. At 2030 a force of 250 bombers reached the capital. AA fire opened up at 2106 as a steady stream of bombers flew over London. The first engagements were visual, but at 2208 permission came from No. 11 Group to activate the Fixed Azimuth (FA) system. The FA system consisted of an array of mobile sound locators positioned out to the east of the capital. These sound locators passed plots to the main London Gun Operations Room. This system produced a predicted path of the raid and future position was deduced and passed to the guns. The box barrage or barrier fire that followed essentially filled a box of sky with a curtain of steel. The object was to force the incoming formation to abandon the attack or disrupt its aim. It was not an accurate system. Sound locators could not distinguish the difference between a hostile bomber or friendly fighter. Only with direct clearance from No. 11 Group could the FA system be used. As the barrage opened up, one raider seemed to fall almost immediately, but after just forty-two shells the barrage was suspended.

The first night attack on London was not AA Command's finest hour. Most of the guns were late into action. Gun-laying radar had proved of little use and the debut of the Fixed Azimuth network was a complete failure.

By mid-September the Luftwaffe began to scale back its large-scale daylight attacks on Britain. Officially known as the "Blitz," the night bombing of British cities would last from September 1940 until May 1941. After the September 7th day and night attacks, 371 guns were rushed to London but for little effect. In the first four night raids, only four aircraft were brought down by gunfire and none by fighters.

Britain's air defense system at the beginning of the war was one of the world's best. Its Achilles' heel, however, was its inability to tackle any raids at night. Most of the pre-war resources went into day-fighters. RAF bombers found navigating at night extremely difficult and assumed German bombers would have the same difficulty. At the beginning of the war, the RAF had no dedicated night-fighters in operation. For the coming Blitz the defense of Britain would rely heavily on the guns of AA Command.

Initially the Luftwaffe night bomber force operated with impunity. Searchlight and gun batteries relied on sound locators to guide them but they were all but useless.

At the beginning of the war, the first gun-laying Mark I (GL I) radars entered service with several AA batteries. In many ways the term *gun-laying* was a misnomer when applied to the GL I. It was more of a gun-assisting radar with limited capabilities. Although it gave accurate ranges, it could not produce good azimuth indications or elevation figures.

On the night of November 14th/15th, one of the most infamous night raids of the period took place. The attack on Coventry by a force of 300 bombers left the city in ruins. Only one Do-17 of KG 3 was shot down by AA fire. In December the AA guns claimed just ten hostiles destroyed. In Colin Dobinson's book *AA Command*, from November 1940 to February 1941, the Luftwaffe "lost more aircraft from accidents over Occupied Europe than from British fire."

Under strong political pressure, AA commander Gen. Frederick Pile henceforth ordered his gunners to fire every possible round using the box barrage method. This was the least effective and most wasteful method of AA fire. The so-called London Barrage

QF 3.7-inch heavy antiaircraft guns firing at night during the Blitz. Critically short of these weapons, the British had to carefully select how many guns each town, city, airfield, and factory would receive. The most numerous were found in and around London and at the Royal Navy base, Scapa Flow.
CHRIS GOSS

chewed up vast amounts of ammunition with little result. What the barrages did provide was a morale boost for those under the bombs. During the month of September, a quarter of a million shells were fired with just twelve enemy bombers shot down.

Improvements were made. The introduction of the "elevation finding" (E/F) attachment to the Mk I gun-laying radar set offered a fair degree of accuracy in both azimuth and elevation. It was an overly sensitive piece of equipment and had to be handled with care. Until the GL Mk II entered service, it was the best thing the gunners had.

During the Blitz London suffered seventy-one major raids. The Luftwaffe's ability to navigate at night did not match the AA Command's capability to shoot them down. Between January and the end of May 1941, AA Command saw improvements but the pace was slow. Six new Ground Controlled Interception (GCI) radars reached operational service. Covering the whole of southern and eastern England, these new sets assisted in laying AA fire and to direct searchlights. Massive efforts were also made in training in the use and care of the new equipment to keep it serviceable. As these improvements flowed through the system, the number of enemy bombers shot down increased. At the beginning of the new year, AA Command held 1,442 heavy guns, 8,148 searchlights, and 245 GL Mk I radars. In March 1941 AA guns were credited with seventeen aircraft hit, followed by 39.5 in April. Between January and May 1941 forty bombers were listed as downed by "cause unknown," with the true causes a combination of AA fire, accidents, and technical failures. Had these results been achieved in September 1940, the Blitz might have been shorter and less destructive.

To supplement the shortage of the 4.5- and 3.7-inch guns, the 3-inch rocket projectile entered service in 1941. Each rocket was 6 feet 4 inches in length. Fin stabilized, these rockets did not rotate in flight and were called "Unrotated Projectiles," UPs for short. Able to engage aircraft at altitudes up to 19,000 feet, the UPs were one-shot weapons. Fired in salvos of 128 rockets in a shotgun pattern, the UPs proved ineffective and were not deployed in large numbers.

Just as the British night-fighter and AA gun defenses began to take a heavy toll on German bombers, Hitler's plan to attack the Soviet Union put an end to their offensive. The bulk of the Luftwaffe bomber force began moving to bases in eastern Germany and Poland. The final raid of the Blitz and the most devastating on London occurred on the night of May 10th/11th when the Luftwaffe flew 541 sorties against London, ending the first large-scale antiaircraft battle of the war. London was hard hit that night with 2,000 fires started and 1,436 people killed, 1,792 badly injured. The AA guns expended 4,510 rounds claiming two bombers shot down. Luftwaffe losses for the night included ten He-111s, one Ju-88, and one Me-110.

From July 1940 until May 1941, AA Command shot down 578 enemy aircraft, with 192 probables and 194 damaged. AA Command's contribution was far greater than just in the numbers of aircraft shot down. During the battle of Britain (July to September 1940), the British estimated that 48 percent of the German bombers turned back because of heavy flak. Even if this estimate is greatly inflated, flak unquestionably had

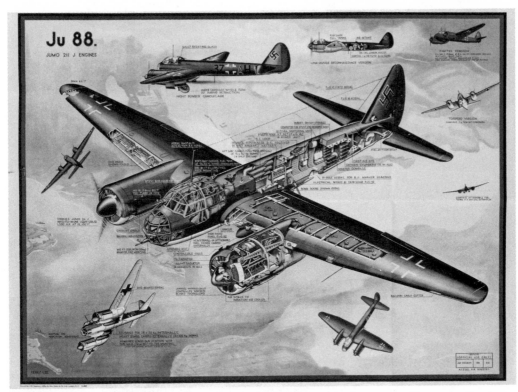

Throughout the battle of Britain and the Blitz, the Ju-88 suffered far fewer casualties per sortie when compared to the He-111 and Do-17. Its good speed, maneuverability, and rugged construction made it the hardest to bring down by either fighters or AA fire. AUTHOR'S COLLECTION

an effect on the Germans' bombing accuracy. Formations were also broken up, causing bombs to be scattered widely. In addition to the effect of flak on accuracy, bombers damaged by flak were often easy prey for fighters. Out of their protective formation, they provided fighter pilots with an easy kill. How many flak-damaged bombers were eventually shot down by fighters is not known.

There were also the hidden effects of flak. Most flak splinters were very small, often capable of causing minor damage to a fuel or oil line. The number of Luftwaffe bombers forced to ditch due to flak damage remains unaccounted for. Serviceability rates for individual bomber units also fell. Flak-damaged aircraft had to be repaired and were unable to participate in the following missions. Flak also killed. German bomber crews suffered accordingly, and when the problem became serious, Göring ordered that only one officer fly per bomber, severely reducing the experience level and efficiency of the crew.

Flak also played a huge role in the psychological reactions of the aircrews forced to face flak on a daily basis. During the battle German pilots regarded the English Channel as the "dirty ditch." It was a morale-sapping psychological syndrome they called *Kanalkrankheit*, or "Channel sickness."

CHAPTER FIVE

Protecting the Fleet

IN SEPTEMBER 1939 THE ROYAL NAVY WAS STILL THE LARGEST IN THE WORLD. THE fleet consisted of fifteen battleships and battle cruisers, seven aircraft carriers, sixty-six cruisers, and 184 destroyers. The HMS *Nelson* and *Rodney* were the only modern battleships in the fleet with the rest consisting of Royal Sovereign and Queen Elizabeth class ships from the First World War. The German Kriegsmarine was in no position to challenge the Royal Navy in any way. With just two modern battleships of the Scharnhorst class and three "pocket" battleships (essentially heavy cruisers) of the Deutschland class, the Kriegsmarine was clearly outnumbered and outgunned. The French navy had seven battleships on strength. Five were older World War I ships with the *Dunkerque* and *Strasbourg* being the most modern, laid down in 1932 and 1934, respectively.

In terms of antiaircraft defenses, both the Rodney and Scharnhorst class battleships represented the best in the world at the time. The HMS *Rodney* was armed with six 4.7-inch heavy AA guns and two eight-barreled 2-pdr pom-pom guns. The *Scharnhorst* in contrast was arguably better equipped with fourteen 105mm guns, sixteen 37mm guns, and ten 20mm cannons.

Its 37mm guns were, however, only semiautomatic with a rate of fire of just thirty rounds per minute. The French Dunkerque class ships were equipped with twelve 130mm dual-purpose guns, five 37mm semiautomatic guns, and eight 13.7mm machine guns. While these ships were heavily armed, it would be the cruisers and destroyers of each nation that would see the majority of action. These smaller ships were even more vulnerable to air attack with fewer guns capable of engaging high-angle divebombing attacks. Most British cruisers and destroyers were equipped with a small numbers of pom-pom guns, Vickers .50-caliber machine guns, and rifle-caliber machine guns. Equivalent German ships would carry a small number of 37mm and 20mm antiaircraft guns. As well equipped as these ships seemed to be, they were not ready for the aerial onslaught they would encounter during the first few years of the war. Each side would suffer heavy losses and each would up gun their ships as the war progressed.

Gunners aboard the German battleship *Gneisenau* man their 105mm/65 AA gun, circa 1938. The *Gneisenau* was armed with fourteen guns in seven twin-gun mountings. Effective range was 19,247 yards. U.S. NAVAL HISTORICAL CENTER

The aerial threat the Royal Navy faced at the beginning of the war was exclusively from land-based bombers. The Germans and Italians did not have any aircraft carriers in service. The range of both Luftwaffe and *Regia Aeronautica* bombers was limited, especially the Ju-87 divebomber when carrying a heavy armor-piercing bomb.

On the eve of war, the "Fighting Instructions" placed the protection of the fleet squarely on shipboard guns. Even though the British had carriers, they didn't have any dedicated fighters. The fighter they did have was the Blackburn Skua: a dual-role fighter/diverbomber. Its performance as a fighter was mediocre at best, and the numbers available on any carrier were limited. Before early warning radar the only alternative was to mount standing patrols, but that was untenable. Using barrage fire from the heavy AA guns, the Royal Navy believed it could disrupt any high-level bombing or low-level torpedo attack. What caught them completely by surprise was the Junkers Ju-87 divebomber, even though they had their own Skua divebomber in service. The number of light and medium guns with high angles of elevation were few and far between. The most effective was the QF 2-pounder (40mm) pom-pom gun with an 80-degree elevation. The gun appeared in single, double, quadruple, and octuple mounts. The octuple mount (eight barrels) could unleash an astounding 920 rounds per minute at an incoming target.

The British pom-pom gun appeared in many variants: single-, twin-, four-, and eight-gun mounts. The Mk VI quad mount was mostly used on destroyers and cruisers. The pom-pom was manufactured in large numbers with 6,691 built in the UK and a further 843 manufactured in Canada. AUTHOR'S COLLECTION

The Kriegsmarine at the beginning of hostilities did not pose any real threat to the might of the British Royal and French navies. Its few surface combatants consisted of just two battleships, two pocket battleships, two heavy cruisers, six light cruisers, and twenty-two destroyers.

During Operation *Weserübung* (the German invasion of Norway in April 1940), the Kriegsmarine committed most of its surface fleet to the task. During the invasion air attacks on ships—both surface combatants and merchantmen—were common. What became abundantly clear was that for any of the antiaircraft defenses to be effective they needed early warning. Without radar all ships depended on human lookouts. Attacks without warning came as a nasty surprise. Early war experience showed the need for constant daylight vigilance, especially at dusk and dawn. It soon became standard procedure to have some part of a ship's AA guns ready to fire on any sector while in the combat zone.

The Kriegsmarine, however, learned this the hard way. On April 8, 1940, the German light cruisers *Konigsberg* and *Koln* and two torpedo boats sailed into Bergen Fjord ready

Two 88mm SK L/45 AA guns on the stern of the light cruiser *Konigsberg* in the 1930s. Each gun was supplied with 400 rounds with a rate of fire of fifteen rounds per minute. U.S. NAVAL HISTORICAL CENTER

to deliver 600 troops from the 69th Infantry division. As they approached their target, the *Konigsberg* was engaged by a Norwegian shore battery that scored three hits. Adrift and unable to maneuver, *Konigsberg* dropped anchor. That night the *Koln* and attendant torpedo boats returned to Germany. The position of the *Konigsberg* was reported to both the Air Ministry and Admiralty. The RAF declared themselves unable to mount an attack. With no carrier in position to fly off a striking force, the mission was almost called off. At the limit of their range (750 miles) and led by Lt. Bill Lucy, sixteen Skuas (five from 800 NAS and eleven of 803 NAS) took off from RNAS Hatston air base in the Orkneys. Each Skua was loaded with a single 500-pound Semi armor-piercing bomb. After a two-plus-hour flight, they caught their prey unawares. Lining up astern the sixteen Skuas began their dives from 8,000 feet.

Surprise was complete. As the first bombs fell, shore-based and AA fire from auxiliary vessels opened up. Armed with twin mounts of 88mm SK C/32 guns and eight 37mm SK C/30 guns, the *Konigsberg* gunners were caught flat-footed. Half of the bombs landed before the gunners returned fire, but by that time it was too late. Three direct hits and two near misses put an end to the *Konigsberg*. Sinking at her moorings, she would make history becoming the first major warship to be sunk by air attack. The Germans would exact some measure of revenge with the attack on the *Scharnhorst* on June 14th. Hit by a torpedo the *Scharnhorst* berthed in Trondheim harbor for emergency repairs. A strike from the HMS *Ark Royal* was hastily laid on. Fully alerted the fifteen Skuas were met by a wall of flak and defending Bf-109 and Me-110 fighters. Eight Skuas were lost for no hits on the *Scharnhorst*.

These two examples graphically illustrated how effective divebombers could be when surprise was complete. It also showed how vulnerable destroyers and cruisers were to aerial attack. During the battle of Norway the Royal Navy lost one cruiser, one destroyer, and one sloop to air attack (the destroyer and sloop were sunk by Ju-87s, the cruiser HMS *Curlew* was sunk by Ju-88s). Both sides would pay heavily with the Royal Navy losing fourteen ships in combat and the Kriegsmarine losing fourteen and eight U-boats.

The lessons learned from the Norway campaign were very clear. Early warning was essential for any effective AA defense. Had the *Konigsberg* gunners been on full alert, the outcome would have been much different.

The Royal Navy also discovered its weapons were relatively ineffective against divebombers. Fortunately the majority of the air attacks were carried out at relatively long range by medium bombers using high-level or glide bombing techniques. British barrage fire was often able to drive off an attack or severely disrupt their aim. The air attack on the *Scharnhorst* clearly showed that a capital ship protected by a mix of fighters and effective AA fire was practically invulnerable.

The British and German experience in Norway clearly showed the need for more and better AA guns for their ships. Moving forward ships were refitted with more guns, but progress was slow. After Norway and Dunkirk the Royal Navy destroyers were given a 3-inch or 4-inch gun in place of the mid-ship torpedo tubes. It was a poor choice and one they would pay dearly for off Crete in 1941.

The sinking of the German battleship *Bismarck* on May 27, 1941, was a great blow to the Kriegsmarine and clearly marked the ascendance of the aircraft carrier over the battleship. It was also a clear vindication of prewar Royal Navy doctrine. When war broke out in 1939, the Royal Navy's fleet structure had been designed mainly to fight the Japanese, not Germany. Fear of Japanese expansion drove British naval aircraft procurement to concentrate on the problems of a decisive fleet battle. During the interwar period the Royal Navy assumed that its aircraft could not sink the enemy's capital ships outright; the best they could do was slow them down and leave it to the battleships to finish them off.

Without the intervention of airpower from both shore-based aircraft and torpedo bombers from the carriers HMS *Victorious* and HMS *Ark Royal*, the mighty German battleship would most likely have escaped destruction. The *Bismarck* was one of the world's most powerful and modern battleships afloat. Its antiaircraft defenses were formidable with sixteen 105mm SK C/33 heavy guns, sixteen 37mm SK C/30 medium guns, ten 20mm MG C/30 single-mount guns, and eight 20mm quad Flak C/38 guns. The 105mm gun fired a fixed-type shell, with a 27.35kg explosive charge. The 105s mounting was

The starboard 105mm/65 AA mounting on the German pocket battleship *Admiral Scheer*. This mount was the primary heavy AA mount for all of the Kriegsmarine's heavy cruisers and battleships. A reasonably good weapon, it had a rather slow training and elevation rate. U.S. NAVAL HISTORICAL CENTER

stabilized to enhance its shooting performance and was electrically trained and elevated. In case of an electrical failure, a hand-operated training and elevating system would be utilized. A fuse-setting device was located on either side of the gun mounting. Total rounds carried numbered 6,800. For close range protection the *Bismarck* depended on the 37mm gun. Like the 105mm guns these guns were single-shot weapons with a rate of fire of just thirty rounds per minute. The round fired was high explosive with a contact fuse and weighed 0.748kg. The *Bismarck*'s magazines held 32,000 rounds. The 20mm guns were among the most widely used German antiaircraft weapons of the war and were recoil operated, air cooled, and fully automatic. On *Bismarck* the single mounts used a 75-round saddle drum, giving each gun a rate of fire of 280–300 rounds per minute. The Flak 38 four-gun mounts used a magazine of either twenty to forty rounds. Delays in reloading meant the quad mounts had a similar rate of fire to the drum-fed single mounts. *Bismarck* carried approximately 36,000 rounds of 20mm. The *Bismarck*'s antiaircraft batteries were controlled by a sophisticated fire-control system. Simple in concept, the fire-control process was highly complex in execution. Once a target was identified, high-angle range finders in the armored cupolas on either side of the forward superstructure were used to gather information on the incoming aircrafts' course, bearing, speed, range, and height. The data gathered would then be relayed to the antiaircraft gunnery officer in one of two flak plotting rooms. The plotting teams would then perform the calculations needed to set up a flak-barrage (*Zonenfeuer*) or direct controlled fire (*Geleitsschiessen*). This information was then fed to the heavy and medium guns.

The *Bismarck* photographed from the heavy cruiser *Prinz Eugen*, May 21, 1941. To the left in the foreground can be seen one of its six twin-gun 37mm/L83 AA guns. Manually loaded, the L83 was a semiautomatic weapon with a rate of fire of just thirty rounds per minute. U.S. NAVAL HISTORICAL CENTER

The *Bismarck* was also heavily armored and well protected against torpedo and naval gunfire. Pitted against this formidable defense was the Fleet Air Arm's Fairey Swordfish torpedo bomber. A large fabric-covered biplane, the Swordfish was a slow but capable torpedo bomber. Often described as obsolete, archaic, or an anachronism to another time, the Swordfish would prove itself to be one of the most successful carrier aircraft of the war.

The pursuit and final sinking of the *Bismarck* would last from May 22nd until May 27th. In that time she would sink the battle cruiser HMS *Hood*, but suffer three hits from the battleship HMS *Prince of Wales* during the battle of the Denmark Straits. On May 24th shortly after the encounter with the *Hood* and *Prince of Wales*, the *Bismarck* would suffer its first aerial attack. At 2300 hours on May 24th, nine Swordfish from No. 825 Squadron took off from the HMS *Victorious* in appalling conditions. After about an hour of flight, the lead Swordfish picked up the *Bismarck* on its AVS Mk II radar. Just after 2330 the attack went in. The *Bismarck* gunners threw everything they had at the incoming attacks. First to open up were the 105mm guns, followed by the bark of the medium 37mm guns and 20mm light flak. The great 15-inch guns as well as the 6-inch secondary guns also added to the chorus. Firing at their lowest possible elevation (-8 degrees), the big guns fired round after round into the sea ahead of the approaching aircraft. As the huge shells splashed into the sea, huge columns of spray rose in front of the incoming aircraft. It was an awesome display, but not enough. As smoke from the guns poured across the battleship's decks and superstructure, *Bismarck* began to turn sharply to avoid the incoming torpedoes. One found its mark hitting on the starboard side, killing one crewman and injuring six more. All nine of the Swordfish managed to land on *Victorious* in the dark, a remarkable achievement.

The second aerial attack occurred on May 26th when fifteen Swordfish of the 810th, 818th, and 820th Squadrons from HMS *Ark Royal* found the *Bismarck*. The attack began at 2045. Once again the *Bismarck* responded with a wall of flak. All fifteen Swordfish managed to launch their torpedoes and return to the *Ark Royal*, but three would crash-land and be pushed overboard as complete wrecks. Many had been hit by flak, but two torpedoes found their mark. One torpedo hit the port side amidship while the other hit in the starboard quarter disabling the *Bismarck*'s steering mechanism, jamming the rudders. It was a mortal hit. At 2140 *Bismarck* reported to the Supreme Command of the Navy (O.K.M.) Group West: "Ship unable to maneuver. We will fight to the last shell. Long live the Fuhrer."

Prewar Royal Navy doctrine had worked perfectly. Slowed by carrier-borne bombers, the *Bismarck* now limped through the waves waiting her fate. On May 27th at 0847, the battleships HMS *Prince of Wales* and *Rodney* opened fire. At 1037 the *Bismarck* succumbed to her wounds and sank.

The two aerial attacks on *Bismarck* were truly historic. For the first time carrier-launched torpedo bombers scored hits on a battleship on the open ocean. For all its

A Fairey Swordfish drops a torpedo during a practice run. The *Bismarck* was hit by three Mk XII aerial torpedoes, which had a speed of 40 knots for 1,500 yards with a warhead of 388 pounds of TNT. U.S. NAVAL HISTORICAL CENTER

defenses and maneuvering, *Bismarck* was unable to avoid being hit. Why? Few of the British pilots on the first attack had ever delivered a torpedo attack, let alone flown into a wall of flak (crews on the May 26th attack were more experienced). The Swordfish also had to launch its torpedo at 90 knots, barely 60 feet above the water making what would seem to be an easy target. Unfortunately for the *Bismarck's* gunners, their inability to shoot down any of the attackers came down to a number of unforgiving factors. Rolling seas and wind caused the ship to pitch and roll, throwing off the gunners' aim. The time of the first attack at close to midnight greatly reduced visibility and the ability of the gunners to track a target accurately. The *Bismarck's* zigzagging only exacerbated the situation, frustrating the gunners even more, and the Swordfish were flying at such low speeds that the *Bismarck's* advanced fire-control system had difficulty tracking them accurately.

In the end the *Bismarck's* formidable antiaircraft defenses alone were unable to keep it safe from aerial attack. The belief, held by most navies, including Adm. Tom Phillips of the Royal Navy and commander of the ill-fated Force Z (battleship HMS *Prince of Wales* and battlecruiser *Repulse*), "that properly-handled capital ships can defend themselves" had been proven false. It was a lesson the British and Americans would learn for themselves in the coming months.

On December 10, 1941, just three days after the Japanese attack on Pearl Harbor, the modern battleship HMS *Prince of Wales*, and the World War I battle cruiser HMS *Repulse* in company with four destroyers, set sail from Singapore, designated as Force Z. Their assignment was to challenge the Japanese invasion fleet off Malaya. At the time *Prince of Wales* had the best available antiaircraft battery with the best available radar and fire-control technology (sixteen QF 5.25-inch heavy guns, four Mk VIII pom-pom mounts with thirty-two barrels, one 40mm Bofors gun, and a number of 20mm Oerlikon and Lewis machine guns). The HMS *Repulse* in comparison was lightly armed with just six 4-inch antiaircraft guns, two eight-barreled Mk VIII pom-pom guns, sixteen .50-caliber Vickers machine guns in four quad gun mounts, and eight 20mm Oerlikon guns.

Unlike the two separate torpedo attacks on *Bismarck* (nine and fifteen Swordfish), Force Z would face an overwhelming force of eighty-eight land-based Japanese twin-engine bombers (Mitsubishi G3M "Nells" and G4M "Bettys"). The crews were also highly trained and determined. The Japanese used a mixed formation of twenty-seven level bombers and sixty-one torpedo bombers. The torpedo bombers were armed with a mix of the Type 91 Model 1 torpedo with a 330-pound warhead and the Model 2 with a warhead weighing 450 pounds. The level bombers carried a single 1,100-pound or two 550-pound bombs.

At 1113 the attack began. As the Japanese bomber formations came into range, the *Prince of Wales* opened fire at 12,000 yards with her 5.25-inch guns. *Repulse* responded with her older and less numerous 4-inch guns at 10,000 yards. Eight high-level bombers flew almost directly over *Prince of Wales* dropping their bombs as they went. Their target, however, was the *Repulse*, which suffered one hit. No serious damage was caused and her

The British battleship HMS *Nelson* passing through the Panama Canal, circa 1930. Two of its six QF 4.7-inch Mk VIII AA guns can be clearly seen. The 4.7-inch gun was similar in performance to the 4-inch long-range AA guns of the HMS *Repulse*. U.S. NAVAL HISTORICAL CENTER

speed was unaffected. The 5.25-inch guns of *Prince of Wales* had fired 108 rounds and the 4-inch guns of *Repulse* thirty-six. None of the attackers were shot down, but no less than five of the eight G3Ms had been hit, two seriously causing them to leave the scene.

At 1140 seventeen G3Ms approached the two ships with eight attacking *Repulse* and nine heading for *Prince of Wales*. Flying steadily toward *Prince of Wales*, the Japanese aircraft presented a good no-deflection target. All eight 5.25-inch guns eventually opened fire, joined by the single 40mm Bofors.

Shortly after, the four sets of eight-barreled pom-poms opened up, followed by the Oerlikons and machine guns. The Japanese released their torpedoes at distances varying between 1,640 yards and 656 yards. After unleashing twelve salvos, the 5.25-inch guns switched from controlled fire to "barrage fire." Shells were fired to explode in a wall directly ahead of the incoming bombers to try to make them drop their torpedoes early. It did not work. Ordinary Seaman W. E. England, acting as a lookout for one of the Lewis guns, had a front row seat: "The planes came on remorselessly as all the pom-poms, machine guns and the Bofors gun opened up. All hell seemed to be let loose at once but

The eight-barreled QF 2-pdr Mk VIII pom-pom gun. A beast of a weapon, the Mk VIII was capable of spewing 920 rounds per minute (115 rpm per barrel). Effective range was 1,200 yards. AUTHOR'S COLLECTION

nothing seemed to stop them and, as they passed over the masts, I could see the faces and goggles of the Japanese pilots looking down at us."

The flak was not enough. While one Nell had been shot down and three damaged, one torpedo found its mark. Like the *Bismarck* the *Prince of Wales* had been hit in one of its most vulnerable places, the outer port propeller shaft. Moments later the ship lost much of its speed, all electrical power failed, and the ship began to list. The loss of electric power was catastrophic. The 5.25-inch guns and pom-pom mounts were now all but useless. Defense of the mighty ship now rested with a single 40mm Bofors, the 20mm Oerlikons, and Lewis machine guns.

The Japanese now turned their attention to *Repulse*. The ship put up a spirited defense but no one had ever claimed *Repulse* was well equipped with antiaircraft guns. Lt. Sadao Takai in the lead formation recalled flying through the flak: "The air was filled with white smoke, bursting shells, and the tracers of anti-aircraft guns and machine guns. As if pushed down by the fierce barrage thrown up by the enemy, I descended to just above the water's surface."

This first attack lasted twenty-three minutes. Twenty-five torpedo bombers and eight high-level bombers managed to achieve two torpedo hits on *Prince of Wales* and one bomb hit on *Repulse* for the loss of one aircraft, two seriously damaged, and ten slightly. *Repulse* managed to dodge fifteen torpedoes. Repair parties managed to restore some power to *Prince of Wales*, but most of its 5.25-inch gun turrets were out of action. The pom-poms mostly remained in action, although each mount was plagued by stoppages due to faulty ammunition belts. Twenty minutes later the Japanese returned.

At 1220 hours a large formation of Japanese bombers was spotted to the east. Twenty-six Mitsubishi G4Ms all carrying the heavier Model 2 torpedo raced toward the British ships, splitting into two groups. *Prince of Wales*, unable to maneuver, stood by ready to fire, but only four 5.25s engaged for no effect. The pom-poms that had power fired back but soon jammed due to the old ammunition faults. Six Japanese bombers dropped their torpedoes. In a matter of seconds, *Prince of Wales* was hit by four torpedoes. The remaining twenty G4Ms now turned their attention to *Repulse*.

Still fully effective *Repulse* began maneuvering and turned into the attack. All her guns fired at the attackers, but after avoiding at least sixteen torpedoes, one finally found its mark. The damage was not serious and *Repulse* continued on, but luck and skill were running out. *Repulse* gunners managed to shoot down two of the G4Ms, but three torpedoes slammed into the ship. One more hit followed sealing the ship's fate. *Repulse* sank at 1233. *Prince of Wales* would linger, finally capsizing at 1320.

The Japanese victory was unprecedented. For the loss of just two aircraft and three seriously damaged, they scored nine torpedo hits—four on *Prince of Wales* and five on *Repulse*. For the first time in aviation history, torpedo bombers alone had destroyed capital ships in full combat maneuver at sea.

This photograph was taken from a Japanese aircraft during the opening attack on Force Z. A salvo of bombs has just exploded around *Repulse*. The dark smoke indicates a direct hit. The wake of HMS *Prince of Wales* (top) indicates a rapid course change ordered by Admiral Phillips. U.S. NAVAL HISTORICAL CENTER

The British had suffered a humiliating defeat. The previous sinking of the *Konigsberg* by divebombers in 1940, and the crippling of the mighty *Bismarck* by a single torpedo in May 1941, had clearly demonstrated how vulnerable surface ships were to air attack. More telling was the damage inflicted on the German pocket battleship *Lutzow* in June 1941 by land-based Coastal Command Beaufort torpedo bombers. Hit by a single torpedo, the *Lutzow* was put in dry dock for seven months. It was a lesson the British admiralty clearly ignored. Incredibly, many of the surviving British officers were astonished when the Japanese carried out their first torpedo attack using land-based aircraft.

In terms of antiaircraft defenses *Prince of Wales* was considered well armed, but in the end its guns did not create the desired effect. First and foremost the gunners' job was to make the attacking pilot drop his bomb or torpedo from a greater range or height than desired, throwing off their aim. Shooting an aircraft down was a bonus. While *Prince of Wales*'s 5.25-inch guns did a commendable job, they were robbed of electrical power early due to the first torpedo hit and subsequent listing of the ship. The pom-pom guns also suffered from the loss of electrical power, and when they did work, jams were constant due to faulty ammunition. The single 40mm Bofors gun and 20mm Oerlikons, being manually operated, remained in action throughout the battle. Incredibly, the pom-poms did not fire tracer ammunition. The Post Action Statement by the gunnery officer of HMS *Prince of Wales* stated, "The tracer fire from the Bofors gun and Oerlikons was definitely seen to make some attacking aircraft jink. The pom poms, although they were seen to hit the enemy, did not frighten him during his approach due to lack of tracer."

It was now clear that the only real defense against air attack required constant fighter cover from both shore-based or carrier-borne fighters *and* more antiaircraft guns like the dependable and hard-hitting 40mm Bofors gun. This equation also applied to the more vulnerable aircraft carrier. Every ship at sea was now vulnerable to air attack. Moving forward the Royal Navy added more and more antiaircraft guns to all their surface vessels.

The expensive battleship with a crew of 1,500 men was now obsolete. Cheap mass-produced aircraft, especially carrier-borne aircraft, could now deliver a load of high explosives more accurately, at a greater range than the big gun battleship. Moving forward the remaining battleships would serve in a secondary role as bombardment ships and anti-aircraft gun platforms. More and more AA guns would be added until ships like the 1944 USS *Missouri* would bristle with twenty 5-inch/38 caliber guns, eighty 40mm Bofors, and forty-nine 20mm Oerlikons.

CHAPTER SIX

Flak over Germany—Defense in Depth

You see the flashes of the guns on the ground and then you sweat the flak burst out, wondering where in hell they're going to crack. You see the ships ahead of you going through the flak barrage and know that you have to go through the same thing.
—B-26 BOMBARDIER LT. RALPH G. MCCONNELL

FLAK, always a major cause of loss and damage, has steadily increased in relative importance to become the greatest single combat hazard in present-day operations. For instance, in June, July and August 1944, data based on interrogation of returning crew members of lost bombers, as well as from crew members who returned safely to base, indicate that many more bombers were lost to flak than to fighters. In the same period, flak damaged 12,687 of our bombers and only 182 were damaged by fighters.
—AN EVALUATION OF DEFENSIVE MEASURES TAKEN TO
PROTECT HEAVY BOMBERS FROM LOSS AND DAMAGE.
OPERATIONAL ANALYSIS SECTION, NOVEMBER 1944

THE AIR BATTLE THAT RAGED OVER GERMAN SKIES DURING WORLD WAR II HAS OFTEN focused on the rise of the fighter and ascendency of the strategic bomber. But what has frequently been missed by historians on all sides was the impact of German antiaircraft defenses (flak). Often dismissed as ineffective and a waste of valuable material and personnel, the German Flak arm in fact made a major contribution to the defense of Germany. The numbers are sobering.

At least half of the American aircraft shot down over Germany met their fate due to flak (5,380 lost to flak, 4,274 by fighters, a further 2,033 were lost due to other causes), and according to the RAF Official History, it was estimated that German flak accounted for 1,229 out of 3,302 of Bomber Command's missing aircraft between July 1942 and April 1945. The numbers speak for themselves, but they also hide other important facts. Antiaircraft fire had two roles to play. One was to shoot down enemy aircraft, and the other, more important one, was to force bombers to drop their bombs sooner or from a higher altitude, thus reducing bombing accuracy. Flak also damaged aircraft causing them to slow down and lose altitude, making them easy pickings for German fighters. Flak damaged thousands of aircraft that required repair and proved deadly, killing and wounding thousands of aircrew.

> Ahead of us a lone B-17 was limping along. A flight of three Messerschmitts were harassing it, darting in and out but not attacking it. Finally all three swooped in and fired for a long time at the bomber. And those three small planes kept attacking that plane receiving no damage to themselves till finally the B-17 caught fire. It was with a hapless feeling that we saw our last ally turn over, spin slightly and then burst into a huge fire ball. —Lt. Harry Crosby, 100th BG, *Wing and a Prayer*

German ground-based defenses played a major role in the defense of Hitler's Reich. By April 1944 the Luftwaffe had 6,387 heavy, 9,333 light flak guns and 5,360 searchlights defending the airspace over Germany. Day after day and night after night, Allied aircrews

A B-17G of the 381st BG runs through an accurate flak barrage. A flak burst in the foreground comes extremely close to the B-17 taking the photograph. NARA

had to fly into this jagged curtain of steel. It was also what they feared the most. Enemy fighters they could shoot back at. There was a sense of control, a way to hit back. Flak on the other hand arrived unannounced, cold, deadly, and indifferent. You had to sit and take it unsure if you would be next.

> All the missions scared me to death. Whether you had fighters or not, you still had to fly through the flak. Flak was what really got you thinking, but I found a way to suck it up and go. —WILLIAM J. HOWARD, B-17 WAIST GUNNER, 351ST SQ, 100TH BG

> We worried more about flak than fighters. When you're flying around 10,000 feet, you're a pretty good target for flak. One time we were hit by flak that took the top off the pilot's Perspex. The wind then howled through the aircraft. The wind was so strong it managed to lift off a large chunk of the bomb-bay door opening, sending it flying through the fuselage and hitting me in the back of the head. —JOE QUELLETE, B-25 WIRELESS AIR GUNNER, 226TH SQ, 2ND TACTICAL AIR FORCE RAF

The air war and flak battle over Germany from 1939 to 1945 was arguably the second longest battle of World War II after the battle of the Atlantic. It was also one of the most costly, for both sides. Long before Allied forces set foot back on continental Europe, Allied commanders liked to portray the bombing campaign as a "second front," one that drew thousands of German troops away from other vital battles. Many historians like to believe that if the over 500,00 flak troops had been available for the defense of Normandy on D-Day, the outcome would have been far different. That may have been true if the 500,000 flak troops were combat-ready men. A closer look at the numbers reveals a different story. At the beginning of 1940 there were 528,000 men serving in flak forces alone and by November 1944 that number had increased to just 573,000 personnel. Of that number auxiliaries constituted from one-third to one-half of all persons manning the guns. At the beginning of 1944 most able-bodied flak personnel had already been transferred to other fronts. From Edward B. Westermann's excellent book, *Flak: German Anti-Aircraft Defenses, 1914–1945*, by April 1945 "fully 44 percent of those serving with the flak arm were either civilians or auxiliaries, including factory workers, prisoners of war, women, foreign nationals and high school students. Furthermore, of the regular service personnel serving with flak, 21 percent were between the ages of thirty-nine and forty-eight, and a further 35 percent were older than forty-eight or medically unfit for combat."

On the Allied ledger the cost of the strategic campaign also robbed the other services of men and resources that arguably could have been used more effectively elsewhere. Allied air forces consumed 40 percent of the armed forces direct military budget. Operationally, air combat required an incredible amount of resources to keep aircraft flying.

According to the AAF The Official Guide to the Army Air Force produced shortly after the war, "If you were to take 150 bombers and 75 escort fighters and put them through a hypothetical daylight bombing mission, the numbers would look something like this: Assume 10 aircraft shot down over enemy territory, 6 force landed at alternate airfields, 25 extensively damaged, 50 moderately damaged, 25 with minor damage (all mostly due to flak), and 109 unscathed. The six forced landings would require 7,200 man hours for maintenance; the 25 extensively damaged would average 450 man hours apiece, totaling 11,250 man hours; the 50 moderately damaged, at an average of 300 man hours, would total 3,750. The total maintenance required for repairs alone (not service) would be 37,200 man hours, or a 48-hour work week for 775 men." By the end of the war the U.S. Eighth Air Force alone would employ 670,000 maintenance personnel.

The strategic bombing of Germany during World War II was not as effective as the prewar airpower proponents had hoped. The reasons were many, but Germany's extensive flak defense was one of the major factors. Weather and the limits of the available Allied bomb-aiming technology also contributed to the ineffectiveness of high-altitude bombing. Unfortunately for the USAAF the weather over Germany often meant targets were covered in clouds, which meant "precision bombing" was out of the question. To compensate the USAAF adopted British area-bombing techniques using H2X ground mapping radar and radio signal navigation aides like *GEE* and *OBOE*. Air Force Operational Research Section reported that "in the last quarter of 1944 some 80 percent of all 8th Air Force missions used blinding-bombing devices, and more than half were judged by the operational analysts to be total or near total failures." For many Allied air commanders it was an article of faith that aerial bombing would transform the nature of the war and lead to an early victory.

As the tempo of bombing increased, German industrial output expanded. Factories were dispersed, camouflaged—some moving underground making them harder to find and destroy. The production of thousands of V-1 and V-2 missiles along with the Messerschmitt Me-262 and Arado Ar-234 jet bombers in 1944 and 1945 is testament to Germany's industrial resiliency. Indeed, the Heinkel aircraft company was able to produce the Heinkel He-162 jet fighter in just a matter of months. As the rest of Germany was crumbling to the ground, a full *Jagdgeschwader* (fighter wing) of He-162, became operational in February 1945! What really hurt Germany was the battle of attrition and its inability to prioritize armament production. The V-1 and V-2 had no impact on the battlefield and were a complete waste of resources. Fighting on three fronts (by June 1944) and the insatiable need for men and equipment for the Russian front robbed Germany of its most valuable commodities—men, space, and time.

When war broke out in 1939, only the Royal Air Force had anything close to what could be called a strategic air force. Equipped with twin-engine Vickers Wellington, Armstrong Whitworth Whitley, Bristol Blenheim, Handley Page Hampden, and single-

By the autumn of 1944 it was estimated a quarter of Eighth Air Force bombers would sustain some flak damage and for every thirteen aircraft damaged one would be lost. The Eighth Air Force would suffer an astounding 54,539 bombers damaged by flak between December 1942 and April 1945. This 508th BS (298004) B-17 was one such aircraft. On September 27, 1944, it was hit by a single 88mm round over Cologne. Severely damaged, it would never fly again, but was never counted as a loss. NATIONAL MUSEUM OF THE USAF

engine Fairey Battles, RAF Bomber Command had twenty-three operational squadrons with just 280 aircraft. This modest force soon began daylight operation against targets in Germany. Warships and airfields were early targets, but the bomber proved extremely vulnerable to fighters and flak with heavy losses. In the opening months of the war, the RAF also flew night missions, but the weapon of choice was the propaganda leaflet.

At the beginning of the war, the Luftwaffe's Flak arm included 657 heavy flak gun batteries, 560 light gun batteries, and 188 searchlight batteries. Early British incursions into German airspace were limited and ineffective. After suffering heavy losses in daylight raids, the RAF switched to night bombing. By the summer of 1940 the RAF realized that German night defenses, both in the air and from the ground, were rudimentary and the greatest threat to RAF bombers was the weather. The reason for the flak's ineffectiveness was simply technical. The sound detectors used by the Luftwaffe were extremely limited in what they could do. Weather conditions adversely affected their performance, and it was very difficult to distinguish between German fighters and British bombers flying at night. As British night raids increased, the Germans rushed into service experimental gun-laying radar. On July 18, 1940, Göring listed gun-laying radar as the highest production priority.

At the start of the war, German forces had only eight Freya radar stations in operation along the northern coast of Germany. The Freya was capable of identifying approaching aircraft at a distance of up to 120 kilometers (74.5 miles), but it did not provide the altitude of the incoming target, a value required for antiaircraft gun operations. During operational tests in the summer of 1940, the Luftwaffe tested two new gun-laying radars: the Lorenz FuMG 40L radar and Telefunken's Wurzburg system. The Lorenz system proved more accurate, while the Wurzburg had double the range. The Air Reporting Service, however, had already placed orders for the Wurzburg system despite its underwhelming accuracy. Telefunken won the contract due mainly to its availability over the Lorenz unit. By the summer of 1941, the Wurzburg radar was the Luftwaffe's standard gun-laying radar. After a series of modifications, accuracy was increased making it effective for aircraft targeting. By December the Wurzburg FuMG 39(T) entered service and remained the standard flak-control radar till the end of the war.

Hitler's personal interest in and involvement with the air defense of the Reich prior to and during the entire war greatly enhanced its effectiveness. In July 1940 he ordered 88mm ammunition production increased to one million shells a month and ordered all captured guns to be used as soon as possible. In response to increased RAF bombing raids, he ordered an additional increase in the size of the flak forces. It should also be remembered that the flak defenses of Germany were both for military and political reasons. Hitler was keenly aware of the public's psychological need to see and hear German flak guns fighting back against the Allied aerial onslaught. The Luftwaffe had to defend the Reich's industrial sectors and urban centers, and that required sizable ground forces and thousands of guns.

At the very beginning of the war, the Germans were already producing some of the most effective antiaircraft guns used in the conflict. The most infamous was the 88mm Flak 18-41. Much has been written about this weapon, much of it nonsense. The 88's performance was comparable to the British 3.7-inch and American 90mm antiaircraft guns. Next in line was the 105mm Flak 38/39 gun. Resembling a scaled-up version of the 88mm gun, the 105 was heavier and a more complex weapon to manufacture. Its performance was only slightly better than the 88. The most effective heavy antiaircraft gun of the war was the massive 128mm Flak 40. In 1944 the 128mm averaged 3,000 rounds per aircraft shot down. (The Germans used this metric to determine the effectiveness of their flak weapons.) This was half as many as the 105 and less than one-fifth

The most numerous heavy Luftwaffe flak gun was the legendary 88mm. The crew is ready to fire its gun at an incoming raid. The gun pit is typical with ammunition racks built into the wall pits. The white bands on the barrel denote eleven planes shot down. NARA

of the older 88 models. When it came to light flak guns, the Germans also excelled. The 20mm Flak 38 was a superb light antiaircraft gun and was employed as a single mount or in the quad (four-barrel) configuration. Motorized versions proved the most effective and were a constant threat to Allied fighter-bombers (between June 1944 and May 1945, Typhoon losses in the 2nd Tactical Air Force amounted to 570 aircraft due to flak). When the 37mm Flak 18/36/37/43 first entered service in 1935, it was regarded as a medium-caliber antiaircraft weapon. Similar to the Swedish 40mm Bofors gun in performance, the 37mm was used extensively by the German army, navy, and air force units. The 37mm Flak 18 was followed by improved models including the 36/37 and twin-barreled 43. The Germans also made wide use of captured Allied guns and equipment. Between 1939 and 1944, the Luftwaffe utilized an amazing 9,504 flak guns and fourteen million rounds of ammunition.

The basic combat formation for heavy flak at the beginning of the war was the gun battery with four guns (*Batterie*). Each battery was equipped with a single *Kommandogerat* 40 gun director. This optical range finder/ballistic computer provided the batteries' guns with precise firing solutions. As the war progressed, German flak batteries came to depend on fire-control radars with two per battery.

Before war broke out in Europe, the Germans had put a greater emphasis on anti-aircraft gun defenses than the Allies. By 1938 the Luftwaffe's gun, searchlight, barrage balloon, and fighter defenses were arguably the best in the world.

In 1937 Maj. Gen. Gunther Rudel released a report, entitled "Development Program for the Flak Artillery, 1937." He listed several "special factors" critical to the effective development of Germany's air defense system. Rudel was one of the few Luftwaffe leaders who piled close attention to the need for future improvements in aircraft performance. First, he called for weapons capable of hurling shells up to 39,000 feet at an aircraft traveling at 375 mph. Second, he knew a method had to be found to engage aircraft flying on instruments (flying at night, in clouds). He also recognized that protective armor would increase, making it more difficult to shoot down a contemporary aircraft. The Germans also kept close tabs on both British and American aviation developments prior to the war. The Reich Air Defense League followed the development of the Boeing B-17 with great interest, featuring the YB-17B prototype on the cover of its November 1937 issue of *The Siren*. Rudel's forecasts about aircraft performance and flak defense requirements proved prescient, and unfortunately for Allied aircrew his work would be their nightmare.

In 1939 the Air Defense Zone was created in order to defend the Ruhr from bomber attack. Built along Germany's western border, the West Wall was created to mount an aerial barrier into which waves of British and French bombers would be savaged by both flak and swarms of fighters. It was one of the very first attempts to create an integrated air defense network using ground-based defenses working in conjunction with a force of fighter interceptors. By the fall of 1939, 197 sites for heavy flak guns and

As the war progressed, the number of guns in each flak battery increased. This photograph shows part of a twelve-gun 105mm gun battery. The basic six-gun battery is in the middle, with a second ring of gun pits radiating farther away from the center. The outer gun pits are empty. NARA

forty-eight sites for light guns were complete. This allowed for 788 88mm or 105mm guns and 576 20mm or 37mm guns. The Air Defense Zone consisted of two lines with the first consisting of 20mm and 37mm light guns and the second equipped with 88mm and 105mm guns. It was against this system that both RAF and American bomber units would suffer heavy losses.

At the beginning of 1941, RAF Bomber Command was growing in numbers and experience. In February it was able to launch 265 aircraft in a single raid, 56 more than it achieved in September 1940. While the British were increasing their force, the

FLAK IN WORLD WAR II

Germans were reacting as well. Gun-laying radar was steadily equipping flak batteries and providing gunners with the eyes to see at night. Before the introduction of radar, the Flak arm was forced to use "barrier fire" (*Sperrfeuerbatterien*), which while effective in reducing bombing accuracy, resulted in the expenditure of large quantities of ammunition. In the first four months of 1941, the Flak arm was credited with 115 of the 144 enemy aircraft shot down. In fact the British realized that German light flak was far more effective than they had earlier thought. Bomber Command's antiaircraft liaison officer suggested flights between 9,000 and 10,000 feet would be the safest, but Air Comm. J. W. Baker reported that German light flak appeared to be effective up to 16,000 feet, the maximum ceiling for early models of the 37mm Flak 18.

By midsummer of 1941 the frequency and intensity of RAF night attacks began to increase substantially. The British Air Staff and RAF Bomber Command argued for more aircraft to "raise the intensity of our bomber offensive . . . to an intolerable pitch." While calling for more aircraft, RAF also realized just how poorly their efforts were going. Hitting a factory at night was next to impossible. In August 1941 D. M. Butt issued a devastating report. Of some one hundred RAF bombing raids between June 2nd and July 25th, no more than one aircraft in five dropped their bombs within 5 miles of the target! It was a poor trade-off. Unable to hurt the Germans in any substantial way, the RAF lost 181 aircraft in March, and by June that number grew to 541. These results would cement the RAF's area-bombing strategy of "dislocating the German transportation system and destroying the morale of the civilian population as a whole and of the industrial workers in particular." In other words German cities were now the target. The poor accuracy of RAF bombing was the result of several factors. They lacked navigational aides to locate targets at night, and as German fighter and flak defenses increased, RAF loss rates followed.

By the end of September 1941, RAF bomber losses stood at 1,170 aircraft destroyed. These losses included all causes, but German antiaircraft defenses accounted for the vast majority. While the British had adopted night bombing as their preferred method, it quickly became apparent to the crews who flew at night that the inky blackness offered little protection.

> Going into the target, you would become very apprehensive and nervous. The searchlights, flak, the fighters, the danger of collision, the danger of getting hit with your own bombs. If you had time to stop and think about being frightened, you weren't doing your job. Especially when you're flying at night for hours and hours in total darkness and then when you get over the target it was lighter than day. All hell was breaking loose. The Germans knew that we dropped TIs [target indicators] and we all had to fly over those indicators at a designated height and time. The Germans knew this, so they just fired their flak through the bloody TIs. —WARRANT OFFICER SECOND CLASS FRED VINCENT, AIR GUNNER, 189 SQ, 5 GROUP RAF

For RAF bomber crews, being caught in a cone of searchlights was one of their worst fears. An essential element of the night Reich flak defenses were the *Scheinwerfer Regimenteen*, equipped with a variety of searchlights. This 150cm *Fakscheinwerfer* 34 was operated by women of the *Flakhelferinnen*, June 1944. As more men were siphoned off for front-line duty, they were replaced by women, teenage boys, and older men. NARA

During the fall of 1941, Luftwaffe commanders continued to explore new ways to improve the flak defenses. In 1939 bombers were operating at high altitudes calling for a new more capable mobile heavy flak gun. The Rheinmetall firm was awarded a development contract for an improved version of the standard 88mm gun. In 1941 Rheinmetall produced the 88mm/Model 41. The new gun was a great improvement. Its effective engagement altitude was 33,000 feet with a muzzle velocity of 3,315 feet per second. Rate of fire was between twenty and twenty-five rounds per minute, making the new Model 41 20 percent more effective than the previous models of the 88mm gun. In fact it was better than the large-caliber 105mm gun. Pound for pound the new Model 41 emerged as the most effective heavy flak gun of the war.

At the same time, tactical improvements were tested in the form of larger gun batteries. In the fall of 1941, the Luftwaffe experimented with flak units of eight guns per

The last step before a shell could be fired was to set the fuse. German gunners set the time-of-flight fuse settings on their 88mm shells. AUTHOR'S COLLECTION

battery instead of the standard four. Arranged in a circle, seven guns formed a ring around the eighth in the center.

The arrival of the United States Army Air Forces (USAAF) in the spring of 1942 did not immediately tip the balance in the Allies' favor. Now instead of engaging the RAF at night and relying on gun-laying radar, the Luftwaffe flak defenses would soon have a large number of daylight targets, well suited to their optical sights.

The American air force entered the campaign with a certain degree of complacency. Lessons learned from the Spanish Civil War, the battle of France, and the battle of Britain were ignored. They believed they had better planes, better bombsights, and better doctrine. No real thought had been given to the dangers of German antiaircraft fire, however. Everything focused on the self-defending bomber. Well-flown tight formations of B-17s and B-24s would be able to defend themselves against determined fighter attacks, bomb the target, and make it home. Flak was deemed a nuisance.

On February 3, 1942, the 97th, 301st, and 303rd B-17E Bomb Groups were formally activated and assigned to England. This was followed by two B-24 Liberator groups (the 44th and 93rd BGs). More aircraft would arrive including B-26 Marauder medium bombers and P-47 Thunderbolt fighters, forming the nucleus of the U.S. Eighth Air Force in England. Soon after, construction of sixty-seven bases began at a cost of one million pounds each.

By the end of 1942, ground-based air defenses remained a critical cog in the Luftwaffe's air defense system. To meet the new American threat, the number of flak guns within the Reich and Western Front totaled 866 heavy gun batteries, 621 light gun batteries, and 273 searchlight batteries.

On August 17, 1942, the Eighth Air Force launched its first raid. Twelve B-17Es headed for the Rouen Sotteville marshalling yards, in northwestern France. Another six B-17Es acted as a diversionary force heading for St. Omer. The mission was deemed a success with all B-17s returning to base. No losses only verified the soundness of the USAAF's policy of precision bombing of strategic targets, rather than the mass area-bombing tactics of the RAF.

In contrast the USAAF adopted low-level tactics for their B-26 medium bomber units. Based on experience from the Pacific, it was believed to be the best way to surprise German defenses. Like the first B-17 mission, the Marauder's introduction to combat was a success. Its second mission, however, would radically change the Marauder's tactics. On May 14, 1943, twelve B-26s bombed the PEN generating station at Imjuiden, on the Dutch coast. All aircraft returned but most had suffered flak damage. Post-strike photos showed little destruction and a second raid was put on. Three days later eleven B-26s from the 322nd BG took off. One aircraft would abort. Even before they reached their target, the Marauders came under fire from coastal flak batteries. One B-26 went down. Upon reaching their target seven more Marauders were shot down by flak with two shot down by fighters. It was a complete disaster. The Americans learned the hard way that flak at low and medium level was extremely effective. Shortly after, USAAF chief "Hap" Arnold effectively cancelled low-level missions by medium bombers stating, "You cannot fly up and down this coast in a bomber at 50 feet and survive." Flak had done its job forcing the B-26 to fly higher. Henceforth, operations undertaken by B-26 units would be from medium altitudes of between 10,000 and 15,000 feet, and fighter cover was deemed essential for medium bomber operations.

That same month RAF Bomber Command, now led by Air Vice Marshal Arthur Harris, changed their night-bombing tactics. These new tactics caught the Germans by surprise. By February new four-engine bombers like the Short Stirling, Handley Page Halifax, and newer Avro Lancaster were in service. These new bombers could now carry more bombs to more distant targets. At the same time more than one-third of Bomber Command aircraft were fitted with a new radio direction-finding device known as GEE. GEE received signals from three separate transmitters located in the UK. By measuring the differences in time it took to receive each signal, bomber crews were able to fix their position. With a range of about 350 to 400 miles, it was not an aid for precision bombing. It did, however, help crews reach the target area with greater accuracy. Harris also wanted to improve bombing effectiveness by concentrating the bombers over the target. Thus the "bomber stream" was created. This major innovation allowed all bombers to fly a common route, at the same speed to and from the target. Each aircraft was allotted a height band and time slot in the stream to minimize the risk of collision. The hoped for result was that the bomber force would swamp both the German night-fighter and flak defenses and reduce the time over the target.

On the night of May 30th/31st, "Bomber" Harris launched the war's first 1,000-plane raid. To assemble such a force, Harris had to gather crews and aircraft from Training Command and from Operational Training Units (OTU). Led by experienced crews equipped with GEE, 1,047 bombers headed for the city of Cologne. In just ninety minutes 1,455 tons of bombs were dropped, two-thirds being incendiaries. Damage to Cologne was extensive, but the RAF did not come out unscathed. Forty-one aircraft were lost in the raid, a loss rate of 3.9 percent. Twenty-two aircraft were lost over the target—sixteen to flak, four to fighters, and two to collision. Of the 116 bombers damaged, eighty-five were from flak and twelve by fighters. The first 1,000-bomber raid was a success, but a follow-up raid on Essen two nights later was a complete failure with just eleven houses destroyed for the loss of thirty-one bombers.

The 1,000-bomber raids made their mark. The new tactics were mainly successful, with far fewer collisions over the target than estimated. Time over the target would be shortened until 700 to 800 aircraft could drop their loads in less than twenty minutes. It was a major turning point in Bomber Command and a crisis for the Luftwaffe flak defenses. Civilian party officials now demanded more guns and searchlights for their respective towns and cities. The Luftwaffe was now in the unenviable position of having

The most common air search radar system used in support of the Luftwaffe flak forces was the FuMG 65 Wurzburg Riese. Given the designation "Wurzburg Giant" by Allied intelligence, it weighed eleven tons and was usually mounted in a static site. This unit belonged to the 4. Flak-Division and was captured near Bad Godesburg. NARA

to choose which targets had priority. Protecting everything was in effect an exercise in wasted resources, a lesson the Luftwaffe was about to relearn.

In response to the new RAF tactics, the Luftwaffe ordered the construction of more heavy and light railroad flak battalions. These units could move quickly throughout the Reich and became the flak elite, receiving the best equipment and best-trained personnel. The Luftwaffe also accelerated the number of weapons in each heavy gun battery from four to six barrels. This led directly to creation of the "superbatteries" (*Großbatterien*)—three batteries of four guns linked to one centrally located fire director. Equipped with Wurzburg gun-laying radar in 1942, these batteries increased the concentration of directed fire, with a greater probability of hitting an engaged aircraft. But to be effective, these units required well-trained personnel.

Among the most visible responses to the increased strategic bombing offensive were the enormous flak towers found in Berlin, Hamburg, and Vienna. Based on sketches by Hitler himself, the flak towers were actually large air-raid shelters with heavy guns on top.

128mm Flak 40 gun on a flak train. The ammunition storage bins were placed on either side of the gun. Flak trains gave the Luftwaffe a highly effective mobile reserve, which could be moved to various locations at a moment's notice. NATIONAL MUSEUM OF THE USAF

Hitler saw the towers as a visible public reminder of Germany's defiance against Allied bombers. The flak towers came in two basic designs: the basic *Gefechtsturm* (G-Trum) was equipped with the flak battery and the *Leitturm* (L-Trum) provided support with the associated fire-control radar. These towers were all finally equipped with the superb twin 128mm Flakzwilling 40 guns.

These guns were undoubtedly the most lethal antiaircraft guns of the war. Crewed by the Flak arm's elite, these twin mounts were capable of twenty rounds per minute — making a four-gun flak tower unit capable of unleashing eighty rounds per minute. With clear all-around fields of fire, these guns were the most efficient with an average of 3,000 rounds per aircraft shot down. All told Berlin would receive three flak towers, followed by two in Hamburg and two in Vienna. Unfortunately for the RAF their best bombers, the Halifax and Lancaster, had low service ceilings of between 22,000 and 24,000 feet. This was well within reach of the 88, 105, and 128mm guns, exposing them to more rounds and time engaged over the target. Both the Lancaster and Halifax were handicapped by their single-stage supercharged engines. Compared to the Boeing B-17 and Consolidated

The 128mm Flakzwilling 40 was simply two guns mounted side by side provided with mirror loading arrangements. Only thirty-three twin mounts were deployed by 1945 and were used exclusively on the flak towers of Berlin, Hamburg, and Vienna. NARA

B-24, both equipped with turbo superchargers, they had a service ceiling of 31,000 feet and 28,000 feet, respectively.

The RAF knew a fully loaded Halifax had little tactical freedom due to the excessively narrow height band. Some Halifax squadrons reduced their bomb-loads by as much as a ton to gain height. By 1944 reports of "fringe merchants," those who dropped their bombs early or dropped their heaviest bombs over the North Sea to gain height, proliferated.

German flak towers not only bristled with heavy antiaircraft guns, they also carried a supplementary armament of 20mm and 37mm guns. The large Berlin and Hamburg towers were equipped with twenty 20mm Flakvierling 38 automatic cannons. A flak crew mans their gun ready for action. The crewmember on the far right holds a twenty-round magazine. Each magazine was good for six seconds of fire. AUTHOR'S COLLECTION

Equipped with two-stage superchargers, the Lancasters and Halifaxes would have been able to fly higher, thus reducing their exposure to flak and night-fighters.

For RAF crews the black of night did not always mask their presence. Flak's effectiveness at night was greatly aided by the simple searchlight battery. Often overlooked these deadly beams were radar controlled and highly effective. In a three-month period in 1942, British Operational Research reported searchlight-assisted antiaircraft batteries inflicted 70 percent of all flak casualties. A supplemental study found that searchlights increased the number of bombers hit by approximately 50 percent. For RAF bomber crews the number of searchlight batteries would only increase and would also play a vital role in the Luftwaffe's air defense network.

The beginning of 1943 did not bode well for the Third Reich and the Luftwaffe. The defeat in North Africa and the slow asphyxiation of the German Sixth Army at Stalingrad signaled the end of German expansion and conquest. As one veteran put it, "during the first few years of the war the Germans were looking for us, now we were looking for

The Gefechtsturm IV flak tower was the first to be built from the outset with the new 128mm Flak 40 Flakzilling heavy flak guns. Secondary armament consisted of twenty 20mm Flakvierling 38 automatic cannons. Popularly known as the "Holy Ghost Bunker" by local Hamburg residents, it was credited with fifty Allied bombers shot down. NARA

them." The Allied decision at Casablanca to use strategic bombing as a means to destroy German military and economic targets set in motion the greatest aerial conflict the world had ever seen. By March of 1943 the USAAF was able to mount daylight raids of just over one hundred bombers on a consistent basis. RAF Bomber Command was able to send 400-plus bombers deep into Germany. The German Flak arm would now fight its greatest battles. During the first three months of the year, flak units accounted for ninety aircraft shot down compared to ninety-six by fighters. Hitler continued to champion the Flak arm and wanted more guns and more crews to defend targets in the Reich. Because of the loss of personnel in Africa and the Soviet Union, the Germans were now forced to use women and young men in the Flak arm. In 1943, 116,000 young women replaced regular Luftwaffe men employed in air defense duties. The Germans were also forced to shorten their training programs and strip their flak schools of much needed equipment. The scales were beginning to tip, but the Flak arm continued to grow. By the end of June 1943, there were 1,089 heavy flak batteries compared to 659 in January. Flak gun production had almost tripled between 1941 and 1943. The Germans also proved adept at modifying captured enemy flak guns. In January 1943 alone the Luftwaffe modified 285 captured Russian guns.

During the war German forces captured thousands of antiaircraft guns along with millions of rounds of ammunition. Most were put to good use. This Vickers 1-pounder pom-pom gun is seen here at Boulogne airfield, France, during the summer of 1940. This weapon was most likely salvaged from one of the many British destroyers damaged and sunk off of Dunkirk. AUTHOR'S COLLECTION

As one of the most well-defended targets in Germany, Berlin bristled with antiaircraft guns and searchlights. Allied crews quickly learned a trip to Berlin was fraught with danger. On the night of August 23/24, 1943, RAF Bomber Command opened the battle of Berlin using 710 heavy bombers. Wireless operator Flt. Lt. Allan Ball of No. 35 Sq RAF, after flying fifty-eight missions, flew his last over Berlin.

"We arrived eight minutes early; we knew that our Station Commander was there in another aircraft and we wanted to be on time. The pilot flew an orbit to the south before going in. There was no problem with the bomb run, though there was a fierce defense reaction. We took our photograph. Then about a minute later, there was a ginormous 'whumpf.' I was looking out of a small blister just behind H2S set at the time. Something came up at me and smashed my skull open. I remember a blinding light and then there was another explosion, and I finished up with twenty-three holes in me and I have five bits of metal in me still. The worst part was the piece of metal, which went into my brain. Then I heard on the intercom that we had to abandon the aircraft; we were spiraling down."

Sixty-two RAF heavy bombers would be shot down that night.

By the end of May 1943, the RAF bombing campaign against the Ruhr had achieved significant levels of destruction. But it came at a great price. In the second quarter of 1943, German flak units accounted for 229 aircraft shot down compared to 348 by fighters; they also damaged a further 1,496. While it was an admirable achievement, it highlighted a dramatic shift. Only a year earlier such losses would have crippled Bomber Command. But now, replacement crews and new aircraft were in such numbers that Bomber Command actually grew in strength. While doing a good job at shooting down bombers, the Flak arm was also causing many Allied crews to miss their targets. In March Bomber Command reported that only 48 percent of aircrews were placing their bomb-loads within 3 miles of the target. Evasive maneuvering due to flak was to blame. USAAF crews also used evasive actions to avoid flak and this led to an even greater dispersal of bombs. Col. Curtis E. LeMay of the 3rd Air Division castigated his commanders for using evasive action. But once on the bomb run, crews had little choice. For new crews on their first mission, the introduction to flak was both fascinating and frightening.

> Suddenly the Bombardier called out: "Flak nine o'clock low!" Huge puffs of black smoke began to burst around the formation. Because we were on the bomb run it meant we had to fly straight and steady for several minutes to provide a stable platform for the Bombardier and the Norden Bomb Sight. BAM!! The ship rocked and I saw a nearby burst of orange followed by boiling, black smoke. I had been told that the crew would not hear the shell bursts. Well, I heard that one! Mostly I saw only black smoke explode into large globs and heard pieces of shrapnel striking the aircraft. —John Commer, B-17 Flight Engineer, 533rd Sq, 381st BG

On July 24, 1943, RAF Bomber Command launched one of its most successful raids of the war. Almost 800 heavy bombers took off headed for Hamburg. To meet the threat were fifty-four heavy flak batteries, twenty-six light batteries, and twenty-two searchlight batteries.

On this night, however, the RAF would unveil a new method to neutralize the German's flak gun–laying radar. Long-range radar had already spotted the incoming raid, but while still 80 miles from the coast, the lead Path Finder aircraft and main force aircraft began dumping hundreds of bundles in a tactic codenamed WINDOW. Window was the code name for simple strips of aluminum foil and each bundle consisted of 2,200 12-inch strips. Dropped at an interval of one bundle per minute, they created an expanding cloud of radar-reflective material that blinded the ground-based gun-laying radar as well as the night-fighters' built-in aerial interceptor radar. The RAF lost just twelve bombers, 1.5 percent of all aircraft dispatched.

The RAF's use of WINDOW, commonly known as Chaff, had long been expected by the Luftwaffe but surprisingly nothing was done to counter its use. The Luftwaffe had

B-17s of the 457th BG fly through heavy flak over Schweinfurt on February 24, 1944. Despite the heavy flak only eleven B-17s were lost. NARA

tested a similar device in the winter of 1942. The Germans knew if it was used in combat it would blot out both Wurzburg and gun-laying radars. Fearing the Allies would find out, the Germans kept the trials absolutely secret, going so far as to ban all work on countermeasures. Only after the Hamburg raid did the Luftwaffe pursue effective countermeasures, much to the frustration of the gun crews.

Adding to the destruction, Hamburg was attacked the next day by a force of sixty-eight B-17s with another sixty-seven bombing the submarine base at Kiel. On the 26th almost 200 American bombers hit targets in northwest Germany including Hamburg and Hanover. Those two days cost the Eighth Air Force twenty-four bombers with thirteen attributed to fighters, seven to flak, and four to unknown causes for a loss rate of 10 percent. While the flak may have been blinded at night, its daytime vision was as sharp as ever. Chaff's effectiveness would not last long. Anti-jamming devices for the gun-layer radars were soon adopted, giving the Flak arm a boost in performance.

Not until the autumn of 1943 did the Americans introduce active radar jamming countermeasures. By 1944 American Operational Research came to the late conclusion that "FLAK always a major cause of loss and damage, has steadily increased in relative

Introduced in 1941, the Wurzburg D gun-laying radar had a range of up to 25 kilometers and remained the standard flak gun–laying radar through the end of the war. AUTHOR'S COLLECTION

importance to become the greatest single combat hazard in present day operations." The USAAF favored combining WINDOW and active radar jamming. On October 8, 1943, the Eighth Air Force introduced a new airborne jamming device codenamed CARPET I. CARPET I was a "barrage jammer" specifically designed to jam German gun-layer radars. To be effective at least half the bombers in formation needed to be equipped with CARPET. The use of chaff by the Eighth Air Force did not occur until December 20, 1943. By October 1944 special chaff-dispensing formations of six to twelve B-17s or B-24s were regularly being sent ahead of the main force to screen the leading formations. While these new measures did decrease exposure to flak, they were not completely effective. "Unfortunately, until very recently (November 1944) we never had enough CARPET equipments. We often did not have or use enough CARPET or WINDOW to obscure the enemy's radar screen completely, and the way we flew our formations more frequently than not placed the trailing bomber units too far from the source of their protection. Even with these handicaps, there is sufficient evidence that our radio countermeasures often jammed the enemy's radar and that our flak losses and damage were reduced by their use."

The main armament of the flak towers was to be four sets of twin 128mm flak guns. Because they were not ready, the towers were originally armed with four single 105mm flak guns. Here gunners prepare to fire from the Berlin "Zoo Bunker." Although they were called flak towers, these huge structures were actually large air-raid shelters with flak batteries on top. NARA

One of the greatest victories obtained by the German Flak arm during the war was the famous Ploesti Raid. On August 1, 1943, a force of 176 B-24 bombers conducted what was supposed to be a surprise low-level attack on the Ploesti oil facilities in Romania. During the run up to the target, a navigational error alerted the Germans. The fifteen heavy and twelve light flak batteries swung into action and decimated the attacking B-24s. Forty-one heavy bombers were shot down and a further thirteen aircraft failed to return from the mission. In one of the most famous raids of the war, not only did the crews flying into the target see the flak close up, they actually saw the German gun crews firing and loading their guns while they themselves fired back.

> Every thing, but the kitchen sink began to rise from the ground at us. I dived behind a row of trees and told the men in the nose to stand clear. We had to shoot our way in. I lifted over the trees and opened up with the fixed front guns. My tracer streams glanced off the ground a mile ahead. I saw natural looking haystacks unfold like daisies, with guns spouting fire at us. On our right a flak train moved at full speed down the track with guns belching black puffs at us. They were shooting eighty-eights like shot guns, with shells set to go off immediately after they left the gun barrel. —COL. JOHN RILEY KANE, 98TH BG

That same month the Eighth Air Force struck the Ruhr for the very first time with a force of 243 bombers: twenty-five were shot down, a loss rate of 10 percent. This was the only mission flown by the Eighth into the heavily defended Ruhr in all of 1943. The flak defensives over the Ruhr were so intense that Ninth Air Force medium bombers were prohibited from attacking targets in the Ruhr. On October 14th, the Americans returned to Schweinfurt for the second time with a force of 291 bombers: 229 bombed the target but 60 were shot down. Flak was responsible for 22 percent of the aircraft brought down with a further 17 receiving major damage, and 121 were damaged but repairable due to antiaircraft fire.

By late 1943 the science of "flak analysis" was taken seriously. It was clear that German flak was far more effective than originally thought, forcing a change in tactics and the use of electronic countermeasures. In November 1944 Headquarters, Eighth Air Force Operational Analysis Section, produced an in-depth study titled *An Evaluation of Defense Measures Taken to Protect Heavy Bombers from Loss and Damage.* The results were revealing.

Defensive Measures Against Flak

During the past year enemy flak defenses have been concentrated and our bombers faced many more guns. The percentage of bombers lost to or damaged by enemy fighters has declined sharply while the percentage lost to has declined only moderately, and the percentage damaged by flak had remained almost constant. As a result, there had been a steady increase in the relative importance of flak until in June, July and August

17—CLOSING UP IN TRAIL To Reduce The Time Between Attacks Of Successive Bombing Units And Thus Saturate The Enemy Flak Defenses.

FOR EXAMPLE — 9 Bombing Units Spaced 1 Mile Apart, Occupy The Same Space And Have The Same Flak Shell Risk As 3 Bombing Units Spaced 4 Miles Apart. *
(AT 20000 FEET)

NUMBER OF SHELLS THAT CAN BE FIRED ON THE INCOMING COURSE.

NO. SHELLS THAT CAN BE FIRED ON OUTGOING COURSE.

INCOMING COURSE — OUTGOING COURSE

ALTI-TUDE	GROUND SPEED M.P.H.
25000	286
24000	281
23000	276
22000	272
21000	267
20000	262
19000	258
18000	253
17000	249
16000	244
15000	240

BOMBING UNITS FLYING IN TRAIL 4 MILES APART

BOMBING UNITS FLYING IN TRAIL 1 MILE APART

(21000 FEET) (20000 FEET) (19000 FEET)

(21000 FEET) (20000 FEET) (19000 FEET)

POSITION WHERE FIRST EFFECTIVE SHELL CAN BE FIRED

MIDPOINT

GUN LOCATION

30 SECONDS BEYOND THE MIDPOINT (RETRACKING ALLOWANCE)

POSITION WHERE LAST EFFECTIVE SHELL CAN BE FIRED

ASSUMPTIONS

1— 90 M.M. AA GUN, FIRING 1 SHELL EVERY 4 SECONDS
2— GUN CEASES FIRING AT THE MIDPOINT WHENEVER ADDITIONAL BOMBERS ARE WITHIN RANGE ON THE INCOMING COURSE.
3— BOMBERS FLY A MAXIMUM EXPOSURE COURSE TANGENT TO THE DEAD ZONE
4— RETRACKING TIME=30 SECONDS, MAXIMUM FUSE TIME = 31 SECONDS

FLAK SHELL RISK

BOMBING UNIT NO	NUMBER OF UNITS WINGS			
	IN	OUT	TOTAL	TOTAL
1	28	0	28	
2	7	0	7	
3	7	11	18	53
1	28	0	28	
7	14	0	14	
9	0	11	11	53

NO. OF UNITS	1	2	3	5	9	13	17
MILES BETWEEN SUCCESSIVE UNITS	—	8	4	2	1	2/3	1/2
TOTAL MILES	—	8	8	8	8	8	8
TOTAL FLAK SHELLS	40	62	53	55	53	53	53
FLAK SHELLS PER UNIT	40	31	18	11	6	4	3

* OTHER FORMATIONS MAY BE APPRAISED BY THIS SAME TYPE OF FLAKOMETER.

ALTITUDE 20000 FT.

C5-5521,AF

Page 61

OR— The More Bombers We Can Get Within A Given Time Interval The Greater The Reduction In Flak Risk Per Bombing Unit.

By 1944 Operational Research was catching up to the problem of flak. This graphic illustration highlights the need for bomb groups to "close up in trail so as to reduce the time between attacks of successive bombing units and thus saturate the enemy flak defenses when they are employing continuously pointed or predicted concentration fire tactics." AUTHOR'S COLLECTION

1944, flak accounted for about ⅔ of the 700 bombers lost and 98% of the 13,000 bombers damaged.

In numbers, the current rate is startling. From 3360 to 4453 bombers have returned with flak damage in each of the 6 months ending September 1944—a monthly average just about double the total number damaged by flak in the entire first year of operations. All our efforts to reduce flak damage have apparently been offset by the fact that we have increasingly flown over targets defended by more and more guns. Further, enemy equipment, gunnery and ammunition have probably improved. The 60-gun target of a year ago is likely to be defended by 300 guns today. This makes it essential that we increase our efforts to decrease flak risks by re-examining the tactics we have been using and such new tactics as offer real possibilities.

The principal tactics to reduce flak risks are:

1. *Avoid flying over flak defenses en route to and from the target*

2. *Enter and leave the target area on course, which cross over the weakest flak defenses in the shortest time possible, i.e. with allowances for wind vector.*

3. *Fly at the highest altitude consistent with other defensive and offensive considerations.*

4. *Plan the spacing and axes of attack of bombing units to make the fullest use of the radio countermeasures WINDOW and CARPET.*

5. *Minimize the number of bombers flying together as a bombing unit.*

6. *Increase the spread of the entire formation in altitude and breadth to reduce the risk from barrage fire.*

7. *Close up in trail so as to reduce the time between attacks of successive bombing units and thus saturate the enemy flak defenses when they are employing continuously pointed or predicted concentration firing tactics.*

8. *Plan evasive action when flying over known anti-aircraft positions (except on bomb run) to make it difficult or impossible for the enemy to get accurate data for continuously pointed or predicted concentration firing tactics.*

In July 1944 the USAAF experimented for the first time with armor plate to help protect heavy bomber engines from flak.

"In June and July 1944, 25 B-17 aircraft arrived in theater with an experimental installation of engine-nacelle armor plate base in part on a study of engine-nacelle damage made in the Eighth Air Force in July 1943. The armor was installed on the ring cowl curved section, and about 6 inches farther back; on the propeller governor; ignition harness; oil sump;

16 — SPREADING THE ELEMENTS OF OUR PRESENT TIGHT FIGHTER DEFENSIVE FORMATION MINIMIZES THE NUMBER OF BOMBERS FLYING TOGETHER AND THUS REDUCES THE CHANCE THAT FLAK AIMED AT ONE BOMBER MAY HIT ANOTHER.

This is because enemy A.A. shells tend to scatter widely around the aiming point. In fact, at the altitudes we fly the majority of shells are likely to burst outside our 18 A/C formation. Each A/C in the formation therefore runs nearly equal risk of being hit by an A.A. shell aimed at the formation. But if the formation unit is cut from 18 A/C to 6 or to 3 the number of A/C likely to be hit by any one shell aimed at the formation is cut in half.

THE DIAGRAMS BELOW SHOW HOW THE BURSTS FROM 100 INDEPENDENTLY AIMED FLAK SHELLS ARE LIKELY TO BE DISPERSED AROUND THE AIMING POINT AT 18,000 FEET ALTITUDE BASED ON A STUDY MADE BY THE BRITISH OF THEIR EXPERIENCE IN FIRING THEIR OWN A.A. GUNS.

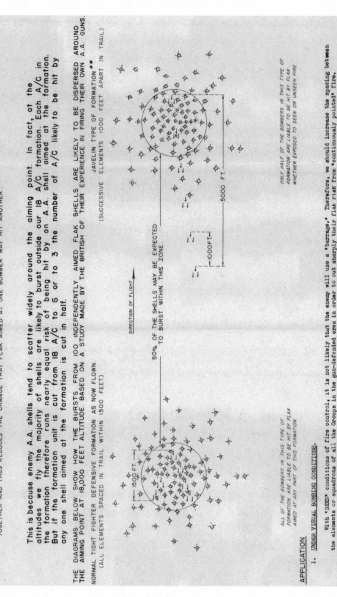

NORMAL TIGHT FIGHTER DEFENSIVE FORMATION AS NOW FLOWN.
(ALL ELEMENTS SPACED IN TRAIL WITHIN 1500 FEET)

JAVELIN TYPE OF FORMATION **
(SUCCESSIVE ELEMENTS 1000 FEET APART IN TRAIL.)

DIRECTION OF FLIGHT

50% OF THE SHELLS MAY BE EXPECTED TO BURST WITHIN THIS ZONE.

1000 FT.

1500 FT.

5000 FT

ALL OF THE BOMBERS IN THIS TYPE OF FORMATION ARE LIABLE TO BE HIT BY FLAK AIMED AT ANY PART OF THIS FORMATION

ONLY HALF OF THE BOMBERS IN THIS TYPE OF FORMATION ARE LIABLE TO BE HIT BY FLAK WHETHER EXPOSED TO SEEN OR UNSEEN FIRE

APPLICATION

1. UNDER VISUAL BOMBING CONDITIONS.

   With "SEEN" conditions of fire control, it is not likely that the enemy will use a "barrage." Therefore, we should increase the spacing between the elements or squadrons of all the Groups in the gun-defended area in order to cut sharply their flak risk from "continuously pointed" fire.

2. UNDER BLIND BOMBING CONDITIONS.

   With "UNSEEN" conditions of fire control, the enemy will only be forced to resort to "barrage" fire if our radio countermeasures are effective --
   if radio countermeasures are not available or are not used effectively -- ALL OF THE GROUPS IN THE ATTACKING FORCE will cut their flak risks from
   "continuous pointed" fire by using a spread-out type of formation as illustrated above -- if WINDOW alone is available and used effectively, then
   THE LEADING GROUP IS THE ONLY GROUP that will be exposed to "continuously pointed" fire and the only group that will cut its flak risk sharply by using
   a spread-out type of formation.
   If CARPET AND WINDOW are available and used effectively to force the enemy to resort to "barrage" fire against all Groups, then NO GROUP will cut
   its flak risk by using a spread-out type of formation.

3. IN ALL CASES WHERE FLAK RISKS CAN BE CUT SHARPLY BY USING A SPREAD-OUT TYPE OF FORMATION, it must also be decided that we can bomb with sufficient
   accuracy by elements or by squadrons and that we can afford this poorer defense against enemy fighters in the target area.

* Using "Continuously pointed" fire
  or "Predicted Concentrations"

** Other types of formations equally spaced in trail
   will achieve at least as much flak risk reduction

05-5SC14F
Page 60

Early tight fighter defensive bombing formations of twelve or eighteen aircraft were found to be vulnerable to flak. This diagram illustrates the benefits of spreading the formation out. "If the elements of a 12-18 aircraft bombing unit were spread out 1000 feet apart in trail, we would greatly reduce the chance that flak aimed at one bomber would hit another." AUTHOR'S COLLECTION

carburetor; gasoline strainers; oil temperature regulator assemblies; and booster pump tear drops. While not enough time has elapsed for a thorough test of these ships in combat, some data are available which confirm the desirability of engine-nacelle armor plate.

"The planes with the experimental installation flew a total of 292 sorties, and suffered 17 hits on the armor plate, 3 from small spent flak fragments, 13 from heavier, high velocity flak fragments, and 1 from a 20mm cannon shell. Eleven of the flak fragments were stopped by the armor. The cannon shell, and 5 of the 13 heavier, high velocity flak fragments, penetrated the armor plate, but were slowed and deflected so that the engine itself was not damaged. This confirms the desirability of engine-nacelle armor plate."

Just as the Americans took steps to add armor plate to improve survivability against flak, the Germans introduced a new antiaircraft shell.

"In May 1944, evidence first appeared that the enemy was using A.A. shells serrated externally to produce controlled fragmentation. Most fragments of these shells found in aircraft have been $1 \times 2 \times 6$ cm. weighing about 5 oz.

"Should such a shell replace the standard A.A. casing on a large scale, a few dozen large fragments would be more lethal to a bomber than the hundreds of small fragments from the standard shell and, moreover, would penetrate light armor plate and flak pads and suits."

In the final weeks of the war, the Luftwaffe began testing a new and highly effective antiaircraft round. In 1944 the *Reichsluftfahrtministerium* (RLM) produced a study that showed contact/time-fused shells revealed a considerable theoretical superiority over the regular time-fused type. Critical ammunition shortages led the Luftwaffe to test the new contact/time the fused shells (*Doppelzunder*). Beginning on April 9, 1945, a number of flak batteries in Munich began testing the round. Thirteen aircraft were shot down for

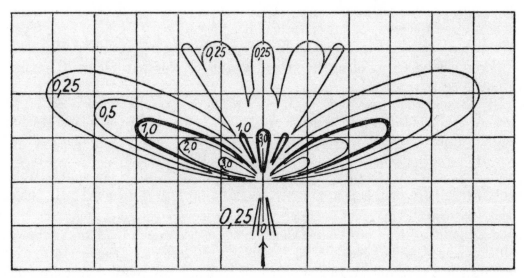

This diagram, taken from a German 88mm flak manual, shows the splinter distribution of an 88mm flak shell. The numbers indicate the number of effective fragments per square meter. AUTHOR'S COLLECTION

just 370 rounds per shoot down. When compared to the existing average of 4,500 rounds, it was an extraordinary result. Fortunately for Allied bomber crews the new rounds never made it into widespread use and the end of the war was just weeks away.

What the RAF and USAAF did not do during the war was mount any sustained attacks on German flak positions. From the very beginning their defense strategy focused on attacks from opposing fighters. Flak was a secondary concern and one that was given very little thought. Finding a specific target like a flak battery at night was beyond the RAF's technical capabilities. They did, however, attempt "flak-busting" missions early in the war. Bomber Command also experimented by dropping antipersonnel bombs on German flak positions during a raid on Hamburg in July 1943. The tactical air forces also played a role, but the number of flak-busting sorties was small.

Not until April 1945 did the Fifteenth Air Force attack German flak batteries northeast of Venice from high altitude (24,000 to 26,000 feet). The weapon of choice was the M-81 260-pound fragmentation bomb equipped with variable time fuses. On April 1, thirty-six B-24s each carrying eighteen M-81 bombs attacked gun batteries near Grisolera, Italy. According to the official Fifteenth Air Force report, "All batteries attacked by the first wave ceased firing when the bombs exploded, even though one of the batteries was missed by several hundred yards. The second was attacked fifteen minutes later and reported that all firing ceased as the bombs exploded. Both waves received scant, inaccurate ground fire on their bomb runs, which were made between 24,000 and 26,000 feet. No damage or losses were sustained. Bomb strike photos show many near misses on gun positions. Ground sources indicated that 22 soldiers were killed, 18 were wounded, and one 20 mm gun was destroyed."

The report concluded, "Bombers at high altitude can identify flak positions and drop 260-pound fragmentation bombs with VT fuses accurately enough to cause diminution of accuracy and intensity of AA opposition. Bomber crews are very enthusiastic about anti-flak missions since they are afforded an opportunity to fight back at the AA gunner."

Unfortunately for Allied aircrews those direct attacks didn't occur until the last full month of the war.

For bomber crews based in England, flak was not only a problem over the target, it was often encountered as soon as they crossed the enemy coast. One of the main routes into Germany was over the Netherlands, the "bomber Autobahn." In 1942 a flak belt was established in the Low Countries. Flak batteries along the coast came under Kriegsmarine command. Most of the Marineflak were deployed in heavily fortified bunkers and were mostly equipped with the Rheinmetall-Borsig 105mm SK C/32 guns. These units were soon incorporated into Hitler's Atlantikwall effort with gun batteries running from Denmark to Normandy. On the Dutch coast alone, twenty-three Marineflak heavy batteries were built. The building of the Atlantikwall also incorporated an extensive array of Luftwaffe early warning radar and signals interception posts. Allied intelligence soon found the "gaps" and each bombing mission was carefully planned to avoid the most con-

With the No. 2 engine damaged by flak, a Consolidated B-24 Liberator of the Fifteenth Air Force comes through an intense and accurate barrage over Vienna on October 15, 1944. "The most vulnerable part of the bomber is the power plant. About 50% of all bombers lost were due to disabled engines." NATIONAL MUSEUM OF THE USAF

centrated AA defense zones. For individual stragglers these flak batteries posed a serious threat and many crews fell victim.

February 1944 would see the Luftwaffe's ground-based defenses swell to a wartime high of 13,500 heavy flak guns, 21,000 light flak guns, 7,000 searchlights, and 2,400 barrage balloons. The highest concentration of weapons could be found in Germany and the Western Front. The southeastern front in Romania and Greece had the fewest weapons. The increase in the numbers of weapons did not necessarily translate directly to more aircraft being shot down. Part of the reason was the increased use by the Allies of electronic countermeasures like WINDOW or chaff and active radar jamming. The Germans were also beginning to suffer shortages of antiaircraft ammunition. Production could not keep up with the number of new guns entering service, and personnel to man the guns became a major problem as well. With the huge losses on the eastern and southern fronts, the Flak arm was forced to rely heavily on foreign volunteers, the largest group coming from Croatia and Italy. They also pressed into service 51,000 Soviet prisoners of war. By 1944

As soon as Allied bombers crossed the coast of occupied Europe, they would often be met by a salvo of flak from the Kriegsmarine. Extensively deployed along the coasts of Holland and France were numerous batteries of Kriegsmarine 105 SKC C/32 guns. These guns were usually equipped with an armored cupola. This battery was stationed near Toulon and had numerous engagements with the bombers of the Fifteenth Air Force. NARA

the Flak arm was not the elite formation it once was. It was also no longer a major pool of replacement troops for front-line units fighting in Russia and Italy. By the end of the war, 35 percent of the personnel manning guns consisted of men of at least forty-nine years of age who had earlier been medically unfit for service in the *Wehrmacht*.

At the beginning of 1944 a new player entered the stage and would provide the USAAF with the means of striking deep into Germany without heavy losses. The introduction of the long-range P-38, P-47, and P-51 with long-range drop tanks tipped the balance and sealed the fate of the German fighter air defenses.

The introduction of the long-range escort fighter quickly took its toll on the German fighter arm. Already exhausted from years of operations, the fighter arm was forced to use hastily trained pilots who could do little more than take off and land their aircraft. To meet the Soviet threat in the East, many fighter units were transferred to the Russian front, reducing further the number of fighters available for the defense of Germany. The burden of the German defense now fell to the Flak arm. In response to the daylight threat, the Germans increased the number of superbatteries throughout the Reich. These batteries consisted of at least twenty-four heavy guns. Most of these batteries were situated around vital targets such as synthetic oil plants. Around Berlin alone there were twenty-four superbatteries including twelve of the formidable two-barreled 128mm flak guns mounted on three massive flak towers. The massed firepower of these batteries greatly improved the effectiveness of the Flak arm in the spring of 1944. During that period (January–April 1944), the Eighth and Fifteenth Air Forces lost 315 bombers shot down by flak and 10,563 damaged. But it was not just the bombers that were suffering. In January 1944 the Eighth Air Force abandoned the "close escort support" of the bombers in favor of "ultimate pursuit." This meant fighters could attack enemy aircraft wherever they could be found, both in the air and on the ground. To encourage their young pilots to attack aircraft on the ground, the USAAF high command decided that aircraft destroyed on the ground would count as a victory, equal to an air-to-air claim. Most of the pilots did not realize how well protected Luftwaffe airfields really were, and as the war progressed, the Germans created numerous flak traps—airfields packed with useless aircraft and lots of antiaircraft guns. Many pilots took the bait and lost their lives in the process. Before this controversial policy was put into place, fighters lost over Germany due to flak before January 1944 stood at just one. After that 2,449 were shot down by flak compared to 1,691 shot down by enemy aircraft. Maj. Edward Giller of the 343rd Fighter Squadron, while flying a mission down the Danube Valley, was hit by flak and was lucky to make it home.

"I had to make a third pass to position myself on a target which I had observed. It turned out to be a Ju 88; I came in on it in the same pattern from south to north, and although I observed many strikes all over the aircraft, I could not get it to burn. As I pulled up from this last pass, a 20mm flak shell came flying through the left side of my canopy and exploded, wounding me in the left shoulder. I was dazed and bleeding rather badly, so I called my flight together and we set course for home."

Each fighter group developed their own methods of attack when it came to ground targets, and all of them learned the hard way.

> Let me stress above all that none of our flights went down on an objective that was not worth the risk of a P-38 and its pilot. This, in my opinion, is the most important lesson we can learn about ground attack. All leaders should constantly be aware of this problem. A questionable target that offers only a small chance of success should be abandoned. It is a hard lesson to learn, but I believed most groups in VIII Fighter Command have learned it. We learned it the hard way on 15 April and again a month or so later. On that day over France, a flight went down to strafe an airfield. No aircraft were visible, but the attack was made anyhow. Out of the four aircraft attacking, three were lost, including the flight commander, and the fourth was badly shot up and came home on one engine. There were no claims—there had been no target to warrant the attack. —COL. ROY OSBORN, COMMANDING OFFICER, 364TH FG

The D-Day invasion in June 1944 and the subsequent liberation of France signaled the end of the Reich's air defense network. During the Normandy campaign the Luftwaffe was forced to abandon 1,000 flak guns. The loss of territory also robbed the Luftwaffe of its forward-based early-warning radar sites and seriously affected its night-fighter force.

The Reich would now face a withering aerial assault of unprecedented proportions. After the invasion of Normandy, the U.S. Strategic Air Forces (Eighth and Fifteenth Air Forces) turned their attention to German oil facilities and hydrogenation plants. These attacks would represent the last great flak battles of the war. In response the Luftwaffe was forced to move more flak guns to defend these sites. During the summer of 1944, the synthetic oil plant at Leuna received more than 500 flak guns including 150 128mm guns and their well-trained crews.

The crisis was so great the Luftwaffe was forced to move units from Berlin and the Ruhr, and some towns and cities like Eisenach, Weimar, Chemnitz, and Dresden were stripped completely. This led to a sharp increase in the number of USAAF bombers shot down and damaged by flak. During attacks against the Leuna oil facility alone, eighty-two USAAF bombers were shot down. Flak accounted for fifty-nine, while fighters were credited with thirteen and seven were destroyed by accidents. This high percentage clearly showed that concentrated flak in very large numbers within a relatively small area could inflict heavy damage and prevent accurate bombing. After the war the United States Bombing Survey found that the flak defenses around Leuna "undoubtedly contributed to inaccuracy in the bombing of the target." More sobering was the fact that only 10 percent of all bombs dropped fell within the plant grounds. Between June and August 1944 the Eighth and Fifteenth Air Forces lost 654 heavy bombers with 14,329 damaged. At this time flak was inflicting ten times more damage than fighters.

Incredibly, in spite of the massive Allied bombing campaign, the production of anti-aircraft weapons and equipment in the last two quarters of 1944 "exceeded that in the first six months of the year." In terms of numbers 6,437 20mm guns were made in the first quarter, with 11,669 in the fourth. Thirty-six 88mm/model 41 guns were made in the first quarter with 114 built in the fourth. But despite the availability of new guns, getting them to the front-line units proved difficult. Attacks by Allied tactical and strategic air forces restricted the delivery of new guns and available stocks of ammunition to operational units. The need to protect Germany's rail lines and waterways became a top priority. A "flak belt" was established along the entire course of the Rhine River. The Luftwaffe transferred 500 heavy flak guns and a further 350 newly built heavy flak guns for the protection of vital transportation routes.

By January 1945 the end of the war was clearly in sight. Allied forces were squeezing Germany on three fronts with the Russians heading for Berlin. The Allies now had complete air superiority, but ironically the flak defenses were themselves battling both air and ground forces. In the last eight months of the war, the Luftwaffe transferred 555 heavy and 175 medium/light flak batteries to the fighting fronts. This left huge areas of Germany with no flak protection whatsoever. Even Berlin was not immune. In January the Luftwaffe ordered the transfer of thirty heavy and thirteen light flak batteries to bolster Wehrmacht defenses against the Russians. These reinforcements did very little to stem the tide, suffering heavy losses in the process. As Germany was running out of time, it was also running out of men. In a desperate move the Luftwaffe began training fifty flak

Strafing missions were extremely hazardous. This gun camera image shows He-177 bombers strafed by marauding P-51s. By 1945 an He-177 caught on the ground was a low-value target. Lack of fuel and pilots had all but grounded the entire He-177 fleet. NARA

The German 128mm Flak 40 was arguably the best heavy flak gun of the war. Entering service in 1942, the Flak 40 was costly and complex to make with just 570 in service by January 1945. This gun belonged to the 14. Flak Division defending the infamous Leuna refinery. NARA

A captured 105mm Flak 39 gun. Much heavier and bulkier than the standard 88mm gun, the 105 was assigned to static emplacements and railway flak trains. NARA

batteries consisting entirely of women trained for combat. Only ten completed the course and were used in the defense of Berlin.

By March 1945 the entire Wehrmacht was suffering from a critical shortage of ammunition. Even in this state the Flak arm could still deal a deadly blow.

In the last great airborne operation of the war, the Allies had set their sights on crossing the Rhine. Operation Varsity was conceived as a massive airborne and river

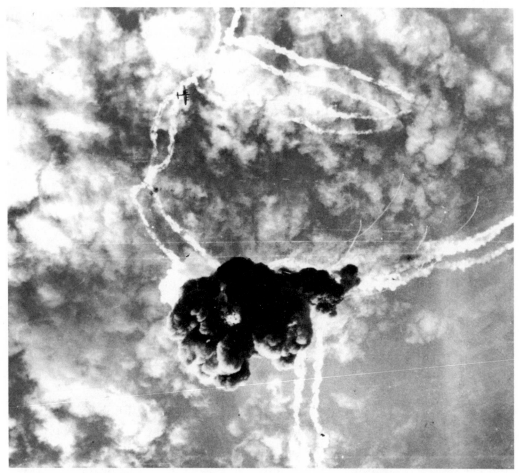

Direct hit. This is one of a handful of photographs that show an aircraft blowing up in midair. This No. 3 Group Lancaster was lost, most likely hit by flak, over Wesel on February 19, 1945. From the size of the explosion, it appears the bombs were still on board. Of the 168 Lancasters sent out, it was the only one lost. ARCHIVES CANADA

assault across the Rhine for late March 1945. Lessons from previous airborne assaults called for the suppression of antiaircraft defenses. Prior to the assault British and U.S. medium bombers and fighters pounded German antiaircraft sites. And three days before the assault RAF fighter-bombers from 83 and 84 Groups flew 1,500 sorties. Right up to the moment of the parachute landing, British fighter-bombers were attacking flak positions. The Germans countered this by moving, changing and adding new gun sites on a continuous basis. By the time of the assault, the Allies estimated the Germans had 712 light and 114 heavy guns in the battle zone.

On the morning of March 24, 1945, one of the greatest airborne operations of the Second World War was launched. Flying in 1,795 troop transports and 1,305 gliders towed by 1,050 tugs were just over 14,000 troops from the British 6th and American 17th

Airborne Divisions. Providing escort were 889 fighters, plus 2,596 heavy and medium bombers attacked airfields, bridges, rail yards, and other targets throughout Germany. The sky was bright and clear as the first troop transports arrived over the drop zones, and then came the flak. In the next ten minutes more than 8,000 British and American airborne troops were dropped; this was followed minutes later by the 2,355 tugs and gliders. Despite the anti-flak program and preliminary artillery bombardment, the response from German antiaircraft guns was devastating. As the slow lumbering transports and gliders made their way to their drop zones, the Germans gunners had hundreds of targets to choose from and all were low and slow. The transports and gliders were raked with machine-gun and cannon fire. Many of the transports were shot down in the first few minutes and the helpless gliders simply folded up under the withering fire.

> Along with the regular flak-type stuff, the Germans were using a phosphorous-type shell. This phosphorous shell was responsible for catching quite a few gliders on fire, because if it hit the wing it would just stay there and start smoldering in the wood. In building the main spars on some of the gliders, they had not done much of a job of cleaning the sawdust out. That sawdust came out of there like little fireflies as the phosphorous was burning. There were four gliders in our squadron that burnt the fabric clear off, all except a little around the nose. —GLIDER PILOT 2ND LT. F. TIPTON RANDOLPH, 80TH SQUADRON, 436TH U.S. TROOP CARRIER GROUP

On this day the Allied air forces flew 7,700 sorties for a loss of fifty-six aircraft and eighty gliders, which included fifteen B-24s shot down on the follow-up supply drop. And once the troops had landed, the flak units soon turned their guns toward the lightly armed airborne soldiers. It was only after the airborne troops achieved their objectives did the flak cease. Even at this late stage of the war, the German Flak arm was still capable of inflicting heavy damage.

The number of Allied aircraft shot down or damaged by German ground defenses during World War II was extensive and far greater than many historians have given credit. Between July 1942 and April 1945, RAF Bomber Command lost an estimated 1,345 bombers during night sorties due to flak. Luftwaffe night-fighters accounted for an estimated 2,278 for a ratio of 1.69 to 1 over the Flak arm. Where flak was more effective was in the number of aircraft damaged. Between February 1942 and April 1945, Luftwaffe flak defenses damaged 8,842, which included 151 beyond repair, while fighters accounted for just 1,731 including 163 bombers beyond repair. Approximately 125,000 aircrew served with Bomber Command during the war. Nearly 60 percent would become casualties with 47,268 killed in action or died while prisoners of war with a further 9,838 listed as prisoners of war.

American losses due to flak were equally staggering. Over half of the USAAF's combat losses during the war in Europe were due to flak. Almost 5,400 aircraft were

Two B-24s of the 67th BG/44th BG fly between a burst of predicted fire over Augsberg, March 1, 1944. Less effective than continuously pointed fire, it was used when clouds prevented visual fire control or when radar information was of low quality. Firing short barrages, gunners placed a barrage at a point in the sky through which it was predicted a target aircraft would pass. NARA

shot down by ground-based guns compared to 4,300 shot down by Luftwaffe fighters. The Eighth Air Force alone lost 1,798 aircraft to flak with an astonishing 54,539 damaged between December 1942 and April 1945. In human terms American bomber crew casualties in Europe totaled 73,000, including 29,000 killed. The Fifteenth Air Force lost 1,046 heavy bombers to flak between November 1943 and May 1945. Approximately 10 percent of those losses were the result of attacks on the Ploesti oil fields, the majority due to flak. A further 11,954 bombers were damaged by flak. Most of the damage, however, was superficial and required little time to repair. It was the "seriously damaged" aircraft that told the real story. Between May 1944 and March 1945, the 1st Bombardment Division alone listed 4,115 aircraft as "seriously damaged" out of a total of 15,042 damaged by flak. Seriously damaged aircraft required extensive repairs and thousands of man-hours to put back in service.

Luftwaffe leaders always measured flak's effectiveness by the number of aircraft shot down. Many were guilty of evaluating the performance of the flak by comparing the

A Siebel Ferry Flak barge of the Kriegsmarine mounting two 88mm guns. Originally designed for Operation Sealion (the invasion of Britain in 1940), these barges would serve throughout the war. Like the railway flak trains, the Siebel Ferry Flak barge gave the Luftwaffe the ability to move guns along coastal waters and the numerous waterways throughout Germany. SK-KUVA

number of aircraft shot down by flak to those shot down by fighters. This narrow focus led the Luftwaffe's leadership to ignore or grossly underestimate the effectiveness of the ground-based defenses. Allied intelligence officers were just as guilty, but as the war progressed, operational analysis changed their view. In the areas of damage and bombing accuracy, flak's hidden effects were harder to measure, but the results were hard to ignore.

Flak damage alone caused hundreds of bombers to divert to neutral countries like Sweden and Switzerland. By 1944 almost 200 bomber crews chose this option. Others often headed their damaged aircraft out over the North Sea and English Channel hoping for a successful ditching and rescue by the Air Sea Rescue Service. During the war 5,721 aircrew were rescued, enough to operate 572 B-17s or 817 Lancasters. For American crews one of their greatest fears was falling out of formation. These flak-damaged stragglers often fell victim to fighter attack and were not considered a shared credit. Many Luftwaffe fighter pilots built up their scores by simply going after damaged bombers.

While the number of aircraft shot down and damaged by flak was impressive, it must be remembered that the first job of antiaircraft fire was to prevent incoming bombers from hitting their target. When using that metric the Luftwaffe flak defenses were highly effective. Driving bomber formations to higher altitudes decreased bombing accuracy and in some cases whole formations were broken up before they reached their target. Intense flak over the target caused British and American bomber pilots to use evasive action, which greatly reduced accuracy. Others bombed early, wasting their bombs (called "creep back" in the RAF). By March 1945 General Spaatz, Commander of the U.S. Strategic Air Forces, stated that flak was the "biggest factor" affecting bombing accuracy. Postwar analysis went even further calculating a 39.7 percent radial bombing error due to a combination of evasive action, nerves, and combat fatigue due to flak. An additional study added another 21.7 percent to the radial error because of the increased altitude to avoid flak. When added up it came to a 61.4 percent radial bombing error directly due to flak alone.

In the end the German flak defenses could not by themselves successfully defend German airspace. While high expectations had been placed on the Flak arm by Hitler and the Luftwaffe, its valuable contributions cannot be overlooked. Without the thousands of heavy and light flak guns defending the Reich, German cities and factories would have been quickly blasted into ruin. Instead German ground-based defenses helped Germany stay in the war far longer than Allied air commanders had hoped.

While the Allied air forces contributed a great deal to final victory, they never conquered the German flak artillery. In the end the defeat of Germany required the massive armies of the Soviet Union in concert with the combined armies of the western Allies and their air forces.

CHAPTER SEVEN

Tactical Air—Flak over the Battlefield

If it flies, it dies.
—AMERICAN AA GUNNER'S SLOGAN, NORMANDY 1944

For equal numbers engaged, four times as many pilots of the Command are lost on ground attack as in aerial combat. Light flak will ring an airfield, or a marshalling yard. Flak cars will open up in the middle of a train. A truck convoy, with sufficient warning, may be a hornet's nest. Every target of special value to the enemy will be heavily defended, and may exact its price.
—FRANCIS H. GRISWOLD, BRIGADIER GENERAL,
COMMANDING VIII FIGHTER COMMAND, SEPTEMBER 1944

AT THE BEGINNING OF WORLD WAR II, THERE WERE FOUR TACTICAL AIR FORCES (OF the major combatants): the Luftwaffe, the Soviet air force, the Imperial Japanese Army Air Force (IJAAF), and the U.S. Marine Corps. All four air forces were designed and largely equipped to support ground forces (the USMC Air Corps had a dual role). On the Allied side tactical airpower was anathema to those who believed that the strategic bomber would be the decisive weapon in the next war. Using aircraft in support of a ground army was a waste of time and resources. Unfortunately for the Americans and British, the strategic bombing campaign against Germany was a costly affair. High-altitude flak had proven itself to be not only effective, but a deadly killer.

Compared to the strategic air campaign, tactical air was a medium, low-level affair. Early low-level missions showed light and medium flak to be extremely effective with no real countermeasures.

A foreshadowing of what was to come occurred during the war between Finland and the Soviets—the Winter War of 1939. In August 1939 Germany and the Soviet Union signed a non-aggression pact, a surprise to many western states. A secret protocol to this agreement allowed the Soviets to seize the small Baltic states including Finland during the German invasion of Poland. In the face of the Communists' threats, the Finns prepared for the worst and mobilized their small but well-trained army. After unsuccessful negotiations the Soviets attacked on November 28, 1939. It was a truly David and Goliath affair. Facing some 3,253 Soviet fighters and bombers, the Finnish air force mustered just thirty-six Fokker D.XXIs and ten obsolete Bristol Bulldog IVs. The antiaircraft gun defenses were also small in number with just ten heavy aircraft batteries, 2.5 light batteries, two machine-gun companies, and sixteen separate AA platoons. The number of barrels available was just twenty-eight 76mm heavy Bofors guns, fifty-three 40mm Bofors guns, thirty 20mm guns, and 125 7.62mm machine guns. While small in numbers the guns were all modern with well-trained crews. They were also greatly aided by a well-established early warning system.

The early warning system consisted of a large number of surveillance stations connected to a number of Air Defense Command Centers. Located on roofs, church towers, and high hills, or in specially built wooden towers, these surveillance stations were equipped with binoculars and simple direction-finding devices. Early warning was critical for any antiaircraft defense, and for the Finns it worked very well. During the Winter War Finnish antiaircraft guns were credited with an impressive 314 Soviet aircraft shot down. Finnish fighter pilots added another 207 for a loss of 53 of their own.

The Continuation War, which started on June 25, 1941, found the Finnish antiaircraft forces far more numerous and far better equipped. When hostilities ceased on September 9, 1944, Finnish antiaircraft troops took a heavy toll of Russian aircraft, including 759 fighters, 248 bombers, and twenty-four other aircraft for a total of 1,031.

In addition units of the Finnish navy (Fleet and Coastal Defense) also contributed with sixty-three fighters and twelve bombers, seventy-five planes total.

For the British and French the tactical air battle fought during the Winter War was all but ignored. The performance of the Finnish antiaircraft gunners was superb, and one of the keys to their success was the establishment of an effective early warning system. When the Germans launched their tactical air war in May 1940, both the British and French suffered greatly by their lack of just such a system.

The battlefield air support provided by the Luftwaffe was a revelation to Allied commanders. Designed from the beginning to be on the sharp end, Luftwaffe doctrine focused, from the outset, on supporting the army in the field. And it did it very well. Equipped with specialized aircraft like the Junkers Ju-87 divebomber, the Luftwaffe was able to attack pinpoint targets with great effect. Medium bombers like the Heinkel He-111, Dornier Do-17, and Junkers Ju-88 were assigned to bigger targets such as rail yards, supply depots, and airfields. Preceding these attacks would be fighter sweeps by

Bf-109s and Me-110s. The Luftwaffe also knew that its fighters could not be present at all times. To fill the gap both infantry and Panzer units were well equipped with both attached Luftwaffe flak units and their own organic flak guns. A typical Panzer division in 1940 was equipped with six towed 88mm flak guns, thirty-two towed 20mm guns, nine 37mm towed guns, and numerous 7.92mm machine guns both on vehicles and antiaircraft mounts. The army units were not as well equipped as their Luftwaffe counterparts and suffered from a shortage of fire directors and advanced aircraft-tracking systems.

In essence the Luftwaffe provided its armies with accurate long-range artillery along with a robust antiaircraft defense. This combined arms approach proved devastating, and

The 20mm Flak 30 was a Rheinmetall-Borsig design that entered service in 1935. Due to its low rate of fire of 280 rpm, it was replaced by the 20mm Flak 38 version in late 1940. Even though it was replaced on the production line by the Flak 38, the Flak 30s remained in service until they were worn out or lost to enemy action. NARA

with the stunning victories over Holland, Belgium, France, and Britain in 1940, the Germans began to believe their own propaganda. Confident in victory Hitler soon turned his gaze toward the Soviet Union.

On June 22, 1941, Operation Barbarossa was launched, with 3,200,000 German troops committed to the invasion in 148 divisions. This force was augmented by divisions from other Axis countries: sixteen Finnish, two Slovakian, three Italian, and fifteen Romanian. Sixty-five percent of the Luftwaffe's strength was deployed in support: 2,770 combat aircraft in all. Luftwaffe antiaircraft strength consisted of the II Flak Corps (three regiments) with thirteen mixed (light and heavy) AA battalions and four light AA battalions (Army Group South); and I Flak Corps (three regiments) with sixteen mixed AA battalions, seven light AA battalions (Army Group Center), and three AA regiments with eight mixed AA battalions and three light AA battalions (Army Group North). This represented 3,769 heavy, medium, and light guns—23.1 percent of the Luftwaffe's total antiaircraft gun strength. Prior to the invasion the Wehrmacht created six to eight motorized army flak batteries composed of a staff battery, two 88mm flak gun batteries, and one 20mm flak gun battery.

To meet the onslaught the Soviets deployed 3,310,000 men in 304 divisions with some 12,482 tanks and more than 8,000 aircraft. Tactical antiaircraft organizations were part of the Red Army and were formed in divisions assigned to a front area. Fronts were similar to German army groups. A normal Soviet AA division was equipped with the following: three to eight regiments with sixteen 76mm or 85mm guns, one light regiment with varying numbers of 37mm guns, and one to three regiments of 12.7mm AA machine guns. In total the Soviets would field 5,833 heavy, light, and medium guns representing 67.8 percent of its total force.

At 0415 on June 22, 1940, the Luftwaffe took to the air. In one of the most devastating preemptive airstrikes of all time, Luftwaffe fighters and bombers attacked over sixty-six Soviet airfields with impressive results. By dusk on the first day the Soviet losses included 322 aircraft lost to fighters and flak with another 814 destroyed on the ground (1,136 total). This figure would rise to 4,017 by the end of the first week for a loss of just 179 Luftwaffe aircraft.

During the opening phase of the war, AA guns for Russian airfields were too few and hard to obtain. Satellite fields were usually protected by a battery or two of light guns supplemented by machine guns taken from wrecked aircraft. Main bases had the benefit of a number of medium and heavy guns along with 12.7mm and 7.62mm machine guns. Accuracy was not highly rated by the Germans. But early on Luftwaffe pilots encountered intensive ground fire from small arms. Russian soldiers and airmen were well trained in the "everyone shoot" technique. Luftwaffe attacks at low level often met a hail of bullets. Soviet troops shot at all low-flying aircraft with what ever was at hand, rifles, submachine guns and pistols. From Osprey's Focke Wulf Aces of the Russia Front an unknown Fw 190 commented, "They just blazed away with everything they'd got; machine guns, rifles, even pistols."

Two Soviet quad mount M1910 7.62mm machine guns unleash a stream of tracer into the night sky. Each quad mount was capable of producing 1,800 rounds per minute. The M1910 was used throughout the war in single, double, and AA quad mounts. AUTHOR'S COLLECTION

While Luftwaffe losses were light, the number of damaged aircraft continued to rise. After their first sortie against a Russian airfield, the Ju-88s of 7./KG 51 had just two serviceable planes ready for their second sortie. The rest had been damaged by flak and small arms fire. Losses from small arms fire would plague the Luftwaffe for the duration of the war.

Luftwaffe flak doctrine divided battlefield defense, including air bases, as a cooperative responsibility between fighters and flak guns. Attacking enemy airfields directly was considered the best defense against aerial attack, and this worked extremely well in the first weeks and months of Operation Barbarossa. Indeed, by the end of 1941 thirty mixed flak battalions and eleven light flak battalions were given credit for the destruction of 1,891 aircraft, 926 tanks, and 583 bunkers destroyed.

This success, however, was a mixed blessing when the Wehrmacht failed to achieve the rapid victory envisioned by Hitler. By 1942 the war in the East transformed into a battle of attrition. As Soviet forces grew in strength, the Wehrmacht began to rely heavily on the flak forces of the Luftwaffe, as well as their own organic flak battalions. These guns were used in the antitank, artillery-support, and direct-fire roles. The Eastern Front's voracious hunger for men and guns caused local commanders to hastily form their own flak units consisting of ground personnel, construction crews, and signal corps, mixed with regular flak forces.

The only theater where specialized ground attack aircraft dominated the battlefield was on the Eastern Front. The two most well known were the Junkers Ju-87 Stuka and the Ilyushin Il-2 Shturmovik, or "armored attacker." The Ju-87 was first and foremost a divebomber (later equipped in the antitank role with two 37mm BK 3.7 [Flak 18] guns) while the Il-2 was a specialized ground attack aircraft. Both were heavily armored but the Il-2 more so. From the outset the Il-2 was designed to operate in the low-level regime and to take hits from small arms fire and glancing blows from larger-caliber ammunition. Nicknamed the "Flying Tank," the Il-2 had an armored tub that surrounded the engine, pilot, and rear gunner. The windscreen was 55mm thick, the pilot's rear plate and protection for the gunner were 13mm thick, the canopy side panels 8mm, and the engine cowling armor 6mm. At the beginning of Operation Barbarossa, the Soviet air force (VVS) had just 249 single seat Il-2s on strength. Capable of 251 mph and armed with two 23mm cannons and two 7.62mm machine guns, the Il-2 was capable of carrying 1,320 pounds of rockets and bombs. Early in the campaign Il-2 losses were heavy, but in the first half of 1942, production of the new Il-2M3 with a rear gunner reached 2,620 and output was more than doubled during the second half of the year with 5,596 completed.

For the Luftwaffe there were never enough fighters to intercept all Shturmovik attacks. Their low-level tactics often meant surprise was on their side. German armored formations quickly adapted by establishing early warning radio links. Any approaching Il-2 formation would be reported and passed along to neighboring units. They also increased their firepower. By the end of 1941, German mechanized troops began to receive their first towed 20mm Flakvierling 38 four-barreled antiaircraft guns. Soviet pilots soon learned to dread these highly effective weapons.

The increasing threat of Shturmovik attacks led to the formation of the Flakpanzer, mobile guns capable of moving with the tanks. Early variants included the 20mm Flakpanzer (38) on a Czech-built PzKw 38 (t) chassis and the Flakpanzer I with a single 20mm Flak 38 on a Panzer I chassis. Other mobile guns would follow including the 20mm Flakvierling 38 or a single 37mm Flak 43 mounted on a SdKfz 7/1 half-track, and the Panzer IV tank chassis.

By May 1943 the Luftwaffe had just 454 fighters available for combat along a 1,800-mile front. Flak guns soon became the main line of defense against the relentless low-level Soviet attacks.

Soviet low-level antiaircraft defenses centered on the quadruple 7.62mm Maxim machine gun, three-barreled PV-1 7.62mm machine gun, and the towed 37mm M39 antiaircraft gun. Like the Il-2 the Junkers Ju-87 Stuka was armored, but not as heavily as the Shturmovik. In 1943 the Luftwaffe introduced the Ju-87D tank buster. Armed with two 37mm B.K. 3.7 cannons, the new Ju-87D proved effective, but could not be flown in well-established combat zones. The Soviets were well equipped with light and medium

A Flakvierling 38 antiaircraft gun mounted on a SdKfz 7/1 half-track. The four-barreled Flak 38 was an extremely effective weapon against low-flying Allied fighter-bombers. The 20mm cannon had a maximum horizontal range of 5,320 yards and a maximum vertical range of 12,500 feet. Effective range, however, was closer to 7,000 feet. The Flak 38 was capable of firing 1,400 rounds per minute. AUTHOR'S COLLECTION

Soviet troops ready their M1910 Maxim quad mount gun. The M1910 machine gun was recoil operated, water cooled, and used 250-round belts. AUTHOR'S COLLECTION

flak guns, and their tactic of shooting with every available small arm made low-level attacks suicidal. Operationally the Ju-87D was only effective when the ground situation was fluid or when Soviet mechanized units were involved in a breakthrough operation. The only other way would have been to neutralize some of the antiaircraft defenses with a group of Fw-190 fighter-bombers. It was a luxury, however, the Luftwaffe could ill afford.

For medium- and high-altitude defense, the Soviets relied on the 85mm M39 antiaircraft gun. Equal in performance to the German 88mm Flak 36 gun, the M39 proved effective during the defense of Moscow. One of the main objectives of Operation Barbarossa was the capture of Moscow. As German forces closed in on the capital, Russian resistance stiffened considerably. To speed the process Hitler ordered Hermann Göring to destroy Moscow. To make it happen a large part of the Luftwaffe's medium bomber fleet was diverted from the battlefield to attack the city. It was a costly mistake. Even though the Russians had suffered grievous losses up to that point, the defense of Moscow was robust and underestimated by the Germans. To defend the city the Russians had 585 single-seat fighters, 1,044 heavy antiaircraft guns, and 336 machine guns. It also had radar coverage and 612 observation posts. The first raid against the Soviet capital was launched on the evening of July 21st, with 195 bombers taking part including Ju-88s, He-111s, and a small number of Do-17s. VVS fighters claimed approximately three bombers shot down with the flak defenses adding four more. The number of bombers damaged by flak is unknown, but the raid by 115 aircraft on the following night clearly shows the lower serviceability rate was most likely due to AA fire. On that night Soviet fighters and flak claimed the destruction of fifteen bombers. The third raid on July 24th was conducted by just one hundred bombers. The strong Russian defense and the demands for air support at the front quickly diminished the Luftwaffe bombers' force. Following raids rapidly decreased in size going from fifty to just fifteen. From July 1941 until April 1942, the Luftwaffe launched eighty-seven raids on the Soviet capital for no tactical or strategic result.

Luftwaffe flak gunners in the East were forced to fight a two-front war. When not engaging aircraft, 88mm flak batteries were constantly used in the antitank role and light/medium flak was used to support infantry and mechanized units, mostly in defense. The Eastern Front's insatiable hunger for guns and manpower was a graveyard for the Luftwaffe Flak arm. As the Soviet armies crossed Poland in 1944 and into German territory, more and more heavy flak batteries were transferred from the Reich to the Eastern Front. During the last week of January 1945, the Luftwaffe transferred 110 heavy and 58 medium and light flak batteries to battle the Soviets, followed by 327 heavy and 110 medium/light batteries in February. In the end the massive flak tower–mounted 128mm flak guns would be used as artillery against advancing Soviet troops during the final battle for Berlin.

On the Russian front light and medium flak played a crucial role, but in the defense of Germany and the occupied countries, its role was not as prevalent. Early low-level

The Soviet Model 1939 85mm antiaircraft gun was developed from the 76.2mm series and proved highly effective. The 85mm was much prized by the Germans with all captured examples being shipped to Germany and designated as the 85mm Flak M.39(r) and 85mm Flak M.44(r). Here Soviet troops man their gun in Smolensk. AUTHOR'S COLLECTION

attacks by Allied medium bombers proved disastrous, forcing them to fly higher out of the reach of the 20mm and 37mm guns. Even though low-level Allied attacks were infrequent, the Luftwaffe still had 1,048 light/medium flak batteries in the occupied countries and Germany.

In January 1944 Germany's light/medium flak guns would have a revival. When Maj. Gen. James Doolittle assumed command of the U.S. Eighth Air Force in January 1944, there was a change in fighter doctrine. Up to that point the P-51s, P-47s, and P-38s of VIII Fighter Command were used exclusively in the long-range escort role. Now they were instructed to destroy all Luftwaffe aircraft both in the air and on the ground. On February 8, 1944, the pilots of VIII Fighter Command received a new directive. "If bombers are not being attacked, groups will detach one or two squadrons to range out searching for enemy aircraft. Upon withdrawal, if endurance permits, groups will search for and destroy enemy aircraft in the air and on the ground." To encourage more pilots to engage in combat, the command stated that enemy aircraft destroyed on the ground would count the same as those destroyed in the air. For many young pilots the road to becoming an ace was now far easier than air-to-air combat. What they didn't realize was how well protected the Luftwaffe's airfields really were and that a single rifle-caliber machine-gun bullet could cause their demise. By the end of the war, light and medium flak would account for many more Eighth Air Force fighter pilots shot down than those lost to air-to-air combat.

By January 1944 the Luftwaffe was a spent force. Front-line fighter strength for the defense of Germany stood at just 400 single-engine and eighty twin-engine fighters. In contrast both the U.S. Eighth and Fifteenth Air Forces could put into the air more than 800 long-range escort fighters at any one time. The RAF 2nd Tactical Air Force alone had more than 600 front-line single-engine fighters operating over northern France in preparation for the D-Day landings. As the Allied air campaign increased, the air defense of Germany now fell to the guns of the Flak Corps.

In preparation for the D-Day invasion, the USAAF launched Operation Pointblank. The mission was to smash the Luftwaffe's ability to mount any resistance. As the number of attacks on Luftwaffe airfields increased, the Flak arm quickly moved a large number of idle light and medium flak batteries in defense. Just as VIII Fighter Command began hunting the Luftwaffe on the ground, the fighter-bombers of the British 2nd Tactical Air Force and U.S. Ninth Tactical Air Force began attacking targets in support of D-Day. Most of the targets were well defended. Spitfire pilot Flt. Lt. Bill McRae of 401 Squadron, Royal Canadian Air Force (RCAF), experienced low-level flak firsthand and quickly understood its dangers and hidden effects.

"It was light flak which caused the majority of our losses leading up to and during the Normandy campaign. Because the small caliber weapons had a high rate of fire, the guns were often mounted as multiple units, and as we were attacking down to very low levels, the odds of being hit were quite high. There was also a psychological factor, which came into play since most of these guns used tracer ammunition. It was rather unnerving to be diving at a target from which streams of red or white ping pong balls were floating up at you, seemingly right at you. Usually these would arc down before reaching you, having been fired out of range. Other times they would have the range but not the line and the pyrotechnics would sail by on either side. Not very comforting, knowing that just one of those things hitting your Achilles heel, the radiator, and your flying days would be over.

"Statistics for total loss of aircraft and pilots reflect only a small percentage of the number of Spitfires which were damaged but able to return safely. I recall one day when 401 Sq was unable to mount any operations during the afternoon due to an insufficient number of serviceable machines."

126 Wing RCAF (for which 401 Sq belonged) ORB (Operational Record Book) for June 27th states in part: "Flak opposition through the day was quite heavy, especially while strafing, and the Wing suffered 12 aircraft temporarily out of action from this cause."

From January 1944 to May 1945, strafing attacks on German airfields were constant and unrelenting. For German flak gunners it was a target-rich environment. In 1943 a typical permanent Luftwaffe base like Achmer in Germany was equipped with four 88mm flak guns, twelve 20mm guns, and several 20mm flak towers.

To provide clear fields of fire for light flak guns around airfields or forested areas, the Luftwaffe built hundreds of elevated platforms. This improvised timber structure is equipped with a single Flak 38 20mm cannon. NARA

Exposed to more and accurate flak, individual USAAF fighter squadrons and groups developed their own tactics to minimize their losses. P-47 pilot Maj. Bolek "Mike" Gladych of the 61st FS/56th FG wrote down the "Ten Commandments of Ground Strafing":

1. Before you make an attack be sure there are no enemy aircraft in the vicinity.

2. Make an approach into the wind, because sound is killed.

3. Watch out for the gun positions, and remember they are difficult to spot before they open fire—study your own gun positions, as they are much the same.

4. The closer to the gun you fly, the safer you are.

5. Pick out the target, give full throttle, half-a-ring elevation, aim steadily and open fire from about 1000 yards.

6. At 300 yards cease fire and get as close to the ground as you dare. Forget about the target and concentrate on flying only.

7. When attacking a gun remember that you have the advantage of fire power. Concentrate on one gun at a time. Go in and kill the crew.

8. Take the initiative and strike first—don't wait for them to open fire.

9. Don't become over confident because you are not hit in the first attack. At first the enemy gunners usually under-estimate your speed, but it doesn't take them long to spot their error.

10. Never spend all your ammunition.

The Germans quickly devised their own defensive tactics as well. Dummy airfields (flak traps) with surplus aircraft were established to draw fighters away from main bases. Operational fields used decoy aircraft and added more elevated flak stands (*Flakhochstanden*) equipped with the quadruple 20mm Flak 38 Flakvierling guns or a 37mm Flak 36 gun. The Germans also began flying from well-camouflaged secondary airstrips, which were well protected by up to a battalion of light flak guns. German fighters could take off and land under a curtain of protective fire and were extremely costly to attack.

Some U.S. group commanders questioned the value of strafing German airfields. Many of the aircraft destroyed were unused bombers, transports, and communication aircraft. They were essentially killing dead targets. Trading a well-trained fighter pilot for a useless Ju-88 was seen by some as a waste.

German fighters destroyed on the ground were quickly replaced. During 1944 German industry produced an incredible 14,212 Bf-109s. What the Luftwaffe wasn't producing was enough fighter pilots. The attrition rate far outpaced the replacement rate, and those new pilots that did arrive were poorly trained and easily shot down.

Ground strafing was not for the faint hearted or heavy handed. Flying at treetop level at better than 300 miles per hour, picking out a target, and hitting it took a great deal of skill, split-second timing, and almost instantaneous physical reaction. Avoiding flak was next to impossible. Bailing out of a damaged aircraft was not an option, and those aircraft that were hit and did not crash immediately often belly-landed a short distance from the airfield they were strafing.

The aircraft themselves were not well suited to the task. All of the Allied fighters assigned to the ground attack role had been designed as high-altitude fighters. The P-38,

German gunners ready for action aboard a flak barge in Germany. The 37mm Flak 36 was produced in large numbers and by August 1944 the Luftwaffe had 4,211 in service. Rate of fire was 120 rounds per minute with an effective range of 6,500 feet. NARA

P-51, Spitfire, Typhoon, and Tempest all had liquid-cooled engines and were extremely vulnerable to flak damage.

> If a P-51 got so much as one hole in the coolant system from just one machine gun bullet, even a little machine gun bullet, the Eighth Air Force might just as well chalk up one more fighter pilot MIA.
> —COL. JOHN B. HENRY, COMMANDING OFFICER, 339TH FG

Nothing was done to add any extra armor to protect the most vulnerable areas (cockpit sides, coolant tank, oil tank, radiators) on these fighters.

In February 1944 the USAAF changed tactics. Escort fighters were now tasked with the job of strafing Luftwaffe airfields. To add more guns the Germans developed the FlaSL 151, an inexpensive pedestal mount armed with three MG 151 15mm aircraft cannon. NARA

To minimize the losses to ground fire, the Eighth set up flak intelligence sections. Their job was to provide as much up-to-date information as possible (photo reconnaissance, flak maps, combat reports) regarding the defenses for each intended target. Armed with this information squadrons could plan their attacks in detail to avoid the heaviest concentration of guns. Squadrons and groups also assigned a certain number of fighters to the flak suppression role, finding and strafing known flak positions. Unfortunately many pilots found the antiaircraft information to be old and of little use. According to the USAAF 1944 strafing manual titled 'Down to Earth': 'The increasing use of mobile flak has made this problem increasingly difficult."

Beginning in May 1944 the Eighth Air Force Fighter Command began targeting transportation targets in France and Germany. They were joined by the RAF 2nd TAF and the U.S. Ninth TAF and XIX TAF already in the process. In Italy the Mediterranean Allied Air Force was already well versed in the art of ground attack, interdicting targets since 1943. The losses would be heavy. Between May 22nd and July 1st, the Eighth Air

Many Flak 36/37s were mounted on the versatile Sd.Kfz. 6 half-track. Like all Luftwaffe flak guns, they often provided direct fire support for ground troops. This version was captured by Allied troops in Italy. NARA

Force alone lost eighty fighters—fifty-nine to light flak, five to heavy flak, and sixteen to small arms fire.

By February 1944 German intelligence had correctly guessed the Allies would invade in the spring. Once the invasion began Luftwaffe plans called for the transfer of two railroad flak regiments, forty-three heavy flak batteries, and twenty-three light flak batteries to the battle area. Prior to the invasion German ground forces had also increased the number of light flak guns in each army division. A typical infantry division now had at least eighty-four 20mm guns, while a Panzer division, the type encountered in Normandy, was equipped at full strength with up to twenty-one self-propelled, fifty-five towed, and thirty-two truck- or half-track mounted flak guns. In both formations the addition of hundreds of lighter-caliber machine guns only added to their lethality.

The D-Day landings at Normandy on June 6th caught the Germans by surprise. Elaborate Allied decoy plans succeeded in leading many German commanders to believe that enemy troops would land at the Pas de Calais. Hitler, using his well-known "intuition," remained undecided, believing the Normandy landings to be a gigantic feint. Despite the obvious, Hitler rejected the pleas of his ground commanders and refused to release Panzer units from other sectors to contain the beachhead. In sharp contrast the Luftwaffe reacted quickly, sending 140 heavy and 50 light flak batteries into France. This force was complemented by no fewer than 15 Jadgruppen of Bf-109s and Fw-190s. To protect their vital supply routes, the Luftwaffe quickly formed "Road Protection Regiments." Equipped with machine guns and light cannons, these were mostly horse drawn and suffered from a lack of manpower. For the protection of railway traffic, railway transport protection battalions (*Eisenbahntransport schutzflakbaterien*) were formed. Each troop consisted of two gun trucks, equipped with either a single 20mm gun or a quadruple 20mm unit. These formations were very effective and successful air attacks on protected trains were very rare.

Allied air cover over the Normandy beaches was overwhelming with a twenty to one advantage over the Luftwaffe. On the first day of the invasion, the combined Allied fighter force flew 1,547 sorties over the beachhead with a further 1,800 flown as escort and fighter-bomber operations. By the end of the day, the Allies lost 127 aircraft mostly to flak, with Luftwaffe pilots claiming just sixteen of the total shot down. While German flak accounted for the vast majority of Allied losses over the beaches, friendly fire also contributed to that number. Pilots and gunners on both sides during the war did not have very good aircraft recognition skills. In most situations gunners had just seconds to identify whether an aircraft

The towed version of the 20mm Flak 38 gun. In comparison to Soviet and Allied armies, the German army was the least mechanized. Right up until the end of the war, they relied on thousands of horses for transport and many flak guns would have been towed in this way. NARA

was friend or foe. The safest place for Allied aircraft during and after the invasion was at high altitude, well away from the ships and beaches. Flt. Lt. Bill McRae of 401 Squadron RCAF recalled: "It was not always enemy flak causing the damage. A few days after D-Day, 126 Wing, attempting to cross the beaches to take up patrol, were fired on by the Royal Navy. After several unsuccessful attempts, in which one pilot was killed, another wounded, and six aircraft damaged, the Wing gave up and returned to Tangmere." The Royal Navy wasn't the only guilty party. As the Allied forces pushed out from the beachhead, the Luftwaffe mounted more and more fighter-bomber attacks. To meet these ground attacks both Commonwealth and American ground forces were well equipped with a mix of 37mm, 40mm Bofors, 20mm Polsten guns, and .50-caliber and .303-inch Bren machine guns.

The Swedish Bofors 40mm antiaircraft gun was the best medium gun of the war. It would serve on every front and was highly effective against low-flying aircraft. Here Canadian troops man their 40mm L/60 gun in Normandy. Firing a 2-pound high-explosive shell, it had an effective range of 6,000 feet. AUTHOR'S COLLECTION

For Allied pilots flying near the front line, being fired on by their own guns was not unusual. In fairness to the Allied gunners, an approaching Spitfire looked similar to a Bf-109 and a P-47 looked very much like an Fw-190. For the gunners of the 3rd Canadian Light Anti-Aircraft Regiment, the similarities ended in tragedy. On July 12th at 1400 hours, "six Messerschmitt 109Gs appeared from the same direction (south west) and banked sharply north at the same place as they did on the day previous. Three were immediately shot down; the others continued, but two of them were smoking badly when last seen. The pilot of one machine bailed out but drifted down into his own lines near the Orne River to the south of the gun positions. Later in the day two Spitfires following the same course as the enemy and machine gunning as they came passed over the gun positions. Both were shot down. A Court of Inquiry was convened to investigate the tactics of the Spitfire pilots and the Regiment was relieved of all blame."

After the successful landing and expansion of the beachhead, the Allies' first priority was the construction of landing strips. The first constructed were Emergency Landing Strips (ELS) used for aircraft in trouble, then Refueling and Re-arming strips (R&Rs), and then Advanced Landing Grounds (ALG), capable of operating a full wing of fighters.

Any German aircraft that ventured over the Normandy front was usually met with a hail of antiaircraft fire. Allied ground troops were well equipped with AA guns of all calibers from machine guns to 90mm and 3.7-inch heavy antiaircraft guns. AUTHOR'S COLLECTION

The Polsten 20mm antiaircraft gun entered service with the British and Canadian armies in 1944. Less complicated than the Oerlikon 20mm gun, the Polsten appeared in single, double, and triple mounts. Here Canadian troops man their towed Polsten gun in Normandy. AUTHOR'S COLLECTION

In the British sector the airfields were well protected by a range of weapons including British Bren guns, 20mm Polsten guns, and 40mm Bofors. In the American sector half-track-mounted M15A1 37mm M1 and two M2 .50-caliber machine guns, 40mm Bofors guns, the M45 quad mount .50-caliber machine gun, and single .50-caliber machine guns defended the strips. The heavier guns, the British 3.7-inch and American 90mm guns, saw limited service, engaging mostly nocturnal raiders over the beachhead.

As the Allies built up their strength, Luftwaffe reinforcements poured into Normandy. By June 8th, 1,000 aircraft had arrived. None of the bombers (Ju-88s, He-177s, and Do-217s) were used during the day but carried out night raids with heavy losses.

The Luftwaffe fighters that did arrive were pressed into the Jagdbomber (fighter-bomber) role. Instead of being used to attack Allied fighters and gain air superiority over the battlefield, Wehrmacht commanders insisted they be used in the ground attack role. Those that were able to penetrate the vigilant Spitfire and Mustang patrols did not survive the intense flak over the battlefield and made little impression. Indeed, during the Normandy campaign from June 7th to June 30th, U.S. First Army antiaircraft gunners alone were credited with ninety-six aircraft shot down of 682 engaged. Following Operation Cobra and the breakout from the beachhead, between July 31st and August 6th, the Luftwaffe launched over a thousand raids for a loss of fifty-eight aircraft due to flak. Not one bridge, road junction, or vital target was hit.

Protection of German ground forces now fell exclusively to the guns of the Flak Corps. After the D-Day landings Flak Corps III moved to bolster German ground defenses and help seal off the Normandy beachhead. They played a key role in slowing the Allied advance in June and July. As Allied pressure increased, the Flak Corps was

The Bofors's relatively light weight offered great mobility and the ability to set up quickly. Here American gunners ready their gun in Germany sometime in March 1945. The swastikas on the side of the gun denote the number of kills, making this one an ace. NARA

Fighters flying low-level missions did not just have light and medium flak to worry about. During a divebombing mission in March 1945, Lt. Hoyt Benge's P-47 suffered the effects of an 88mm flak burst. He managed to land his P-47 but it was a complete write-off. NATIONAL MUSEUM OF THE USAF

forced to concentrate its heavy batteries (88mm and 105mm guns) for artillery and direct antitank support. Allied armor would pay a heavy price with 60 percent of tank losses due to a single round from a 75mm or 88mm gun.

The Allied victory in Normandy has been attributed to the numerical superiority and the paralyzing effects of both strategic and tactical air power. While the Allies did have complete control of the skies, it never fully translated to decisive destruction on the battlefield. Ground attacks by Allied fighter-bombers were not as effective as some histories have made out. There are a number of reasons for this, but the three most important were the presence of flak, the inaccuracy of the air-to-ground weapons used, and the fact the aircraft used were fighters and not divebombers. None of the Allied fighters that used the divebombing method were modified to carry dive brakes. Dive brakes allowed a divebomber to maintain a set speed during a dive, thus increasing accuracy. When a fighter like the P-47 or Spitfire went into a dive, it gained speed rapidly. For the pilot to have sufficient time to pull out of the dive, that meant a higher release point, usually around 4,000 feet.

RCAF Spitfire pilot Flt. Lt. Bill McRae describes the physically taxing pull-up maneuver and how sometimes it proved deadly. "On our first dive-bombing show I went through the procedure, pulled out with great difficulty, blacked out, to recover back up

The Spitfire did many things very well, but as a fighter-bomber, it was lackluster. Capable of carrying 1,000 pounds of bombs, as seen here, it was extremely vulnerable to ground fire. The big radiators under the wings and the oil tank, located directly under the front of the engine, had no armor plate. A single machine-gun bullet in one these two areas often led to the loss of the aircraft. AUTHOR'S COLLECTION

about where I started. I believe the training we had with small smoke bombs was inadequate, especially since we were not told what to expect when dealing with the real thing. Consequently we each had our own idea how to go about it. Initially I trimmed out for the dive then tried to trim out while pulling out of the dive. It usually took both hands on the stick, pulling with all my strength to get out of the dive. A day later I watched as another of our pilots appeared to be pulling out, then the dive steepened, past the vertical, and he plowed right into the ground.

"In my opinion our efforts at dive-bombing were almost a complete failure; we were unable to achieve the precise bombing that our small targets called for. Had we been given area targets, such as marshalling yards or troop concentrations, we could have made a better contribution."

The primary weapons used by the Allied tactical air forces were the free-falling bomb (500-pound, 1,000-pound, and cluster munitions) and the 3-inch air-to-ground rocket projectile (RP). Operational Research (OR) studies prior to D-Day clearly showed bombs dropped from fighters in a dive were found to hit a viaduct 500 yards long and 85 yards wide just once in eighty-two attempts. The "tank-busting" rocket-firing Typhoon was just as inaccurate. During an RAF trial in 1944, it was shown that one rocket could destroy or seriously damage a Panther tank (when the rocket hit the side armor), but it took sixty-four rockets to achieve three hits on a stationary target. The presence of flak decreased accuracy even further. To achieve a 50 percent chance of an RP hit, the following effort had to be made.

- Small gun position   44 Sorties 350 RPs fired
- Panther tank   18 Sorties 140 RPs fired
- Large gun position   11 Sorties 88 RPs fired
- Army hut   3 Sorties 24 RPs fired
- Large building   1 Sortie 8 RPs fired

The fighter-bomber's most effective accurate weapons were its machine guns and cannon. The P-47 was armed with eight .50-caliber Browning machine guns while the Typhoon and Tempest carried four 20mm Hispano cannons. Against soft-skin or lightly armored vehicles, they were devastating.

Fighter-bomber pilots faced a highly dangerous low-level environment. In the autumn of 1944, Typhoon squadron leader Charles Demoulin calculated that the average survival rate for a rocket-Typhoon pilot was about seventeen missions—and the reason was flak and small arms fire. Demoulin recognized the supremacy of German flak and gave the odds in favor of the Germans at four to one. The odds soon caught up to Demoulin when he was shot down by flak on December 5, 1944, near Ede, Holland. He survived as a POW.

While aircraft such as the Typhoon and P-47 Thunderbolt were rugged, they were nonetheless vulnerable to a direct hit from flak. Most numerous was the 20mm single-barrel Flak 38 and the 20mm four-barreled Flakvierling. The rate of fire for these weapons was high with the Flak 38 capable of 450 rounds per minute and the Flakvierling an impressive 1,800 rounds per minute. These weapons were supported by the heavier 37mm Flak 36/43 (150 and 500 rpm) and the twin-barrel Flakzwilling capable of 500 rounds per minute. A single hit by a 37mm was almost always fatal and a well-aimed 20mm hit would do the same. The chances of taking a hit from a well-defended target were high. To press home their attacks, Allied fighters often found themselves diving through a curtain of flak (3,000 to 6,000 feet).

German flak lethality was confirmed by 2nd TAF Operational Research Section (ORS), which concluded that "practically all damage sustained on operations due to enemy action was caused by light flak."

On July 25, 1944, Operation Cobra began, signaling the American breakout from Normandy. The American offensive made rapid advances to the south and southeast led by the Third U.S. Army. This was followed by Operation, TOTALIZE (August 7th)

The positioning of an antiaircraft gun was critical to its overall effectiveness. This well-positioned 37mm Flak 43 has a clear field of fire over the bridge it was assigned to protect. Rate of fire was 180 rounds per minute. This version was introduced in early 1944 to replace the Flak 36/37 gun. NARA

and TRACTABLE (August 12th), launched by the First Canadian Army and British divisions of the 21st Army Group. By August 8th the Allied armies were ordered to converge on the Falaise-Chambois area to trap German Army Group B. The U.S. First Army formed the southern army, the British Second Army the base, with the First Canadian Army squeezing the north arm of the encirclement. As the Germans began their retreat, tactical airpower—most effective against ground forces already defeated and in full retreat—came into its own. Allied fighter-bombers proved devastating, destroying hundreds of trucks and lightly armored vehicles. But it came at a price. Fighting to keep their escape routes open, German flak crews continued to inflict heavy casualties. On August 18th the pocket was finally closed. During the last two days of the battle, the 2nd TAF lost thirty aircraft due to flak with many more damaged. It was also the greatest loss of Typhoons in a single day—seventeen destroyed and four badly damaged.

From July 25th to August 7th, the U.S. Ninth TAC lost eighty aircraft, 49 percent to flak, 7 percent to enemy aircraft, 24 percent to small arms fire, and 20 percent from unknown causes (most likely flak). Protecting German forces in the Falaise Pocket fell to

To suppress German antiaircraft defenses, Typhoons from the British 2nd Tactical Air Force began to use the No. 23 cluster bomb in 1944. This Typhoon carries two bombs, which contain twenty-six 20-pound fragmentation bombs. DND

the guns of the III Flak Corps. Wolfgang Pickert, a General der Flak-Artillerie in charge of the III Flak korps, reported that in "fighter-bomber weather . . . the movement of large vehicles during the hours of daylight was practically tantamount to their certain loss." But when light antiaircraft forces were present in sufficient strength (a rarity in Normandy), "fighter-bombers had hardly any successes, or only with heavy losses."

The type of missions flown by the tactical air forces had a direct bearing on losses sustained by flak. During the European campaign the tactical air forces flew five types of missions: fighter sweep, close air support, divebombing (as close air support and targets behind the front line), armed reconnaissance, and fighter escort. Armed reconnaissance and attacks on specific targets beyond the battlefield, rather than close air support, created the most flak casualties. Flak at the front line, except in support of heavily defended key positions, was far lighter than encountered beyond the battle zone, because the Germans concentrated their flak assets on their vital transportation networks, airfields, headquarters, and supply dumps. The tactical air forces flew more armed reconnaissance missions than close air support and in turn lost more aircraft. Even in the last full month of the

European war, German flak was still effective. In April 1945 No. 83 Group RAF 2nd TAF mounted 5,443 armed reconnaissance sorties for the loss of eighty-three fighters and sixty-nine pilots lost. In contrast 7,393 close air support and fighter patrols were also flown for the loss of thirty-three fighters and twenty-seven pilots.

On January 1, 1945, one of the last great flak battles of the war took place. On the evening of December 31, 1944, Luftwaffe fighter units in the West were readied for Operation Bodenplatte ("Baseplate")—a massive attack on Allied airfields (twelve British and four American) throughout Belgium, southern Holland, and France. II. Jagdkorps had 986 (Bf-109s and Fw-190s) aircraft available, as well as twenty-four Me-262 and six Ar-234B jet bombers. The attack was to be a surprise, catching the Allied air forces on the ground. Unfortunately for the many and inexperienced Luftwaffe fighter pilots, considerable numbers of 2nd TAF and U.S. Ninth Air Force aircraft were already airborne engaging the incoming enemy formations. As the German fighters began their attacks, the AA gunners of the RAF Regiment, Canadian Army, and U.S. Army responded with intense and accurate fire. The majority of the guns employed were the superb 40mm Bofors, augmented on American airfields by the quad .50-caliber mounts and on the British and Canadian airfields by the Bren .303-inch machine guns.

Wherever American troops were found, the M45 heavy-barreled .50-caliber quad mount AA gun was present. From their towed trailer American gunners scan the sky. The M45 was capable of firing 1,600 to 2,200 rounds per minute. NARA

Ground personnel also joined in with their side arms, rifles, and Sten guns. It was now the Germans' turn to experience just how effective light and medium flak over the battlefield really was. Indeed, even before the German fighters reached the Allied lines, they had to run the gauntlet of their own flak defenses. All German flak units were usually warned of Luftwaffe sorties planned for each day, but on January 1, 1945, in order to keep the raid secret, they were not informed. Even before the attack began, the Luftwaffe suffered its first losses. Some estimates put the number shot down by friendly fire as seventeen. Coming in at treetop level, the Luftwaffe attacks were not well coordinated and their shooting was poor. Wing leader Johnnie Johnson described their marksmanship as "atrocious."

Operation Bodenplatte was a complete failure. Hoping to destroy 400 to 500 Allied aircraft, the Luftwaffe fell well short of its plan and suffered grievous losses. Allied losses amounted to approximately 300 aircraft. The attack lasted no more than a half hour, but in the end the Luftwaffe lost 271 aircraft shot down and 65 damaged, 143 pilots dead or missing, 70 taken prisoner, and 21 wounded. Allied fighters shot down between 60 and

This posed photo clearly shows the effective M54 combination mount, consisting of one 37mm M1A2 gun and two .50-caliber machine guns. Because machine guns were ballistically similar to the 37mm gun, the gunners could use their tracer fire to correct their aim before firing the main gun.
AUTHOR'S COLLECTION

80 German aircraft leaving the rest to the AA gunners. The RAF Regiment alone claimed 47 aircraft shot down.

In the last few months of the war, German flak continued to take its toll. On April 1, 1945, the 2nd TAF alone lost thirty aircraft to flak.

Even with air superiority the battle in Europe was essentially an infantry war with huge losses. Beginning in the Normandy campaign, Britain, Canada, and the United States all suffered far higher casualty rates than projected. Manpower shortfalls became a real problem. Like the Germans the Allies quickly turned to their AA units to make good the shortfalls in infantrymen.

Light and medium flak proved extremely effective during the Second World War. Losses of aircraft and crewmen numbered in the thousands. The U.S. Ninth and Twelfth Tactical Air Forces sacrificed 2,415 medium bombers and fighters to flak. From June 6, 1944, to May 1945, the RAF's 2nd Tactical Air Force lost 1,617 aircraft, the vast majority to flak. The U.S. VIII Fighter Command's tactics of ground strafing cost them 890 fighters; the Fifteenth would add another 236 fighters. The greatest carnage occurred on the Russian front. During four years of war, the Soviets lost an estimated 17,000 aircraft to Luftwaffe, army, navy, and SS flak defenses in the East.

A captured 37mm flak gun. This emplacement was the standard configuration with the outer wall of planks and the space in between filled in with dirt. Ammunition lockers were placed on the periphery of the gun pit, with one locker used for equipment storage. NARA

CHAPTER EIGHT

Battling the V-1 Flying Bomb

The mountain hath groaned and brought forth a mouse.
—LORD CHERWELL, CHIEF SCIENTIFIC ADVISOR TO THE PRIME MINISTER

ON JUNE 13, 1944, AT 0350 HOURS NEAR HESDIN, NORTHERN FRANCE, ONE OF THE FIRST V-1s (*Vergeltungswaffe 1*—Revenge Weapon No. 1) aimed at England was fully fuelled and ready for launch. After engine start and seven seconds to maximum thrust, the missile was released. Accelerating rapidly up the 156-foot launch ramp, it flew off at about 250 mph. Six minutes later the missile reached its cruising altitude of approximately 3,000 feet headed for London. Of the ten missiles launched that night, four crashed immediately or shortly after takeoff. At 0410 hours British radar near Dover caught their first glimpse of this new type of aerial warfare. It was the beginning of a unique antiaircraft battle that would be one of the longest of the war.

After the battle of Britain and the Blitz, Britain continued to battle the Luftwaffe for a long period of time. The bomber raids were not nearly as large, but required a constant vigilance and an improved AA defense. By the late spring of 1941, Britain's AA defenses had undergone a complete transformation. Gun-laying radar in the form of the GL Mk II contributed greatly to the accuracy of AA fire and increased enemy losses for any nocturnal raid. By 1942 the gun-laying Mk III radar, designed and built in Canada, was introduced, improving accuracy even more, allowing for the employment of continuously pointed fire at night and through cloud cover.

Hitler's turn to the east and the invasion of the Soviet Union in June 1941 left the Luftwaffe bomber force in the West with about 200 bombers. In response to the RAF's devastating attack on the city of Lubeck in March 1942, Hitler ordered reprisal on British cities. From April to May 1942 the Luftwaffe struck a number of cities killing 1,637 civilians for heavy losses. At the same time the Luftwaffe launched their "tip and run"

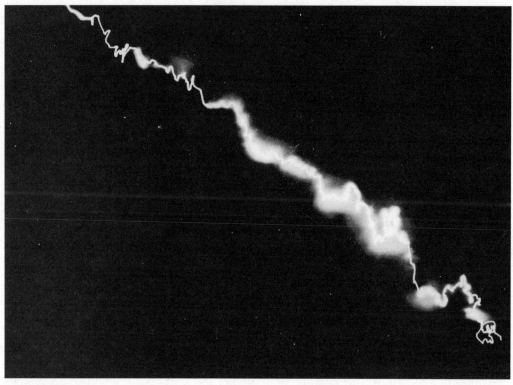

A V-1 leaves a fiery trail in the night sky over England. The V-1 was a twenty-four-hour bombardment weapon, and for those living in the threatened areas, they quickly learned to recognize the distinctive rumble of its pulse jet engine. NARA

fighter-bomber raids along the south coast of England. Skimming the wave tops at about 50 feet, fast-flying Bf-109s and Fw-190s were impossible to detect let alone shoot down. These raids were more of an annoyance and had no military significance, but had to be addressed. To battle this new menace, AA Command was forced to deploy 115 40mm Bofors guns and hundreds of .303-caliber Lewis machine guns along the coast. During the fifteen-month campaign AA Command was credited with twenty-eight fighters shot down with RAF fighters adding another twenty-eight. While the raids had no military impact, they did give the light AA gunners a taste of what was to come.

In January 1944 Hitler ordered the last direct revenge attacks on London and southern coastal cities. The Luftwaffe committed 500 bombers to the task, codenamed Operation *Steinbock*. London was well equipped to meet the threat with 284 heavy guns, which included 3.7-inch and 4.5-inch guns along with sixteen 5.25-inch guns and GL Mk III radar. From January to May 1944 the Luftwaffe lost more than 300 bombers to the defenses with AA Command credited with 49½ bombers shot down, plus two probables and ten damaged.

By 1944 Hitler's hope for final victory lay with the new V-1 and V-2 missiles, or Vergeltungswaffe. British Intelligence was well aware of the German long-range rocket program, and initial plans for an effective defense began. To delay the deployment of these new weapons, the Allies launched Operation Crossbow (the destruction of the missile and storage sites in France).

On December 5, 1943, the Crossbow campaign began. This effort was shared by RAF Bomber Command, US Eighth and Ninth Army Air Forces, and the 2nd Tactical Air Force. The campaign, while costly in aircraft and crews lost (the majority to flak), did manage to pulverize most if not all of the permanent sites, and it was believed at the time to have delayed the start of the missile attack on London by six months. This forced the Germans to build "modified sites" that were easier to construct and more difficult to locate and destroy.

In parallel with Operation Crossbow, the plan to defend Britain against V-1 attack was codenamed Diver. Planning for this defense fell to Air Marshal Sir Roderic Hill, head of the Air Defense of Great Britain, and Maj. Gen. Sir Frederick Pile of AA Command. Believing the Germans would be able to launch two V-1s per hour from existing sites toward London, the British devised a defensive plan that incorporated a mix of heavy and light antiaircraft guns, searchlights, barrage balloons, and both day- and night-fighters.

On June 8, 1944, two days after the successful D-Day landings, Major General Pile received word that the flying bomb threat had "entirely disappeared" and Operation Diver would not be implemented. At eighteen minutes past four in the morning on June 13th, the first flying bomb to strike Britain came crashing to earth at Stone, near Dartford, exploding harmlessly on agricultural land. This was quickly followed by three more, which struck sequentially in Sussex, at Bethnal Green, and near Sevenoaks in Kent. The Chiefs of Staff believed "these were only tests," but between the evening of June 15 and midday on the 16th, 244 V-1s were launched toward London with seventy-three reaching greater London and a further fifty or so into the area around Southampton. The "testing" was over; the battle had begun, an antiaircraft campaign that would last until March 29, 1945.

The first line of defense consisted of nine squadrons of Spitfire, Tempest, and Typhoon day-fighters and two squadrons of Mosquito night-fighters. These fighters flew standing patrols along three lines: the first line was positioned 20 miles off the southern coast, one above the coastline itself, and the last one 15 miles inland. Behind the fighter patrol lines was the gun zone known as the Kentish Gun Belt. Packed into the belt were 192 3.7-inch guns, 246 40mm Bofors guns, and 216 searchlights. The heavy 3.7-inch guns were supported by gun-laying Mk III radars and Vickers Predictors using time-fused shells. A wall of 480 barrage balloons just outside of London served as the last line of defense.

The guns came into action almost immediately, and over the first three weeks of the campaign, many additional guns arrived in North Downs south of London. Reinforcements came from training units, the Royal Marines, and the U.S. Army. In the first week of July, there were 373 heavy barrels along with 592 40mm Bofors guns. A week later these would be augmented by a further 500 RAF Regiment guns (mostly 20mm). By the end of July the Diver AA defense had ballooned to 373 3.7-inch guns, 776 40mm Bofors, and 422 20mm guns.

The increase in the number of guns was in direct response to the increased intensity of the V-1 bombardment. By the end of the day on July 15, 1944, the Germans had launched no fewer than 4,361 V-1s against Britain. Of those, 2,934 were logged by the defenses, 1,693 escaping destruction and 1,270 landing somewhere in the London Civil Defense Region. The defenses responded by destroying 1,241 flying bombs. Of those only 261⅓ were credited to the AA guns on the North Downs, 924 credited to the fighters, and 55 to balloons. Despite the huge effort to mobilize and place 1,400 heavy and light guns, by far the greater proportion of the V-1s destroyed fell to the guns of the fighters. By July 15th it was obvious the guns were not performing as expected.

The reasons for this were many. The V-1 was a tiny target. Its small size and high speed (350 to 400 mph) made it hard to pick up visually. For AA gunners attempting to shoot down a V-1 approaching head-on, the presentation area was less than 16 square feet, compared with 45 square feet for the Focke Wulf Fw-190. The V-1 also represented a new type of target. As a pilotless cruise missile, the V-1 was not deterred by AA fire. For the first time AA gunners had to destroy their target outright to be successful. Causing it to explode in the air was the desired effect. Since all antiaircraft gunnery was based on a target flying straight and level at a constant speed, the V-1 should have been an easy target. It was not.

For the heavy guns the V-1s' low approach heights (between 1,000 and 3,000 feet) defeated the traverse rate of the mobile 3.7-inch gun. For the light guns the height put the V-1s at the limit of their effectiveness. The power-operated static 3.7-inch guns worked best with their smoother and faster rates of tracking. Static guns had the benefit of being bolted down in concrete; the mobiles were simply placed on level ground. With the mobiles being more numerous, a way had to be found to improve their performance. The solution was the "Pile Platform." Devised by Brigadier General Burls, chief mechanical engineer of AA Command, the new platform was a combination of railway sleepers and rails in the form of a cross, buried in rubble and quick-setting concrete.

The existing radar sets also did not work as well as hoped. To avoid enemy jamming the radars were located in folds and hollows of the Downs, resulting in a stream of spurious contacts. Fighters chasing a V-1 into the gun belt force were often damaged, forcing the guns to cease firing.

On one occasion AA gunners had trouble identifying Britain's first jet fighter, employed specifically to battle the V-1. Gunner Ron Ford remembers:

"Control told us that there was a fast target approaching at 3,000 feet. I had seen a Meteor a few days earlier but before I could shout a warning the guns started to fire. No one noticed that it had two engines and was much bigger than a V-1, they thought it was a German aircraft. The pilot gave a remarkable display of the aircraft's maneuverability and every other gun opened up on it as it took evasive action and escaped."

By mid-July the decision had been made to abandon the Kentish Gun Belt and move everything to the coast to provide an unrestricted field of fire. In a herculean task begun on July 14th and completed in just four days, 23,000 personnel and 30,000 tons worth of

ammunition were moved to their new positions. The new gun belt now ran from Cuck-
mere Haven to St. Margaret's Bay, with a secondary cordon known as the Diver Box (208
heavy and 578 light guns) formed along the Thames Estuary to protect London from air-
launched V-1s approaching from the east. By July 19th the new coastal gun belt was in
action. The great advantage of the new location was unrestricted firing over the sea. This
allowed 2-inch rocket launchers to be added to the guns. It was a formidable concentration
of guns and rocket launchers with 412 heavy guns, which included 16 90mm U.S. Army
guns, 572 light guns, 584 light guns from the RAF Regiment, and 200 rocket launchers.

As the world's first cruise missile, the V-1 was powered by the most basic of jet
engines and was a crude and inaccurate bombardment weapon. From a technical stand-
point the V-1 could have been in service during the battle of Britain. With a maximum
range of 160 miles, its flight time was between twenty and twenty-five minutes and the
longer it flew the slower it went.

At the time of the V-1 campaign, the standard British gun-laying radar was GL Mk
III, which produced a range, a bearing, and an angle of elevation to the target, all manually
tracked by the radar operator, transmitted to the predictor, which then produced the gun

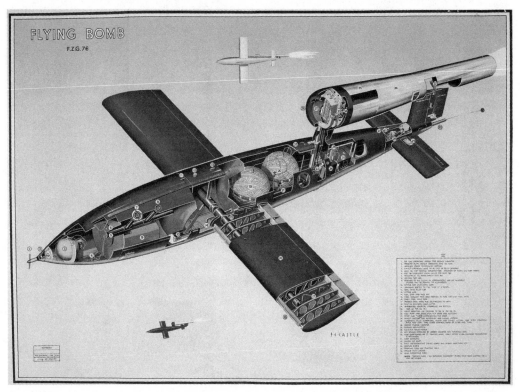

This Air Intelligence cutaway drawing shows the inner workings of the V-1 flying bomb. At launch the
V-1 weighed 4,858 pounds of which 1,185 was fuel and 1,988 pounds was the warhead. AUTHOR'S
COLLECTION

The American SCR-584 radar played a vital role in the V-1 defense. The SCR-584 offered fully automatic tracking and aiming with no need for manual intervention once the target had been locked on, feeding its information directly to the guns. NARA

data. And just as the gunners found their range, two important technical developments tilted the battle well into their favor.

General Pile knew the flying bombs would present a very inviting target for his guns. Its "robotic" character (with no pilot to take evasion action) made it the perfect target. To make his gunners' aim even more accurate, Pile requested the supply of American SCR-584 radars.

The new radar, when presented with a target, automatically locked on and followed it more smoothly than any human operator. The information was then electrically fed to the new No. 10 Predictor system, which delivered the output data and was capable of driving a power-operated gun. This new system could now point the gun and follow it smoothly and accurately without human intervention. All the gunners had to do was load and fire as fast as possible.

The second and most technically advanced improvement was the proximity or VT fuse. (For many years the letters *VT* were often said to mean "variable time." This was encouraged to hide the real nature of the fuse, and in fact the letters came about because the new shell was developed by Section V of the Navy Bureau of Ordnance and designated as "Project T"). As far back as 1938, radar scientists were well aware of the errors inherent when aiming and setting fuses for effective antiaircraft fire. One suggestion was to develop a fuse with a simple receiver capable of picking up the radar signals reflected from the target by either early-warning radar or a ground-laying set. Once in range the reflected energy would cause the shell to explode. But the signal strengths were too weak. The next step was to put a complete radio transmitter/receiver unit into the fuse itself. In 1940 work on the new fuse began led by the U.S. Navy. The first development was the VT fuse Mk 32 for the U.S. Navy's 5-inch/38 gun. This was followed by other variants for U.S. Army and British army and navy antiaircraft guns.

In August 1942 the new proximity-fused 5-inch/38 shells were test fired with good results. Designated as the Mk 32, the new projectile was delivered to the U.S. Fleet during November and December 1942. Shortly after, VT shells from the cruiser USS *Helena* shot down the first of many Japanese aircraft in January 1943. In mid-1944 the first VT T98 fuse for the British 3.7-inch AA gun came off the production line.

By the end of June, AA Command was now well equipped and supplied with the new SCR-584 radars and VT shells. In conjunction with the proven 3.7-inch guns and the freedom of action over the water, experienced gunners saw their accuracy increase rapidly. During the first week on the coast, the guns destroyed just 17 percent of all flying bombs entering the gun belt. That figure increased to 60 percent by August 23 and 74 percent in the last week of the month. In one extraordinary day the gunners destroyed 82 percent of all targets available to the guns. On average the heavy guns were expending just 156 shells per V-1 shot down, an unprecedented low figure.

At the beginning of September, the first phase of the V-1 antiaircraft campaign came to an end. As the Allied armies cleared the Pas de Calais area, the V-1 launch sites were overrun and the bombardment ceased. From June 13th to September 5th, the Luftwaffe sent 8,617 ground-launched and 400 air-launched V-1 missiles toward Britain. Of the 9,017 V-1s in all, the guns were credited with 1,459 destroyed. Fighters added 1,771 and the balloons chipped in with 231. Approximately 2,450 hit London. For General Pile and his men, it was a satisfying victory: "More was learnt about the potentialities of antiaircraft work in 80 days than had been learned in the previous 30 years."

While the worst was over the battle continued. On September 16th the second phase began, and for the gunners it would be an ordeal like no other, as the Luftwaffe began air launching their V-1s in earnest. Flying across the North Sea, they managed to outflank the AA guns south and east of London. In response to the new threat, a new "Diver Strip" running north from the River Blackwater extending up to Great Yarmouth was set up. On September 21st the guns were ordered to move from Kent and Sussex up to the coast of Essex and Suffolk. It was a difficult and dreary affair. Unlike the good road networks in Kent and Sussex, the roads to the Essex and Suffolk coast were poor and unmaintained. The terrain also proved hostile being made up of below sea level marshes and dunes. Two

This film capture shows British gunners loading their 3.7-inch Mk III with VT proximity-fused shells. The number of gunners ready with shells clearly displays how efficient the guns were during the V-1 campaign. With the SCR-584 radar and VT proximity-fused shell, all the gunners had to do was to load and fire the gun as fast as possible. AUTHOR'S COLLECTION

A small number of American M1A1 90mm AA guns were added to the defense against the V-1 threat. A gun crew prepare their gun for firing in southern England, 1944. Used in all U.S. theaters of war, a total of 7,831 90mm guns were produced by August 1945. NARA

hundred miles of road was built. Accommodation for 50,000 men and 10,000 women was needed, requiring 4,000 Nissen huts to be dismantled and moved from all over Britain. The move did not go well. Along the narrow and twisting roads convoys, often blocked each other causing huge traffic jams. Orders were often contradictory and vague. Men found themselves without accommodation, rations, or essential equipment. It was a logistical nightmare and AA Command's most embarrassing moment of the war.

By October 13th and despite the appalling difficulties, the gunners of AA Command redeployed 300 guns all by themselves. By the end of the month, that increased to 542 heavy and 503 medium guns ready for action.

Launched from low-flying Heinkel He-111s, the air-dropped V-1 presented a very different target. Flying no higher than 1,000 feet and always at night, these flying bombs often followed the same tracks used by returning RAF Bomber Command aircraft. To meet these novel tactics, the SCR-584 radars were provided with specially designed mesh screens to eliminate ground clutter. More searchlights were also added to illuminate the V-1s at such low levels.

This second phase ended in the middle of January 1945. Of the 1,200 V-1s released toward British targets, 638 were observed by the defenses with AA Command credited with 331½ and fighters 71½. Of the 235 that eluded the defenses, only 66 hit London. The hit rate in the Box and Strip gun zones reached an impressive 82 percent of all flying bombs coming within range.

The end of the air-launched V-1 campaign was not, in fact, the end of Operation Diver. On March 3, 1945, the third phase of the flying bomb campaign against Britain began. The Luftwaffe introduced the new Fi-103E-1 long-range version of the V-1, launched from ground sites in Holland. Forewarned, AA Command had already redeployed their guns, forming a line between the Isle of Sheppey and Orford Ness. Of the 275 V-1s launched, the guns were credited with 87 of the 125 detected by the defenses. Fighters added just four. Thirteen reached London and on March 29th the last V-1 to reach Britain was blasted from the sky by the heavy guns near Orford Ness.

London, Southampton, Portsmouth, and Manchester were subjected to the V-1 attack, but they were not the only cities targeted by the Germans during the Second World War. In September 1944 British Intelligence knew the Germans were planning a V-1 attack against the Belgium port of Antwerp. The defense known as "Antwerp X" has been often overlooked and was not publicly revealed until after the war.

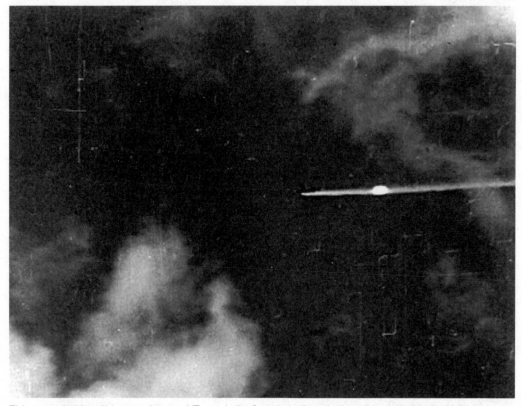

This remarkable still image shows a VT proximity-fused shell exploding directly behind a V-1 over the English coast. Shrapnel from the shell has punctured the fuel tank. Moments later the V-1 would crash into the Channel. AUTHOR'S COLLECTION

Antwerp was vital for Allied victory in Europe. While the port of Cherbourg in Normandy was fully operational in September 1944, it could only support twenty-one divisions and required a great deal of motor transport. Located on the Scheldt River and 50 miles from the North Sea, Antwerp was one of the world's great ports, comparable to New York, Rotterdam, and Hamburg. Antwerp could supply fifty-four divisions all by rail and could handle more cargo in one day than the artificial ports on the beaches of Normandy and Cherbourg combined. The Germans realized the importance of Antwerp and planned for a two-pronged defense (defense of the river approach to the city and aerial bombardment by V-1 and V-2 rockets). After the breakout from Normandy, the swift advance of the British 21st Army caught the Germans by surprise. Antwerp was captured completely intact. It was one of the war's great prizes, but the river approaches to the city were still in German hands. Before those approaches were cleared, Antwerp was all but useless.

The clearing of the Scheldt Estuary and the antiaircraft battle over Antwerp were two of the most critical and forgotten battles of the war. In the words of General Bradley, "all plans for future operations always led back to the fact that in order to supply an operation of any size beyond the Rhine, the port of Antwerp is essential." The clearing of the north bank of the Scheldt was assigned to the Canadian army. Beginning on October 3, 1944, the battle would last until November 8th. It would take the Royal Navy a further eighteen days to clear mines with the first ship docking on November 28th.

Though Antwerp was the Allies' most important port installation, the early preparations for the defense were surprisingly sparse. Requests for RAF fighter squadrons were all but ignored even though they had a number of idle fighter squadrons in the UK. The AA troops in the British 21st Army Group were equipped with mobile 3.7-inch guns and GL Mk III radars. They had no SCR-584 radars, American M-9 Predictors, or proximity fuses. With the bulk of British AA forces assigned to the defense of Brussels, the 21st Army turned to the Americans for help. On October 22nd advanced elements of the U.S. 30th AA Group arrived in Antwerp to reinforce the British 80th AA Brigade.

The antiaircraft battle of Antwerp had three phases. Phase I began on October 27th with the first V-1 shot down by the 90mm guns of D Battery, U.S. 126th Battalion. Three minutes later another V-1 was dispatched. The first launching sites were known to be near the city of Cologne, coming in from the southeast, with the guns aligned accordingly. The guns were deployed in three belts, two of heavy guns, followed by a belt of light AA guns. Each was sufficiently spaced to allow for all the guns to get a chance at any one target.

Phase II began on December 15, 1944, lasting until January 27, 1945. By this time Antwerp's gun defenses consisted of twelve heavy gun battalions and three automatic gun battalions. The V-1s were now coming from the northeast, requiring a change in the guns' positions. The second phase coincided with the Germans' surprise attack in the Ardennes, what became known as the Battle of the Bulge. One of the main objectives of the Ardennes offensive was the capture of Antwerp itself, the Allies' most important

American gunners man their M-9 Predictor in Belgium. In combination with the SCR-584 radar and the VT proximity fuse, the gun defenses of Antwerp destroyed 70 percent of all targets engaged. When compared to other Allied gun defenses, it was an outstanding result. NARA

strategic port. Seven U.S. AA battalion units were quickly transferred to meet the new German offense. To fill the holes more British AA units were brought in.

Phase III began on January 28, 1945, with V-1 attacks now coming from sites located to the north in the Hague, Holland. With the range greatly reduced, the reaction time was greatly reduced, improving the V-1's accuracy. February and March saw the worst period of the attack. During one twenty-four-hour period, 160 V-1s were launched and on several nights ammunition expenditure exceeded 15,000 rounds. The last V-1 detected was launched on March 30, 1945.

The most numerous guns used in Antwerp's defense were the U.S. M1A1 90mm heavy antiaircraft gun and the British 3.7-inch Mk III gun. Augmenting the heavy guns was the superb 40mm Bofors gun and the M45 quad-mounted American .50-caliber machine guns. The .50-caliber guns were the last line of defense and were aimed optically.

While the American and British AA units were organized differently, they used the same equipment. Both the British and Americans used the SCR-584 gun-laying radar and the M-9 Predictor. All of the light battalions were equipped with the 40mm Bofors gun and the M-9 Predictor. As the M-9 operator tracked a target optically, each individual 40mm gun, connected electrically, automatically positioned itself in azimuth and elevation for firing.

Initially the heavy guns used time-fused high-explosive shells. The 40mm guns used contact fuse shells and the .50-caliber guns were equipped with standard ball, armor-piercing, and armor-piercing incendiary shells. Once the Ardennes offensive began on December 16th, the heavy guns quickly received the highly effective VT radar proximity-fused shells. Because of its physical characteristics and small size, the V-1 was a difficult target to shoot down. Its simple flight control system and primitive pulse jet engine made it less vulnerable to antiaircraft fire than the typical combat aircraft.

The 90mm and 3.7-inch guns were however the most effective weapons against the flying bomb. The V-1 was vulnerable to both 3.7-inch and 90mm shell fragments. A burst 80 feet from the target meant 300–400 fragments were capable of piercing the petrol tank, and 200 of perforating the compressed air bottles. A small number of fragments had sufficient velocity to explode or damage the warhead. Some 45 percent of AA kills exploded in the air, a distinct advantage when defending a city the size of Antwerp.

As with all good antiaircraft defenses, early detection was one of the keys to success. The high-speed and low-altitude approach of the V-1 limited the gun's engagement time, thereby reducing the total number of rounds fired. Early warning was provided by British-operated surveillance radars and ground observers. British observers were positioned 50 miles in front of the guns with American observers 15 miles from the guns. The arrangement allowed for maximum detection and centralized control. These three lines of detection communicated directly with two Antiaircraft Operations Rooms. These in turn disseminated information directly to the fire units.

The antiaircraft defense of Antwerp was unique. For the first time radar technology matched with excellent weapons turned the antiaircraft gun into a true aircraft killer. If the Germans had developed their own VT radar proximity-fused shell, the strategic bombing of Germany would have been impossible to sustain.

Antwerp's importance was highlighted by the Germans' desire to destroy or capture the port. That it was given a strictly antiaircraft defense without fighter protection was truly rare in the Second World War, but the numbers speak for themselves.

From October 1944 to March 30, 1945, the guns completed their mission. Of the 4,883 V-1s detected by the Antwerp defense, only 4.5 percent (211 V-1s) fell within the target area. Of those 211 V-1s that got through, 55 were not engaged due to the proximity of Allied aircraft; the other 156 were fired on but escaped. It was an outstanding attrition rate and testament to the effectiveness of the organization, tactics, training, and weaponry used in the port's defense.

While the defense against the V-1 flying bomb was very effective, it could not stop the V-2 ballistic missile. In concert with the V-1, the Germans fired more V-2s at Ant-

These three film stills clearly show how accurate the VT proximity-fused AA shell really was. A tight burst explodes the V-1 in midair. For the gunners this was the best result. Simply damaging a V-1 only to have it crash into the ground could still result in death and damage. AUTHOR'S COLLECTION

werp than London. On average Antwerp received three V-2s per day with 1,600 falling on the city during the campaign. Both missiles were highly inaccurate with the V-2 sinking just one ship and damaging sixteen others. The harbor facilities were never seriously affected during the entire bombardment.

Antwerp's strategic importance was vital for Allied victory in the West. Fortunately for the Allies the German decision to use its V-1 and V-2 missiles as the sole means to subdue the city was a critical error. The inaccuracy of both systems and the Allies' robust antiaircraft defenses all but guaranteed the port remained open. Had the Germans changed their January 1, 1945, Bodenplatte surprise attack plan and used that attacking force (986 Bf-109s and Fw-190s as well as Me-262 jet fighter-bombers and six Arado Ar-234 jet bombers) to attack Antwerp harbor instead, the results could have been devastating. With no fighter defense and with the antiaircraft defense caught out of place, the Germans could have scored a major victory. In the end the battle did take a terrible toll with more than 30,000 people killed or injured.

The commanding general of General Headquarters AA Troops, 21st Army Group put it succinctly: "This is a great victory; perhaps not heralded or understood by the world at large in the same way as they would appreciate a victory by other arms. The victories of other arms have territorial gains to show. You have not, but nevertheless this does not make it less important than any other form of major military success in its effect on the final outcome of the war. It has been a perfect example of technical and tactical skill assisted by the harmonious co-operation by all ranks of both nations, commanded by yourself."

CHAPTER NINE

Armageddon in the Pacific

The Island of Oahu, due to its fortification, its garrison, and its physical characteristics, is believed to be the strongest fortress in the world. With our heavy bombers and our fine pursuit planes, the land force could put up such a defense that the Japs wouldn't dare attack Hawaii, particularly such a long distance from home.
—GEN. GEORGE C. MARSHALL, FEBRUARY 1941

ON DECEMBER 7, 1941, THE JAPANESE LAUNCHED ONE OF THE MOST AUDACIOUS attacks of World War II. The Japanese caught the Americans completely by surprise, but not totally unprepared for what would be the first large-scale antiaircraft action of the war in the Pacific.

As far back as 1921, the Americans knew that war with Japan was a distinct possibility. Because of the Limitations of Armament Treaty of 1921, the Americans were barred from constructing any new defenses to the west of Hawaii. As a result, Pearl Harbor assumed an ever-increasing strategic importance. The U.S. Army was given primary responsibility for protecting Pearl Harbor and the island chain from invasion. This was augmented with the antiaircraft guns from three USMC defense battalions. In 1937 a fresh survey of the island's defenses was conducted by Col. Edward M. Markham. Markham's prescience was remarkable. His understanding of the advances in aircraft design and range since the World War I era led him to the most prophetic forecast of the prewar years:

"War with Japan will be precipitated without notice. One of the most obvious and vital lessons of history is that Japan will pick her own time for conflict. The very form of its government lends itself to such action in that its military and naval forces can, under the pretext of an emergency, initiate and prosecute military and naval operations independently of civil control. . . . If and when hostilities develop between the United States and Japan, there can be little doubt that the Hawaiian Islands will be the initial scene of action, and that Japan will apply her available man-power and resources in powerful and determined attacks against these islands."

American military authorities knew that the nearest Japanese airfield was 2,100 miles away, well beyond the range of any existing bomber. But it could be reached by aircraft carriers, of which Japan had six in operation by August 1939 with two more under construction. In January 1938 Colonel Markham knew how easy it would be for carrier-based planes to approach Pearl Harbor from the northeast and deliver a surprise attack. To meet the threat Markham recommended an increase in AA defenses and 350 planes for interception and long-range reconnaissance. By 1941 the USAAF had just 115 combat aircraft on Hawaii, and most were obsolete and best suited to training. There was also a call for more antiaircraft guns. Since 1921 AA artillery had played an important part in the defense planning and preparation. By 1941 the War Department had assigned an impressive number of guns to the defense of Hawaii: eighty-four mobile and twenty-six fixed 3-inch M3 guns for high-altitude work; 144 37mm M1A2 light guns; and 516 .50-caliber machine guns for low-flying aircraft. Four AA regiments were assigned to the island's defense with a fifth coming at the end of 1941. But many of the guns had not yet been delivered by December 1941, and in truth the AA defenses were not in a good state of readiness. The four regiments present were half strength and the equipment on hand was considerably less than allotted with just sixty mobile and twenty-six fixed 3-inch guns, 109 .50-caliber machine guns, and only twenty 37mm guns. Ammunition was also in short supply with the 37mm guns receiving their first supply on December 5, 1941. Machine-gun ammunition was also in short supply leaving little if any for practice. The 3-inch guns were no better. Half of the mobile 3-inch guns were located on private property, leaving the gun crews to stay on nearby roads to avoid trespassing, and after May 1941 all of their ammunition remained in the ordnance depot. Only the fixed 3-inch guns had ammunition close to hand and ready for immediate action. In the event of an alert, most of the guns would require several hours advance warning to get ready.

Ironically, by early December 1941 the army was installing the island's first aircraft warning system. In September the first five SCR-270 mobile radar sets arrived in Hawaii. This was followed by three fixed sets in November. By the end of November, six of the mobile units were operating at temporary locations around Oahu.

These mobile radars had a dependable range of between 75 and 125 miles seaward. Early exercises demonstrated their ability to detect a group of carrier planes 80 miles away, time enough for the army's pursuit planes (fighters) to scramble and intercept. It was also more than enough time for the AA guns to prepare. These tests, while promising, did not indicate the radar's true readiness. Prior to the Japanese attack, these sets were used solely for training. A shortage of spare parts and the absence of a dependable power supply limited their use to just a few hours a day.

Even with the new mobile radar sets, the Americans were still firm in their belief that a carrier-borne attack was the least of their worries. As late as September 17, 1941, the War Department listed the forms of possible enemy attack in the following order of probability.

1. Submarine-torpedo and mine

2. Sabotage

3. Disguised merchant ship attack. Blocking channels by mines or by air or surface craft.

4. Air raids, carrier based

5. Surface ship raids

6. Major combined attack, absence the U.S. Fleet

By December 1941 Army Air Force in Hawaii consisted of the 18th Bombardment Wing at Hickam Field and the 14th Pursuit (fighter) Wing at Wheeler Field.

Although extensively reinforced, the U.S. Army defenses of Oahu were not ready to detect the approach (through long-range aerial reconnaissance or radar detection) of a Japanese carrier attack or to react in any significant way. While the 14th Pursuit (fighter) Wing was equipped with thirty-nine P-36A, eighty-seven P-40B, and twelve P-40C fighters, most were unarmed and not fully equipped for combat.

While the air defense of Hawaii and Pearl Harbor was the responsibility of the U.S. Army, the AA assets in the harbor itself were formidable. Aboard the various ships there were 353 large-caliber guns (5-inch/25, some 5-inch/38, and 3-inch/50 guns) and over 400 machine guns (.30- and .50-caliber). The most numerous heavy gun was the 5-inch/25 antiaircraft gun. Most if not all of the battleships present during the attack had their antiaircraft armament upgraded in the late 1930s to include eight 5-inch/25 guns and four water-cooled M2 .50-caliber machine guns.

The 5-inch/25 naval gun was the first heavy weapon specifically designed for anti-aircraft use. The lightweight mount and short barrel enabled the gun to traverse quickly, a highly desirable trait when tracking a fast-moving torpedo bomber. The 5-inch/25 replaced the old 3-inch/50 antiaircraft guns and was mounted on capital ships and cruisers between 1926 and 1940. Capable of firing fifteen to twenty rounds per minute, it was a vast improvement over the older 3-inch weapon.

Defense against divebombers was assigned to the M2 water-cooled .50-caliber machine gun. With a high rate of fire—450 to 600 rounds a minute—it had an effective range of approximately 1,500 yards. An approaching aircraft flying at 200 knots would be under fire for about fourteen seconds and subject to about a hundred rounds. The approach and diving speed of a divebomber made that even shorter. And because the M2 did not fire an explosive shell, the chances of it damaging or shooting down an incoming divebomber were slim.

The Japanese Carrier Striking Task Force, or 1st Air Fleet, was a truly formidable force: six fast fleet carriers escorted by two fast battleships, two heavy cruisers, six destroyers, and three submarines. Aboard the carriers were more than 360 planes. From a position 200 miles north of Oahu, the carriers turned into the wind. At 0740 on December 7, 1941, 183 aircraft (forty-nine high-level bombers, fifty-one divebombers, forty-three fighters, and forty torpedo planes) of the first attack wave passed just north of Kahuku Point. At 0751 bombs began to fall on Wheeler Field. Shortly after at 0755 the first of eighty-nine Nakajima B5N2 "Kate" torpedos and high-level bombers began their runs. As the torpedoes raced to their targets, the bombs began to fall. Surprise was devastating and complete. Within minutes of the first bombs hitting home, "general quarters" was sounded around the fleet. Amid the confusion and chaos gun crews manned their guns and began to fight back. Within five minutes the many ships in harbor managed to get their .50-caliber machine guns into action. One of the first ships to return fire was the USS *Maryland*. Inboard of the battleship USS *Oklahoma*,

A Japanese Zero-sen trails smoke after being hit by machine-gun antiaircraft fire over Pearl Harbor. Japanese aircraft were lightly constructed and not nearly as rugged as American aircraft, and were easily damaged by .50-caliber machine-gun fire. U.S. NAVAL HISTORICAL CENTER

A crew man their .30-caliber machine gun during or soon after the Japanese attack on Pearl Harbor.
U.S. NAVAL HISTORICAL CENTER

the *Maryland* was protected against torpedo attack and managed to bring all her anti-aircraft guns into action. The torpedo attacks proved the most devastating with eight battleships, three light cruisers, three destroyers, and four other naval vessels either sunk or severely damaged.

The first wave caused the most damage and loss of life. While the AA response had been quick and intense, it did not inflict a great deal of damage with just nine Japanese aircraft shot down and forty-six damaged. The vast majority of these planes were shot down and damaged by machine-gun fire.

The second wave, launched one hour and fifteen minutes after the first, arrived on target shortly before 0900. Consisting of fifty-four high-level B5N2 bombers, eighty D3A divebombers, and thirty-six A6M2 fighters, this second attack met a much stiffer and accurate antiaircraft defense. This wave now faced both 5-inch/25 fire and even more machine-gun fire and small arms fire. The high-level bombers and divebombers were largely met with barrage fire from the 5-inch/25 guns. Low-level strafing fighters and divebombers encountered more and accurate .50-caliber and .30-caliber machine-gun fire. Across the harbor and at the numerous army airfields and naval air stations, individuals with machine guns, rifles, BARS (Browning automatic rifles), and pistols fought back.

At Kaneohe Naval Air Station, Chief Ordnanceman John William Finn and 2nd Class Petty Officer Robert Peterson set up to a .30-caliber and .50-caliber machine gun and began filling the air with lead. Completely exposed to the strafing Zeros, Finn managed to shoot down one Zero and damage several others. At 0945 the bombing and strafing came to an end.

Twenty (fourteen D3As and six A6M2s) second-wave aircraft were shot down with two claimed by U.S. Army fighters. More remarkable were the sixteen B3N2s, forty-one D3As, and eight A6M2s damaged by AA fire. As the Japanese returned to their carriers, it is believed another twenty aircraft were considered a total loss and pushed over the side. The confirmed loss of twenty-nine aircraft represented 8 percent of the total engaged and not surprisingly was close to the average loss then being sustained by air raids of similar size in Europe against alerted AA defenses.

The U.S. Army's antiaircraft performance during the attack was almost nonexistent. None of the mobile 3-inch batteries were at their assigned positions and ammunition was still in the ordnance depots. At 0810 the Hawaiian Coast Artillery Command alerted all units and within minutes the antiaircraft batteries at Fort Kamehameha (next to Hickman Field) and at Fort Weaver (close to the harbor's entrance) opened fire with small arms. Finally at 0830 a fixed 3-inch battery at Weaver made a contribution, followed by guns at Kamehameha and on Sand Island in Honolulu, claiming two aircraft. Antiaircraft

A panoramic view of Pearl Harbor during the second attack. The AA shell bursts show that the 5- and 3-inch guns had joined the battle, putting up what looks to be a box barrage above the fleet. U.S. NAVAL HISTORICAL CENTER

troops at Camp Molekoli and Schofield Barracks fired BARS and rifles at the enemy, claiming one plane. This contribution was in the end insignificant when compared with the barrage and machine-gun fire thrown up by the guns of the Pacific Fleet.

The damage to the Pacific Fleet and surrounding air bases was devastating. Twenty-one ships were sunk or damaged: five battleships, one mine layer, three destroyers, two service craft, and an auxiliary sunk; one cruiser and one auxiliary severely damaged; three battleships, two cruisers, one destroyer, and one auxiliary moderately damaged. The United States also lost 171 aircraft and 159 damaged. The loss of life was staggering: 2,390 killed and 1,178 wounded.

Japanese losses were minimal—just sixty-four killed for the loss of fifteen D3A dive-bombers, nine A6M2 fighters, and five B3N2 torpedo and high-level bombers. What's more telling is that forty-six aircraft were damaged in the first wave and sixty-five in the second. That means fifty-five of the first wave of 183 aircraft and eighty-five of the second wave of 167 were lost or damaged to AA fire—a pretty good performance for a defense that was taken completely by surprise.

The reinforcement of Hawaii was almost immediate. Three battleships and one carrier were transferred from the Atlantic while the antiaircraft defenses were increased. With Japanese troops storming ashore in the Philippines, Borneo, and Wake Island shortly after the Pearl Harbor attack, the U.S. military was convinced the invasion of Oahu would be Japan's next move. The air defense of Pearl Harbor was now a top priority.

Shipping guns from the mainland would take time, so to bolster the defenses the battleships *Arizona* and *West Virginia* were stripped of "anything useful." Ships that were crippled or dead in the water (*Nevada* and *California*) were supplied with power from shore or salvage ships to maintain their 5-inch/25 batteries and machine guns. Salvaging guns from the ships damaged during the attack received high priority. Eight 5-inch/25 guns were removed from the *West Virginia*, four of which formed an antiaircraft battery at West Loch. Nine emergency antiaircraft batteries (four guns each) were proposed for the harbor defense. Four of these early batteries were equipped using salvaged 5-inch/25 and 5-inch/38 guns. By the end of October 1942, the heavy antiaircraft defense of Pearl Harbor stood at thirty-six 5-inch guns in nine batteries.

The air attack and antiaircraft battle over Pearl Harbor set in motion a new type of warfare. Ironically, neither the Americans nor the Japanese foresaw a Pacific war in which carrier airpower would play a decisive role. While carriers were important, the battleship remained the centerpiece for any future deciding battle. This illusion was shattered by the air attack on Pearl Harbor and the subsequent clash of carriers during the battle of the Coral Sea at the beginning of May 1942.

The battle of the Coral Sea was the first naval battle in which the participating ships never sighted or fired directly at each other. It would also be the first test in which the anti-aircraft defenses of both sides would be subject to both torpedo and divebombing attacks on the open sea. After Pearl Harbor the Imperial Japanese Navy's (IJN) carrier fleet was the most powerful in the world. Its aircrews were highly trained and well equipped, but there were a number of deficiencies. Early detection was vital for any effective antiaircraft defense, but unlike American carriers the Japanese ships had no radar. During the early months of the war, the Japanese relied heavily on standing fighter patrols for their first line of defense. Usually three were airborne with six ready to scramble. Without radar or good radio communication, the Zero-sen fighters were virtually impossible to control and guide to any incoming raid. Fortunately for the Americans the IJN's shipboard gun defenses were also inadequate and would remain so for the duration of the war. Japanese shipboard anti-aircraft gunnery proved largely ineffective in defending their carriers against determined American air attacks. IJN doctrine relied heavily on maneuver and airborne fighters for defense. When under attack Japanese carriers maneuvered independently of their escort. The Americans were also free to maneuver but their escorts were required to stay close enough to the carrier to provide antiaircraft support.

In terms of firepower Japanese antiaircraft weaponry and fire control did not compare well to that of the U.S. Navy. The standard 5-inch Type 89/40 dual-mount high-angle antiaircraft gun was a respectable weapon, but its Type 94 fire-control director had dif-ficulty tracking fast targets. As a result, Japanese gunners used barrage fire (Americans used aimed fire). Against horizontal bombers flying at a predictable speed and course, it was effective, but it was all but useless against more maneuverable carrier-based torpedo bombers and divebombers. For intermediate- and short-range defense, the Japanese relied heavily on the Type 96 25mm gun in single and triple mounts. It was a poor choice. Against high-speed targets it could not be trained or elevated fast enough and its sights were inadequate for the job. Excessive vibration and muzzle blast also hindered accurate fire and its magazines carried too few shells to maintain high rates of fire. And when the gunners did manage to hit an oncoming plane, its small weight of shell (0.6 pound) was largely ineffective against the rugged American carrier aircraft. The Japanese carriers involved in the battle were the fleet carrier *Shokaku* armed with sixteen 5-inch guns in eight twin mountings along with twelve triple-mounted 25mm guns; the *Zuikaku* armed with sixteen 5-inch guns and thirty-six 25mm guns; and the light carrier *Shoho* armed with just four twin 5-inch mounts and four triple 25mm mounts.

In comparison the American carriers and escorting ships were much better prepared and equipped to defend against aerial attack. Like the Japanese the U.S. Navy assigned half of its fighters for fleet defense. Standing combat air patrols were standard operating procedure with fighters ready on deck for immediate launch. Equipped with radar and reliable radios, the Americans had a distinct advantage over their Japanese counterparts. Radar provided the much-needed early warning vital for any effective defense. Fighters in sufficient numbers could be scrambled in time to meet an incoming attack and gunners had time to prepare. It also gave the escorting vessels good warning, bringing more barrels to bear. At the time of battle the USS *Yorktown* was equipped with the CXAM-1 radar,

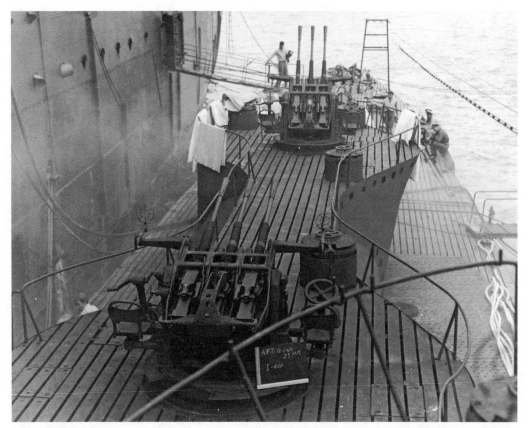

Triple-mount 25mm guns on the deck of an I-400 Japanese submarine. The Type 96 25mm was a failure for the Japanese. U.S. NAVAL HISTORICAL CENTER

which was capable of detecting a large aircraft or a formation of aircraft at 10,000 feet at 70 nautical miles.

If fighters were considered the outer ring of defense, the antiaircraft guns aboard the carrier and escorting battleships, cruisers, and destroyers were the inner ring. First in line was the long-range 5-inch/25 and 38 guns. The newer 5-inch/38 gun was an accurate weapon with a high rate of fire. A well-trained crew could get off twenty rounds a minute out to a maximum range of 18,220 yards. The older 5-inch/25 gun had a shorter range of 14,500 yards. To meet the short- and intermediate-range needs, the U.S. Navy relied on a mix of guns, which included the .50-caliber machine gun and the new quadruple 1.1 inch/.75-caliber machine cannon.

In the mid-1930s senior U.S. officers had become increasingly concerned by the appearance of the new divebomber. Most knew the divebomber would be a difficult target. Rear Adm. Luke McNamee cautioned, "Even if the defensive fire begins at the earliest possible instant only about 30 seconds of actual firing times are available to get

Water-cooled .50-caliber machine guns in action against attacking Japanese planes during a U.S. carrier raid on the Marshall Islands, February 1, 1942. The water-cooled .50-caliber gun had a rate of fire of 450–600 rounds per minute. U.S. NAVAL HISTORICAL CENTER

on the attacking planes and damage them sufficiently to prevent the attack from being completed." None of the guns then in service was designed for the purpose.

Introduced in 1937 the 1.1-inch quad gun was found to be difficult to maintain and prone to failure. Both the gun and mount suffered from a number of problems including overheating and jamming as the weapon warmed up. Its rate of fire, however, was impressive at 600 rounds per minute (150 rpm per barrel). Even with these deficiencies the 1.1-inch guns were a welcome addition to the fleet carriers and would play an important role in the upcoming battle.

After Pearl Harbor both the *Yorktown* and *Lexington* (along with all the other ships in the fleet) began replacing their .50-caliber machine guns with Oerlikon 20mm cannons and 1.1-inch quadruple gun mounts. The Oerlikon fired explosive, armor-piercing, and incendiary projectiles at a rate of 450 rounds per minute with an effective range of 2,000 yards. Lightweight, it required no external power and could be mounted anywhere with a clear arc of fire. At the time of the battle of the Coral Sea, both carriers were well

A 1.1-inch (28mm) AA quad gun mount aboard the USS *Enterprise*. The prototype gun first appeared in 1931 with limited production starting in 1934. It did not enter service until 1936 and was not available in quantity until 1940. U.S. NAVAL HISTORICAL CENTER

equipped with long-range, intermediate, and close-in AA weapons. The USS *Lexington* had twelve 5-inch/25 guns, twelve quadruple 1.1-inch mounts, twenty-two Oerlikons, and roughly twenty-four .50-caliber machine guns. The USS *Yorktown* carried eight 5-inch/38 guns, four quad 1.1-inch gun mounts, twenty-four 20mm guns, and twenty-four .50-caliber machine guns.

The battle of the Coral Sea began on May 3, 1942. After the successful invasion of Tulagi island in the southeastern Solomons, aircraft from the USS *Yorktown* attacked, sinking and damaging several Japanese support vessels. In response the Japanese sent the fleet carriers *Shokaku* and *Zuikaku* in search of the U.S. carriers. It did not take them long. On May 7th the two sides exchanged airstrikes. The Americans were first to attack with fifty-three SDB Dauntless divebombers and twenty-two TBD Devastator torpedo bombers, escorted by eighteen F4F Wildcat fighters. The *Shoho* was hit with no fewer than thirteen 1,000-pound bombs and seven torpedoes and sank. It would be the first Japanese carrier lost during the war. On May 8th the main carrier forces traded punches.

In the first carrier battle of the war, both sides suffered heavy casualties. The *Yorktown* was hit first, but was only moderately damaged by a single bomb hit; the *Lexington* suffered from a well-executed attack and succumbed to two bomb and two torpedo hits. The *Shokaku* was hit by three bombs and damaged and the *Zuikaku* was untouched, but losses to her air group were heavy and she would be out of action for a full month. Most importantly, those two carriers were eliminated from the upcoming Midway operation.

The first carrier strikes of May 7th and 8th clearly revealed how deficient both carrier air defenses really were. The huge potential of U.S. radar for early warning and fighter direction was not fully realized. Neither side had enough fighters for both combat air patrols (CAP) and strike escort. Even though the Americans had more AA barrels, their AA fire was equally ineffective in protecting the carriers. Even more ineffective were the defensive efforts of the Japanese, whose AA fire was all but useless. While American antiaircraft fire wasn't sufficient enough in preventing attacks, both fighters and antiaircraft fire did inflict heavy losses. At the end of the battle, the Japanese had lost sixty-six carrier-borne aircraft while the Americans sacrificed thirty-one.

In less than a month, the Japanese and American carriers forces would clash once again during the battle of Midway. For the coming battle the United States had three carriers: USS *Yorktown*, *Hornet*, and *Enterprise*. All three carriers carried radar, and by

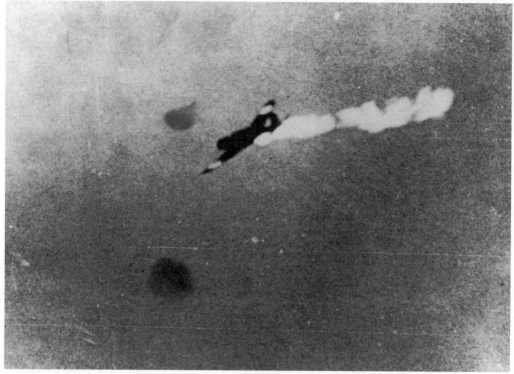

During the battle of the Coral Sea, a Nakajima B5N2 "Kate" torpedo bomber is hit by antiaircraft fire during attacks on U.S. carriers, late morning on May 8, 1942. U.S. NAVAL HISTORICAL CENTER

June 1942 both the *Yorktown* and *Hornet* had each received twenty-four 20mm guns and the *Enterprise* added thirty-two. All three carriers were also equipped with eight of the new 5-inch/38 dual-purpose guns, the best ship-based long-range antiaircraft gun of the war, and four 1.1-inch quad mounts. As the Americans moved quickly to add more AA firepower and improved fighter control with radar, the Japanese did little. As in the battle of the Coral Sea, the Japanese had no radar and relied on lookouts to spot incoming

The Oerlikon 20mm cannon was found on every U.S. warship in service. The U.S. Navy adopted the Swiss-designed cannon in 1941, and it proved a reliable weapon with a high rate of fire of 450 rounds per minute. Note the sixty-round spare gun magazines in the ammunition locker in the foreground. During 1945, at the height of the kamikaze attacks, the 20mm guns of the fleet would expend 1,308,370 rounds and shoot down 297.5 aircraft for a "rounds per bird" of 4,398. U.S. NAVAL HISTORICAL CENTER

aircraft. When aircraft were spotted, escorts would lay smoke or fire their main battery to gain the attention of the overhead combat air patrol (which consisted of three A6M2 Zeros). It was an extremely inefficient system and would play out during the battle when the Japanese were constantly surprised by the appearance of American divebombers.

If attacking American aircraft avoided the CAP, they still had to contend with massed antiaircraft defenses aboard every Japanese fleet carrier. For long-range defense the Japanese relied on their 5-inch guns and for short-range fire the Type 96 25mm gun. Both were ineffective. In fact the carrier *Akagi* was still equipped with the older 4.7-inch gun with a slow rate of fire and inferior elevation.

The other carriers—*Kaga*, *Soryu*, and *Hiryu*—all had the new 5-inch/40 type dual-mount gun. As an example, the *Soryu's* primary armament consisted of six dual-mount 5-inch guns mounted on projected sponsons, three on each side. Effective range was 8,750 yards with a sustained rate of fire of eight rounds per minute. The secondary armament was just fourteen twin-mount 25mm guns. During the battle Japanese antiaircraft fire was so ineffective just five of the 144 American aircraft lost were due to AA fire.

A Japanese heavy cruiser, circa 1937. Note the 5-inch/40 type dual-mount AA gun. Effective range was 8,750 yards. Against aircraft its time-fused shell was considered to have an effective radius of destruction of 62.7 feet. U.S. NAVAL HISTORICAL CENTER

For the upcoming battle Adm. Chester Nimitz decided to operate his carriers in two separate task forces in accordance with existing doctrine. After the battle of the Coral Sea, a single fighter controller, based on the *Enterprise*, would control all fighters. To augment the fighters were the antiaircraft guns of the carriers and escorting vessels. To maximize antiaircraft protection for the carriers, the U.S. Navy placed their carriers inside a ring of escorts, exposing any attacking force to more barrels.

Adding to the ship-based antiaircraft defenses were the guns of 6th Marine Defense Battalion on Midway itself. Armed with 3-inch and .50-caliber machine guns, their task was to defend the air base. At 0620 hours on June 4, the battle for Midway began. Thirty miles from the island, eighteen Marine F-2A Buffalos and six F4F Wildcats intercepted the 108-aircraft Japanese strike force. For the loss of one or two Zeros and three carrier attack planes, the defenders sacrificed thirteen Buffalos and two Wildcats. It was now the turn of the U.S. Marine and Navy antiaircraft gunners to defend their base. At 0630 hours the order "open fire when targets are in range" was issued. At 0631 hours the guns opened up. Almost immediately the Japanese level bombers reported "vicious" antiaircraft fire with two shot down. No American aircraft was caught on the ground but the hangars and support facilities were heavily damaged. The Japanese had failed to meet their objectives and paid a high price. The antiaircraft gunners took a heavy toll with seven shot down (fighters added four for a total of eleven) or ditched en route back to the carriers. Just as important, fourteen aircraft were heavily damaged and rendered non-operational. A further twenty-nine suffered light damage. It was a victory for the guns. In their first attack the Japanese lost twenty-five aircraft (shot down or non-operational) to antiaircraft fire. That was 10 percent of Admiral Nagumo's striking force. As Midway burned, the carriers continued to search each other out.

At 0530 hours the Japanese were spotted. At 0700 hours the *Hornet* and *Enterprise* launched aircraft. Heading toward the Japanese were 116 aircraft that included twenty F4F Wildcat fighters, sixty-seven SBD Dauntless divebombers, and twenty-nine obsolete Douglas TBD-1 Devastator torpedo bombers. They were followed by the *Yorktown*'s strike group of seventeen divebombers, twelve torpedo bombers, and six fighters at 0830 hours.

At Midway Captain Simard launched all his operational bombers. The fifty-one strike aircraft were an interesting mix of U.S. Army, Navy, and Marine Corps aircraft consisting of six TBF Avenger torpedo bombers, four Martin Marauder B-26 medium bombers (armed with torpedoes), eighteen SBD Dauntless, and eleven SB2U Vindicators divebombers. At just past 0700 hours, *Akagi*'s lookouts spotted the approaching aircraft. The Japanese were ready with twenty-nine Zero fighters flying CAP. Without fighter escort the attacking bombers were hacked from the sky. Just two TBFs and a single B-26 were able to launch torpedoes, but only one TBF and two Marauders survived. At 0800 hours the eighteen Marine SBDs from VSMB-241 began their attack against the carrier *Hiryu*. This attack was equally frustrating with eight SBDs shot down for no results. In this case the Japanese

CAP system worked very well with all aircraft losses due to fighters and not antiaircraft guns. These attacks were followed by fourteen B-17s delivering a high-altitude attack on the carriers *Soryu*, *Hiryu*, and *Akagi* for no results, and finally the eleven SB2U Vindicator divebombers attacked the battleship *Haruna* for a loss of three aircraft and no hits.

Strike aircraft from three American carriers were now heading for Nagumo's carriers. Up to this point the A6M2 Zeros flying CAP proved their worth with devastating results. But now they would face a more formidable foe: navy pilots trained in attacking ships. Japanese fighter and antiaircraft gun defenses would now be put to the real test.

At 0915 hours the battle began. The first to strike were the fifteen Devastators from the *Hornet*. Protecting the carriers were eighteen Zeros flying CAP, and as the battle developed eleven more were launched from *Akagi* and *Kaga*. The Devastators did not stand a chance and in short order all were shot down. Next to attack were the fourteen Devastators of VT-6 from *Enterprise*. The Japanese CAP now numbered twenty-seven fighters. For fifteen minutes the Devastators faced a wall of flak from 5-inch and multiple-barreled 25mm guns from the *Kaga*. Then the fighters piled on. Only four bombers survived. By this time forty-one Japanese fighters were airborne, but they were all at low altitude having dealt with the American torpedo attacks. At 1003 hours the twelve Devastators from VT-3 made the last torpedo attack. As the bombers skimmed the waves, the Japanese failed to spot the SBD divebombers approaching at 15,000 feet. Diving down completely unopposed and with no CAP and no return antiaircraft fire, the three squadrons of SBDs delivered a devastating blow. In just over six minutes the carriers *Kaga*, *Akagi*, and *Soryu* were gutted by bomb hits and uncontrollable fires. Only the carrier *Hiryu* remained untouched. As the surviving SBDs made their way back, the *Hiryu* launched a retaliatory attack.

At 1155 hours the Japanese strike force of eighteen Aichi D3A "Val" planes spotted the *Yorktown*. The Wildcat CAP intercepted first, dispatching seven of the attackers. The remaining D3As divided into two groups. To confuse the *Yorktown*'s gunners, the experienced Japanese pilots dove in from different bearings with a small group coming in out of the sun. The antiaircraft gunners responded with the *Yorktown*'s aft 1.1-inch quad gun shooting down the first attacker, but not before the bomb was released hitting the ship. The second D3A was also shot down by AA fire and crashed in *Yorktown*'s wake. Seven divebombers scored three hits and two near misses. Of the eighteen attacking bombers, the Wildcat CAP was credited with seven while the gunners came away with six. The *Hornet* received a serious blow, dead in the water and burning. By 1245 hours the *Hiryu* organized a second strike. It was a formidable force of nineteen B5N2 "Kate" torpedo bombers and six A6M2 Zeros. At 1427 hours radar contact was made, sending the six F4F Wildcats flying CAP into action. After spotting the *Yorktown* the Japanese formation split into two groups of four and five torpedo bombers each. Just two Wildcats were able to intercept, shooting down one before the escorting Zeros shot down both F4Fs. Now the gunners had their chance. Approaching at 200 feet at a speed of 200 knots, the Kates were met with an initial barrage of 5-inch aimed fire. Fighting through the barrage the

Taken from the cruiser *Pensacola*, this photo shows four Japanese B5N2 torpedo bombers flying through a barrage of 5-inch shells heading toward the carrier USS *Yorktown* during the battle of Midway. U.S. NAVAL HISTORICAL CENTER

first four Kates were shot down by fighters with AA fire scoring no hits. The remaining five Kates continued on and at 150 feet came under intense AA fire and fighter attack. Four Kates launched their torpedoes with two finding their mark. Both hit on the *Yorktown*'s port side with devastating effect. Turning away, all five Kates now came under intense 1.1-inch and 20mm gunfire but all survived the intense barrage.

The final aircraft carrier to be sunk was the *Hiryu*. At 1705 hours twenty-four SDB Dauntless divebombers from the *Enterprise* were spotted by the cruiser *Chikuma*. Plunging through a wall of intense antiaircraft fire, four hits were gained for a loss of four SBDs, all to fighters. The Japanese lost four SBDs, all to fighters. Mortally crippled, the *Hiryu* would not survive.

For the Japanese the battle of Midway was a disaster: four carriers sunk, 248 aircraft lost, and 3,057 personnel killed including 110 aircrew. For the Americans it was a major strategic victory with just one carrier and one destroyer sunk, 144 aircraft lost, and 362 personnel killed.

For the naval antiaircraft gunners, the battle left much to be desired. The Japanese came off poorly with just five Americans shot down by AA fire. Their 5-inch/40 guns were unable to track and engage divebombers in a dive, and the Type 96 25mm did not have the range or ability to engage high-speed targets. In his after-action report G. Eders, one of the few Devastator pilots to survive the battle, commented on the AA fire: "In making our torpedo run we were under constant gun fire from the carrier, which appeared to be ineffective."

The Americans' AA fire was a bit more successful, but there were some major problems. The 1.1-inch machine cannon proved disappointing due to continual jams. The 20mm Oerlikons, which had an effective range of 2,000 yards or less, were unable to destroy Japanese torpedo bombers or divebombers before they could release their weapons.

Moving forward the battle of Midway set in motion a number of changes. For the Americans that meant more antiaircraft guns for their ships (a program they had already started) and the replacement of the 1.1-inch machine cannon with the superb Bofors 40mm gun. The Japanese would stagnate. Their answer was to simply add more and more 25mm guns to their ships. It was a poor choice and one they would pay for dearly.

A Bofors 40mm quad mount in action during the USS *Biloxi*'s shakedown cruise in early 1943. As a replacement for the disappointing 1.1-inch quad mount, the 40mm gun was an outstanding weapon. Director-controlled 40mm guns were effective to 3,000 yards. During 1945 the 40mms of the U.S. Fleet fired 718,699 rounds, and shot down 476 aircraft for a rate of 1,508 "rounds per bird." U.S. NAVAL HISTORICAL CENTER

The battle of the Eastern Solomons, August 24, 1942. During the battle this Japanese Aichi D3A "Val" divebomber was shot down by AA fire directly above the carrier USS *Enterprise*. U.S. NAVAL HISTORICAL CENTER

Before 1942 was over the United States and Japan would fight two more carrier battles: the battle of the Eastern Solomons on August 24th and the battle of Santa Cruz on October 26th. During the battle of the Eastern Solomons, the Japanese would suffer heavy aircraft losses: seventy-one shot down—fifty-seven credited to fighters and fourteen to the AA guns. At the battle of Santa Cruz, the improvements to the U.S. Fleet's AA defenses paid big dividends. Of the 203 Japanese aircraft at the start of the battle, almost half (ninety-nine) were destroyed, and for the first time in a carrier battle. the losses were evenly split between American fighters (twenty-six) and AA fire (twenty-five). A further eighteen were operational losses with the rest forced to ditch. In return the Americans lost just twenty aircraft. After four hard-fought carrier battles and other surface operations, U.S. naval AA gunners were credited with 228 enemy aircraft destroyed in 1942.

After twelve months of war, both sides' carrier forces were exhausted. American shipyards, however, were already far ahead of the Japanese with the construction of the war-winning Essex-class carriers. Entering service in 1943, these new ships were well armed with twelve radar-controlled 5-inch/38 guns, seventeen quad Bofors 40mm guns, and sixty-five single 20mm Oerlikon guns, and each one carried up to one hundred aircraft. For the rest of the fleet, the order went out to retrofit every possible warship and combat transport with as many antiaircraft guns as possible.

By the end of 1942 the Americans were also making major improvements to their shipboard AA defenses including:

- Radar direction for 5-inch batteries. (A Fletcher-class destroyer carried five in single mounts; a cruiser carried eight and the new battleships carried ten twin mounts.)

- Increase in ratio of 5-inch/38 guns to 5-inch/25s.

- Production of VT ammunition for 5-inch projectiles.

- Replacement of 1.1-inch quad mounts by 40mm antiaircraft guns in many combatant ships.

- Issue of Mark 14 automatic lead-computing sights to 20mm antiaircraft guns.

- Replacement by the 20mm of nearly all the caliber .30 and .50 machine guns.

- Introduction of Marks 49 and 51 AA directors for control of 40mm mounts.

- Increasing of number of all antiaircraft weapons mounted.

- Proper arming of all merchant vessels and auxiliaries.

Undoubtedly the most important scientific development in the AA battle was the introduction of the VT fuse. The "proximity fuse" was a game changer, making the fleet's AA defenses on par with that of its fighters. Built around a miniature radio transmitter and receiver, the VT fuse overcame the major disadvantage of the "time" and "contact" fuses and was capable of detecting its target and detonating within 75 feet. In 1943 the number of standard 5-inch shells needed for a shot down numbered 508 per aircraft. The VT fuse decreased that to just 155 rounds per bird. This would bode well for the U.S. Navy and the coming kamikaze storm.

The victory at Midway allowed the Americans to gain the strategic initiative, making the landings on Guadalcanal possible. On August 7, 1942, U.S. Marines landed on the islands of Guadalcanal, Tulagi, and Florida in the Solomon island chain. Among the first units ashore were the antiaircraft guns of the Marine Defense Battalions. Once ashore the Marines quickly captured the Japanese airfield under construction (later named Henderson Field) and set up their AA guns. Even before the first Japanese bombing raid, the 3rd Marine Defense Battalion deployed its radar-controlled M1A1 90mm guns, Bofors 40mm, Oerlikon 20mm guns, and .50-caliber machine guns (each battalion had twelve 90mm guns, nineteen 40mm, twenty-eight 20mm, and thirty-five .50-caliber machine guns).

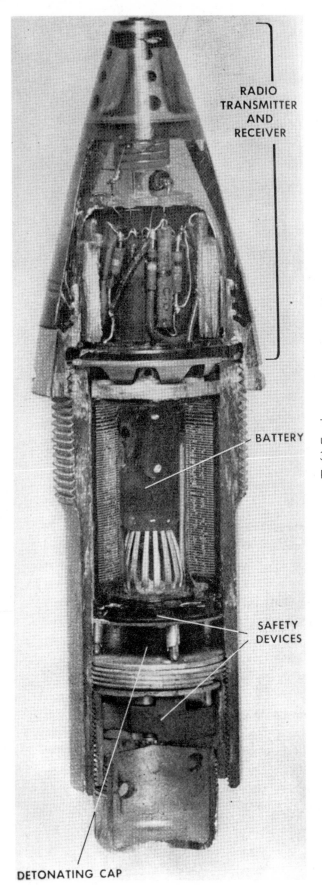

RADIO
TRANSMITTER
AND
RECEIVER

BATTERY

SAFETY
DEVICES

DETONATING CAP

The inner workings of a 3-inch/50 VT fuse head used during World War II. During 1945 the 3-inch/50 gun shot down 30.5 aircraft for a "rounds per bird" of 359. U.S. NAVAL HISTORICAL CENTER

The 3rd Marine Defense Battalion's 90mm guns at "Condition Red," ready to meet an incoming raid on Guadalcanal, 1942. NARA

For the Japanese the antiaircraft defenses on Guadalcanal came as a rude shock. To destroy the Marine airfield, the Imperial Japanese Naval Air Force (IJNAF) deployed the Mitsubishi G4M1 "Betty" bomber. Capable of flying long distances, the G4M1 was extremely vulnerable to AA fire and during the Guadalcanal campaign the aircraft was given the nickname "One-shot Lighter." The Betty, like every other Japanese aircraft early in the war, carried no armor plate or self-sealing fuel tanks. The accuracy and range of the Marine's 90mm guns and the G4M1's incendiary properties forced them to bomb at ever higher altitudes, decreasing their accuracy. Jim Norris, a ground crewman with the army's 76th Squadron recalled the futility of most Betty raids: "I don't think any of us really knew why the enemy bombed from such a high altitude. Maybe they were afraid of our fighters or trying to stay away from flak. But keeping the Japanese at a higher level was a tremendous advantage. The Japanese accuracy at 20,000 feet was very poor. Very often they'd miss everything and the bombs would drop out in the jungle."

The mix of accurate high-altitude AA and a determined fighter defense saved Henderson Field from destruction. After six months of combat and constant aerial bombardment, the Japanese withdrew their forces from Guadalcanal in January 1943.

Marine defense battalions were equipped with the twin-barreled Oerlikon 20mm cannon. This gun defended Henderson Field on Guadalcanal. In the background is a P-39 Airacobra and two P-38 Lightnings. NARA

As the Pacific campaign expanded to both land and sea campaigns, the role of the antiaircraft defenses on both sides only increased. Much has been written detailing the great fighter battles and bombing missions, but very little attention has been paid to the subject of antiaircraft defenses. Indeed some historical accounts continue to say incorrectly, "often batteries never hit a plane." In terms of bomber aircraft shot down, AA fire was almost certainly the greatest killer on both sides. They were also the best weapons for decreasing bombing accuracy. Only AA fire could force a bomber to fly higher. Fighters could destroy a bomber at any altitude. The Allies quickly established a technical and numerical advantage at sea and over land bases. While the Japanese may not have been able to keep pace, they still managed to take a steady toll of Allied bombers.

A graveyard for Allied bombers shot down by AA fire during the war was the Japanese naval and air base at Rabaul. By late summer of 1943 the great Japanese base at Rabaul, on New Britain, stood firmly in the way of any Allied advance up the Solomon island chain.

The Japanese Army Type 98 20mm gun was introduced into service in 1938. The Japanese base at Rabaul had 120 20mm guns in defense of its airfields and harbor facilities. With a rate of fire of 120 rounds per minute, the Type 98 proved to be a hard-hitting weapon. NARA

In 1943 the highest priority was given to Rabaul's antiaircraft defenses. A total of 367 guns were assigned to the defense including 118 heavy, 212 light, and 37 heavy machine guns. Adding to Rabaul's defense were the warships in Simpson Harbor with hundreds of heavy and light weapons. This made Rabaul one of the most heavily defended bases outside of Japan.

From the beginning of 1943, Rabaul drew American bombers and fighters like a magnet. On October 12, 1943, the USAAF's Fifth Air Force and RAF launched the largest attack to date. This was the beginning of the sustained air assault against Rabaul. Over 350 aircraft were committed to the attack—63 B-24 Liberators, 107 B-25 Mitchells, 12 Beaufighters, and 106 P-38 Lightnings as escort. Unlike earlier raids this attack was mounted in daylight and came as a complete surprise. The AA guns were slow to react. On that first day the Fifth Air Force strafers destroyed at least forty Japanese aircraft with one merchant ship sunk and twenty damaged. Just two B-24s and a single Beaufighter were shot down due to AA fire. The Fifth Air Force continued the pressure with more raids until the end of November, but losses mounted considerably with fourteen aircraft lost on November 2nd, most to AA fire. Meanwhile, by the end of October more than a hundred land-based U.S. Navy and Marine Corps SBD Dauntless divebombers and Grumman TBFs commenced their own air offensive against Rabaul. Flying daily strikes for a period of months, the heavily escorted SBDs and TBFs endured heavy flak and lost aircraft on every mission. In concert with continued Fifth and Thirteenth Air Force strikes, Rabaul was slowly reduced. By February 1944 Japan's surviving fighters retreated to Truk, leaving Rabaul's air defense to the AA guns. In February alone the sorties flown against Rabaul were startling: 256 B-24, 263 B-25, 244 TBF, and 573 SBDs. In the end the AA guns shot down more Allied aircraft than the Japanese fighters did. Lt. Gen. Rimpei Kato, chief of staff at Rabaul and head of the antiaircraft effort, estimated the AA guns shot down 400 Allied aircraft during the aerial assault on Rabaul. By his count one hundred fell to fighters and 300 to AA fire, of which 90 percent were SBDs and other single-engine aircraft making ground attacks. Higher than the figures given by U.S. sources (none are in agreement), these numbers show once again the vulnerability of low-flying aircraft against light AA fire, not surprising when the majority of the guns surrounding the harbor and airfields were 25mm, 20mm, and 13.5mm.

The Japanese Type 96 25mm triple mount was used both onshore and aboard ship. The Type 96 suffered many deficiencies. Its small fifteen-round magazines required frequent reloading, reducing its overall rate of fire. With each magazine change the gun stopped firing. NARA

By January 1944 the U.S. Navy had launched eight Essex-class heavy carriers and nine Independence-class light carriers. Each class bristled with 5-inch, 40mm, and 20mm AA guns. Indeed almost every ship in the fleet, from the merchant ship to the lowly mine sweeper, was equipped with some sort of AA weapon. On shore the Marines and army units were also well equipped with radar-guided 90mm, 40mm, 37mm, and 20mm cannon. Add the revolutionary VT proximity-fused shell and the United States had the most formidable AA defenses in the world. In 1944 the Americans would need every bit of it. In 1943 alone U.S. Navy AA gunners were credited with 372 enemy aircraft shot down: 292 Japanese and 80 German and Italian. In the first six months of 1944, Japanese air attacks on surface vessels were increasingly ineffective. Of the 315 Japanese aircraft that made it through the fighter CAP, just 10 percent scored a hit, causing mostly superficial damage. Of those 315 aircraft, an impressive 106 were shot down by antiaircraft fire. The massed AA fire of a U.S. Fast Carrier Task Force was formidable.

The USS *Hornet* and USS *Bon Homme Richard* fire their starboard 5-inch/38 gun batteries during a practice exercise in June 1945. Kamikaze tactics left the 5-inch/38 at a disadvantage and it was not as effective as hoped. It did, however, put up some respectable numbers. During 1945 the 5-inch guns, shooting conventional time-fused shells, expended 108,516 shells and shot down 173 aircraft for a "rounds per bird" of 627. When using the VT proximity-fused shell, 75,961 shells shot down 207.5 aircraft for a "rounds per bird" of just 366. U.S. NAVAL HISTORICAL CENTER

Between November 1943 and June 1944, 195 Japanese aircraft made daylight attacks against the fleet with 40 percent downed by AA fire.

For the Japanese the AA battle against constant Allied air attacks was one of constant pressure, frustration, diminishing resources, and overall lack of effectiveness. A graphic example is the AA battle fought between two of the world's most powerful battleships and the aerial might of the U.S. Navy. In November 1944 the U.S. Navy assembled an overwhelming force for the assault on Leyte in the Philippines. To destroy the U.S. invasion fleet, the Japanese committed six battleships including their super battleships *Yamato* and *Musashi*. These ships would be supported by four carriers (used as decoys only) and fourteen heavy cruisers. To meet the threat the Americans had eight fleet carriers and eight light carriers, along with twelve battleships. To contend with the growing threat of U.S. airpower, the IJN bolted more and more antiaircraft guns to its surface ships. Most were the ineffective 25mm gun. For the upcoming battle *Yamato* and *Musashi* were up gunned with 152 and 130 guns, respectively. For long-range anti-aircraft fire both ships depended on the Type 89 5-inch gun (twenty-four on *Yamato*, twelve on *Musashi*). With a well-trained crew it had a high rate of fire, but its main drawback was its Type 94 High Angle Firing Control Installation. Unable to track the fast-moving U.S. carrier aircraft, the Japanese had to rely on their close-range 25mm gun to defend their ships. The Japanese had also developed an 18.1-inch *San-Shiki* shell, fired by its main armament. The Type 3 incendiary AA shell was filled with 996 25mm x 90mm steel tubes containing an incendiary mixture. Despite its impressive display the Type 3 shell was completely ineffective.

On October 24, 1944, at 1000 hours, the *Musashi*'s radar picked up the first incoming raid: forty-five aircraft—twenty-one F6F Hellcats, twelve SB2C Helldivers, and twelve TBF Avengers. As the Americans pressed home their attack, the *Musashi* opened up with what looked like a wall of impenetrable flak. For the loss of two Avengers, one torpedo hit was registered. At 1200 hours the second strike was more successful with two 1,000-pound hits and three torpedo hits on the port side. During the first two attacks, the *Musashi* fired just 260 5-inch AA shells for little effect.

The third raid consisting of sixteen F6F Hellcats, twenty SB2C-3 Helldivers, and thirty-two TBF-3 Avengers targeted both the *Yamato* and *Musashi*. Four bombs and three torpedoes hit the *Musashi*, dropping its speed to just 16 knots. Amazingly after seven torpedo and six bomb hits, the *Musashi* was not in danger of sinking.

The biggest raid of the day came at 1315 hours with sixty-five aircraft. The *Musashi* was now unable to defend itself. Reduced to just 12 knots and with only about a quarter of its antiaircraft guns remaining in action, the *Musashi* awaited its fate. The results were devastating. Ten bombs found their mark followed by at least four torpedo hits. By this time the *Musashi*'s antiaircraft defenses were so ineffective all of the attacking aircraft returned safely. The last raid of the day consisted of sixteen Hellcats, twelve Helldivers, and just three Avengers causing little if any damage.

Battle of Sibuyan Sea, October 24, 1944. The Japanese battleship *Musashi* under intense attack by Task Force 38. After five hours of attack, the *Musashi* was hit with between eleven and fifteen torpedoes before sinking. The large number of divebomber hits did not seriously damage the ship but they did shred the upper decks, degrading the AA defenses and making it easier for the torpedo bombers. U.S. NAVAL HISTORICAL CENTER

When the smoke cleared U.S. Navy aircraft sank the *Musashi*, torpedoed the cruiser *Myoko*, and hit the *Yamato* with two bombs for the loss of just eighteen aircraft. As powerful as the *Musashi* and *Yamato* were, their antiaircraft defenses were completely ineffective. The Type 3 18.1-inch antiaircraft shell was a complete failure. The Type 89 5-inch guns were not used effectively and the massed fire of the 25mm guns was inaccurate and lacked the range to prevent the divebombers and torpedo bombers from dropping their weapons. Flying into the heaviest concentration of IJN AA fire of the entire war, the U.S. Navy came out relatively unscathed, losing just 6.9 percent of the attacking force, and most if not all of the aircraft shot down were hit after they dropped their ordnance. Unfortunately for the Japanese simply increasing the quantity of 25mm guns did nothing to improve the quality of their AA defenses.

The *Musashi* is targeted by Helldivers from Task Force 38.3. The huge plume of smoke was started by an earlier divebombing attack. U.S. NAVAL HISTORICAL CENTER

For the Japanese the crippling losses suffered during the battle of the Philippine Sea in June (three aircraft carriers and more than 400 aircraft) and the loss of *Musashi* in October 1944 graphically illustrated the ineffectiveness of conventional air and sea attacks against the U.S. Navy's Pacific Fleet. With few options and desperate to stop the invasion of the Philippines, local Japanese commanders opted for a new and terrifying method of attack—the suicide bomber.

For U.S. Navy AA gunners, the introduction of the kamikaze was a terrifying and incomprehensible threat. It also dramatically changed the antiaircraft defense equation and led to the most savage and destructive antiaircraft battles of the war. Like the German V-1 flying bomb, the kamikaze was not deterred by AA fire. The target had to be destroyed outright. Near misses and damaging hits were not enough. Unlike the V-1 (which flew at a set height and in a straight line), the human-guided kamikaze plane could maneuver, making the job of the AA defense even harder.

> The suicide attack represents by far the most difficult antiaircraft problem yet faced by the fleet. The psychological value of AA, which in the past has driven away a large percentage of potential attackers, is inoperative against the suicide plane. If the plane is not shot down or so severely damaged that its control is impaired, it almost inevitably will hit its target. Expert aviation opinion agrees that an unhindered and undamaged plane has virtually a 100 percent chance of crashing a ship of any size regardless of her evasive action. —Anti-Suicide Action Summary August 1945, COMINCH P-0011, United States Fleet Headquarters of the Commander in Chief Navy Dept., Washington, DC

By 1944 the US Navy's foresight and investment in more and better antiaircraft guns paid big dividends and provided the fleet with a high level of protection from conventional attack. The introduction of the kamikaze changed all that. No one had ever considered using an aircraft as a missile with a human as the guidance system. The problems presented were numerous.

As in all good AA defenses, the first requirement for success was detection. Spotting an incoming suicide aircraft with shipboard radar alone proved difficult for a number of reasons. The Japanese quickly learned to take advantage of radar "shadows" caused by nearby islands. They would also latched onto returning U.S. Navy aircraft formations, making it difficult for the radar plotters to identify friend from foe. There were also gaps in the radar coverage. The SK radar, installed on larger ships, performed unevenly, especially against both high- and low-flying aircraft. Capable of detecting incoming aircraft well beyond 50 miles, it would lose them as they came closer to the ship. And once a kamikaze approached the task group, the radar picture worsened with sea clutter and other radar signals blotting out the screens.

The first line of defense was combat air patrol (CAP). Grumman F6F Hellcats, Chance Vought F4U Corsairs, and FM2 Wildcats were assigned to the task. Most CAPs were flown at medium altitudes in order to counter both low- and high-level approaches by Japanese aircraft. Early detection was key, but the radar systems could not provide an accurate altitude making an intercept extremely difficult. The Japanese also adopted both high- and low-altitude approaches to avoid the CAP.

To meet the coming storm the U.S. Navy had hundreds of AA guns ranging from the 5-inch to the 20mm. But there was a basic weakness. Long the mainstay of the fleet's defense, the 20mm and 40mm guns, which had performed very well against conventional attacks, were not powerful enough to stop an incoming kamikaze. Even when multiple hits were registered and the kamikaze was mortally damaged, the kinetic energy of the aircraft often kept it on line to the target, causing a near miss or direct hit. The U.S. Navy AA gunners quickly learned it was "kill or be killed."

The best weapons, capable of destroying a suicide aircraft far enough away, were the proven 5-inch/38 dual-purpose or older 5-inch/25 guns. Both weapons with their fire-control systems could hit an aircraft beyond 1,500 yards (a four-gun 5-inch/38 battery

A Zero-sen crashing near the USS *Essex* off Okinawa, May 14, 1945. After suffering severe damage the Zero's forward momentum carried it toward its intended target. Damaging an attacking kamikaze was not enough; it had to be destroyed completely. U.S. NAVAL HISTORICAL CENTER

under director control was effective to 10,000 yards). But here their power and accuracy were negated by the swift and unpredictable kamikaze. The Mk 32 VT proximity fuse, however, helped redress the balance, giving the 5-inch gun a greatly increased effectiveness. Effective at both short and long ranges, the VT fuse was four times more effective than a regular shell and would be responsible for 56 percent of 5-inch/38 kills. The short detection time often left the 5-inch gun's long-range capabilities unused, leaving the smaller 20mm and 40mm guns to defend the fleet.

Fire control for the 40mm gun was initially provided by the Mk 44 director. The Mk 44 was essentially a dummy weapon manned by three men. By the battle of Okinawa the Mk 44 was replaced by the more complex and effective Mk 51. Hand-slewed, the Mk 51 was mounted away from the vibration of the guns, making it much more effective.

For the short-range 20mm guns, sighting was done with the Mk I eye ball via a ring sight and tracer rounds. The introduction of the Mk 14 gyro-sight improved its accuracy, making it 50 percent more effective.

U.S. Navy tactics helped redress the deficiencies of their guns. First was the sheer number of guns available to the fleet. The standard Fletcher-class destroyer was armed with five 5-inch/38 guns, ten 40mm guns in five twin mounts, and seven 20mm guns. The Iowa-class battleship had twenty 5-inch guns, twenty quad-mount 40mm guns, and forty-nine 20mm guns. To protect the carriers the U.S. Navy used a circular formation as standard antiaircraft defense. This provided a defense in depth and all-around protection. Maneuvering also provided the best means to defeat a kamikaze attack. A U.S. Navy study revealed that when properly executed, only 29 percent of kamikaze attacks succeeded. When the ships were not maneuvering, that figure rose to 47 percent.

On October 25th six A6M3 Zero-sens took off from Mindanao Island. Shortly after, they spotted the four escort carriers of "Taffy 1" and screening ships. Although detected by radar they were not spotted as they approached. Diving through scattered clouds a single Zero-sen caught the escort carrier USS *Santee* by surprise, hitting the ship forward. There was no time for the AA guns to react. Seconds later a second Zero-sen headed for the USS *Suwanee* only to be destroyed by a 5-inch round, splashing into the sea. A third Zero-sen dove for the USS *Petrof Bay* only to be hit by AA fire and missing. The final kamikaze, also hit by AA fire, struck the *Suwannee* forward of the aft elevator. These U.S. carriers had survived the world's first kamikaze attack, but this was just the opening salvo.

Later in the day the escort carriers of "Taffy 3" were targeted. Approaching from low level six Zero-sens with three escorts popped up to attack altitude. Though they detected the Japanese planes by radar, the CAP could not respond fast enough. Three Zero-sens dove on the USS *Kalinin Bay* with two hitting the ship causing little damage and the third missing. Next in line was the USS *Kitkun Bay*, which suffered slight damage being hit on the port side catwalk. The USS *St. Lo* would not be as fortunate. Battling through heavy AA fire a single Zero-sen approached from astern and dropped its bomb before crashing into the flight deck. Penetrating the flight deck the bomb exploded in the han-

October 25, 1944. After being hit by one of the first kamikaze attacks of the war, the USS *St. Lo* suffers an internal explosion, sinking shortly after. U.S. NAVAL HISTORICAL CENTER

gar deck below. A series of explosions followed and in less than thirty minutes the *St. Lo* rolled over and sank.

It was an unqualified success and just the beginning. For the sacrifice of just twelve Zero-sens, the Japanese sank one escort carrier and damaged five more, some of which were forced to retire for repairs. In the days and weeks that followed, the Japanese refined their suicide tactics. More kamikazes were committed to the battle and the frequency of attacks only increased. During the Philippines campaign the Japanese expended 500–600 aircraft damaging 140 ships to various degrees, of which seventeen were sunk or scuttled.

The kamikaze attacks, which began on October 21, 1944, were continuous until August 1945 with the greatest kamikaze battle of the war being fought off Okinawa in 1945. During that campaign alone (April–June 1945), close to 2,000 kamikazes rained death and destruction on the American fleet. For the Japanese the kamikaze was a success. To score a hit using conventional methods it required thirty-seven attacking aircraft, but for a kamikaze attack it was just 3.6 aircraft.

In these two remarkable photos, a kamikaze flies through a storm of exploding 5-inch AA shells only to crash into the cruiser USS *Louisville*, outside of Lingayen Gulf, Philippines, January 5, 1945. U.S. NAVAL HISTORICAL CENTER

With all eyes skyward, gunners aboard the cruiser USS *Phoenix* clearly show the stress and strain of the constant kamikaze attacks. Crewmen at the port side man their 5-inch/25, 20mm, and 40mm antiaircraft guns trying to identify a plane overhead, during the Mindoro invasion, December 18, 1944. U.S. NAVAL HISTORICAL CENTER

For the American gunners the physical and psychological effect of the kamikaze took a heavy toll. Ships in danger areas required their crews to be constantly alert, guns at the ready. Too often there was little warning of an attack, leaving little time to engage the target. For the most part the ship's antiaircraft guns were able to fire, but the savage and incomprehensible nature of the threat was exhausting.

> The potential adverse psychological effect of suicides upon gunnery should not be underestimated. It can be forestalled or overcome by wise leadership devoted to instilling confidence in personnel.
> Assure personnel that their very lives depend upon their best performance, and that the suicide problem resolves itself into one of "kill or be killed"! —ANTIAIRCRAFT ACTION SUMMARY SUICIDE ATTACKS 1945

For the Americans the kamikaze pilots were a constant evolving threat. After their shocking debut in the Philippines, their overall success, however, was in decline by

Crewmen aboard the USS *Nashville* clean up the port side 5-inch/25 gun battery after being hit by a kamikaze on December 13, 1944. The fire damage to the gun and nearby structure is clearly visible.
U.S. NAVAL HISTORICAL CENTER

the time of the Okinawa campaign. More and more novice Japanese pilots were being used, and as U.S. gunnery and interception tactics improved, the number of successes only went up. Between February and May 1945, an estimated 1,100 kamikaze sorties were flown. Of these, the fighter CAP accounted for roughly 500 shot down while the antiaircraft guns were credited with 420. From October 1944 until the end of the war, approximately 3,000 kamikaze missions were flown. Of those, 367 kamikazes hit their target or obtained a near miss.

The U.S. Navy and Allies would lose sixty-six ships or craft sunk or never repaired. The number of killed and wounded was grim with 6,190 killed and 8,760 wounded. Between October 1944 and August 1945, the AA guns were credited with 685 kamikazes shot down—a 68 percent success rate. Add in the 459 conventional attacking aircraft shot down, and the grand total for that period was 1,144. For the period December 1941 to August 1945, U.S. Navy guns were responsible for the destruction of 2,773 Axis aircraft. It should be noted that 50 percent of all antiaircraft kills were scored in the last twelve months of the war.

A direct hit. In this dramatic photo a Japanese Nakajima B6N "Jill" has its tail blown off by a 5-inch shell during the Gilbert Island assault, December 4, 1943. U.S. NAVAL HISTORICAL CENTER

The bulk of the success achieved by the guns fell to the 40mm and 20mm batteries. U.S. Navy data showed that of the kamikazes shot down by guns 50 percent fell to the 40mm guns, 27 percent to the 20mm, with the remainder accounted for by 5-inch/38 guns. It was an impressive performance and a testament to the men who manned the guns and fought against an implacable foe.

Just as the U.S. Navy gunners began battling the unrelenting kamikazes, the last anti-aircraft battle of the war was being waged over Japan.

> Japanese antiaircraft is definitely becoming more effective, and it behooves all who fly over Japan to know as much as possible about the capabilities of their defenses.
>
> Japanese AA has caused approximately 70 percent of all Army (Air Force) battle damage in the Pacific and about 88 percent of the battle damage to US Navy aircraft. —FLAK OVER JAPAN. FLAK INTELLIGENCE MEMORANDUM NUMBER 6, CINPAC – CINCPOA BULLETIN No. 127-45, MAY 30, 1945

Lost in the hail of bursting flak, smoke, and tracers from near misses, a solitary Zero-sen kamikaze roars toward the USS *Missouri* at zero height. The twin 5-inch turret at lower right has its guns pointed straight at the incoming Zero. The attack took place on April 11, 1945, during the battle of Okinawa. The Zero hit the portside with no American casualties. U.S. NAVAL HISTORICAL CENTER

By 1943 the Japanese knew the Boeing B-29 and the coming strategic bombing campaign posed a real and unprecedented threat to the Japanese homeland. In 1944 the IAAF produced a prescient interim report. They knew the B-29 would be pressurized with an operational ceiling of 32,800 feet. Yet in spite of their good intelligence, their lack of preparation and their inability to build up adequate air defenses proved to be some of Japan's greatest failures in the Second World War.

Unlike Britain or Germany, Japan's prewar antiaircraft defensive plans were given a low priority. As late as 1939, just four regiments were deployed in Japan. Part of the reason was the lack of any serious long-range bomber threat from either the Soviet Union or China. The Japanese also espoused an offensive ethos and most officers considered defensive issues with contempt. With the projected war against America, the Imperial Japanese Army (IJA) expanded their AA defenses, going from 12,500 men in 1939 to 68,500 in 1941.

At the outbreak of war with America, Japan's air defenses were not extensive or well equipped, consisting of just 300 AA guns and about a hundred obsolete Type 97 fighters. The Germans by comparison had 2,628 88mm and 105mm guns alone in September 1939. The British had fewer guns with approximately 1,296 heavy guns and an eclectic assortment of some 1,200 light flak guns. Japan's air-raid warning system, however, was basic but extensive, consisting of a network of military and civilian observers. Offshore early warning was dependent on Imperial Japanese Navy (IJN) picket ships stationed about 600 miles from shore. Radar was added in 1941 with a chain of Type A sets, but these were aimed toward the Sea of Japan and any possible threat from the Soviet air force.

On April 18, 1941, Japan was bombed for the first time. Taking off from the carrier USS *Hornet*, sixteen American B-25 Mitchell bombers bombed Tokyo and several other targets. The incoming B-25s were first detected some 70 miles northeast of Tokyo, but it was too late. The B-25s did encounter some light antiaircraft fire, but none were shot down. For the Japanese the raid came as a complete shock. New reforms soon followed with the rapid expansion of the AA regiments and the acquisition of new 88mm and 120mm guns and better radar.

Not until 1944 did the Japanese see another American bomber, but by that time the military antiaircraft brigades were renamed as AAA commands and finally expanded to AAA divisions by the end of 1944. By far the largest was the 1st AAA Division based in Tokyo with a total of 780 guns in 93 regiments.

The main Japanese antiaircraft gun was the Type 88 75mm gun. Adopted in 1928 it was used in both fixed and mobile roles. It had a maximum ceiling of over 26,000 feet, but its effective ceiling was 21,750 feet, well below the B-29's operating altitude. This weapon was the most numerous and was deployed widely, but by 1945 just 869 of these guns were assigned to the Home Islands. Unfortunately its low effective ceiling left it completely useless against the high-flying B-29. The first new design to enter service during the war was the Type 99 88mm gun. Entering service in 1942 the new gun offered mediocre high-altitude performance with an effective ceiling of 26,000 feet.

To overcome the shortcomings of the 75mm Type 88 gun, the Japanese produced the 75mm Type 4 gun, based on the Swedish 75mm Bofors Model 29 captured in China. Only sixty-five were built and all were based on the Home Islands.

On June 15, 1944, the bombing of Japan began—Operation Matterhorn. Taking off from forward bases in China, B-29s from XX Bomber Command bombed the Yawata steelworks on Kyushu. The Japanese claimed seven B-29s shot down by interceptors, but only one was lost. The antiaircraft defense was negligible. The 131st AA Regiment's performance was so poor its commander was swiftly transferred to Manchuria.

Japan's recognition of the need for a more powerful weapon capable of taking on the B-29 at very high altitude led to the development and production of the more powerful 120mm Type 3 gun. Patterned on the navy's 127mm Type 89 gun, it had an effective ceiling over 35,000 feet. Despite its superior range and firepower, only 154 guns were produced. The Japanese also pressed into service a small number (ten mobile units and

The 88mm Type 99 AA gun was used primarily in the defense of the Japanese Home Islands. With a rate of fire of fifteen rounds per minute, its poor high-altitude performance meant it could barely reach the B-29's operating altitude. Just 919 were made during the war. NARA

thirty-six fixed versions) of captured British 3.7-inch guns. How effective they were and how much ammunition was available is not known. By 1945 the IJA's antiaircraft force included 569 batteries with 1,794 heavy guns and 860 small-caliber automatic cannon.

Augmenting the IJA AA gun defenses were the guns of the IJN. For the defense of all major ports and facilities, the IJN deployed some 981 heavy guns and hundreds of the ubiquitous 20mm and 25mm guns. Not only did the Japanese navy face the threat from the B-29, but beginning in 1945 U.S. Navy carrier strikes began hitting targets on the Japanese Home Islands. Incredibly the IJN committed just 15 percent of its total AA gun force to help defend Japan. Many of the guns were simply land-based versions of naval guns, but the navy used a number of army weapons including the 75mm Type 88 (106 in use) and 116 of the older 76.2mm Type 3 (1914) guns. Based on a British Armstrong design, the Type 3 gun was originally designed as a shipboard weapon. The most common IJN AA gun was the old 120mm Type 10 gun. Deployed in a single mount from a fixed concrete position, 377 guns would see service in the Home Islands. The most widely used type was the 127mm Type 89 gun first accepted into service in 1929. It was a dual-purpose gun, but its high-altitude performance was inadequate. To strengthen their ground defenses, the Japanese navy sometimes used turrets from damaged or uncompleted warships. A small number of twin 100mm Type 98 gun turrets were mounted for

The 120mm Type 3 was the best of the IJA's antiaircraft guns and was one of the few weapons capable of reaching the B-29s at high altitude. Too few were built to have any real impact against the B-29s over Japan. NARA

the defense of Yokosuka. The most powerful naval antiaircraft guns deployed by the IJN were a handful of 155mm/60 Type 3 guns that had originally been fitted on the *Mogami* cruisers and then later on the battleships *Yamato* and *Musashi*. In anticipation of the coming Allied airstrikes, the IJN amassed a total of 980 heavy guns and 3,700 20mm, 25mm, and 13.5mm guns. While the number of AA barrels was impressive, the Japanese IJA and IJN had fewer than 200 heavy guns over 100mm capable of reaching the high-flying B-29s (32,000 feet).

While the Japanese had amassed a respectable number of AA guns, the primary problem facing the Japanese AA units was the poor quality of their fire-control equipment. Training was also an issue. In a retrograde move the Japanese actually replaced their complicated Type 97 director with the simpler and cheaper Type 2. Archaic sound locators were also still being used with the Type 95 equipping the searchlight regiments.

During World War II the rapid development of radar technology greatly enhanced the effectiveness of AA defenses. Early warning radar was essential for detecting incoming raids and providing enough time to scramble fighters. Fire-control radars were also

FLAK IN WORLD WAR II

critical. The aiming data they produced enabled the guns to engage enemy bombers in all weather conditions and at night. Japanese radar development at the beginning of the war was not very advanced. By 1945 Japanese radar technology was on the same level U.S. radars had been in 1941.

Fortunately for the Japanese they enjoyed a technical windfall with the capture of British and American gun-layer radars in 1942, as well as a British GL Mk II gun-laying, an American SCR-268 fire-control, and an SCR-270 early-warning radar. The first Japanese radar accurate enough for gun-laying was the Toshiba Tachi-4 radar based on the British GL Mk II technology. In total only 349 fire-control radar sets were produced for the IJA between 1943 and 1945. The IJN used the American SCR-268 fire-control radar to form the basis of their NEC S3 and S24 radars that were used for their land-based guns. Even with these advancements the poor quality and limited quantity available forced the Japanese to rely on unreliable sound locators and searchlights.

On November 24, 1944, XXI Bomber Command mounted the first B-29 daylight raid on the Musashimo aircraft engine factory near Tokyo from their bases on Saipan. Of the 111 B-29s dispatched, ninety-four reached Tokyo. Half of the B-29s dropped their bombs on secondary targets. The Japanese responded with more than a hundred fighters, as well as "moderate flak." In the weeks that followed the raids, the number of B-29s only increased.

The performance of Japanese AA batteries against these early raids was poor. The 75mm Type 88 gun and 88mm Type 99 gun were largely ineffective against targets above 20,000 feet. It was not until the widespread distribution of the 120mm Type 10 gun in November that the AA defenses saw any improvement.

As more raids followed, the supply of new 120mm Type 10 guns was concentrated in the Tokyo area, and by war's end there were eighty-four.

In February 1945 the antiaircraft battle over Japan shifted to the low-level regime. On February 16 the U.S. Navy's Task Force 58 launched airstrikes against Japanese airfields on the Kanto Plain near Tokyo. Navy fighters claimed 190 aircraft destroyed on the ground for the loss of 60 aircraft due to aerial combat and light and medium flak. Up to this point the Japanese had struggled against the high flying B-29, but now for the first time U.S. Navy fighters were over the skies of Japan putting a further strain on the already hard-pressed AA defenses. The AA defense equation would change again. On the night of March 9th/10th, U.S. strategy in the Pacific War took a new turn when 346 B-29s bombed Tokyo at low level (5,000 to 9,000 feet) dropping incendiary bombs. The raid resulted in 16 square miles of Tokyo being burned out completely. The 1st AAA Division claimed eighteen B-29s shot down and sixty-six damaged. U.S. records show only one was shot down by flak.

The introduction of low-level night attacks all but crippled Japan's heavy AA gun defense. The heavy guns found it difficult to swing fast enough to track the fast-moving B-29s below 9,000 feet. The poor quality of Japanese fire-control radar also played a part.

Japanese use of gun-laying radar generally involves some degree of visual tracking. It is believed that radar control which furnishes all the firing data of Japanese heavy guns still is rather uncommon. —Flak Intelligence Memorandum, May 6, 1945

Their 20mm and 25mm guns were all but useless, and the lack of investment in a true medium gun like the Bofors 40mm gun left B-29s relatively immune to flak. The Japanese now faced a three-altitude AA war. B-29 raids would increase in frequency with both high- and medium-altitude daylight raids, and low-altitude night raids. Low-level carrier strikes by U.S. Navy fighters and bombers continued right up until the last day of the war.

The constant pressure and complete collapse of the Japanese war economy greatly reduced the supply of AA ammunition. Guns that normally had 200 rounds to fire were now restricted to just thirty or forty rounds. As weak as the Japanese AA gun defenses were, they still managed to shoot down a good number of U.S. Air Force and Navy aircraft. While the 1st AAA Division alone claimed 193 B-29s shot down, the real number for the entire war was fifty-four. A further nineteen were lost to AA fire and fighters. A total of 414 B-29 were lost to all causes with 147 due to enemy action.

B-29s flying into a well-placed burst of flak. Japanese antiaircraft guns shot down just fifty-four B-29s, but the number of damaged aircraft was far higher. The number of B-29s damaged by flak and fighters was 3,111 with 419 listed as seriously damaged. Without the island of Iwo Jima, B-29 losses would have been much higher. By war's end 2,251 B-29s had made emergency landings there. NARA

Even in the closing weeks of the war, Japanese AA defenses could still deal a stinging blow. In one five-day period (July 24–28), fighters and bombers from carrier Task Force 38 attacked airfields near Nagoya. Flying through heavy flak the navy lost 133 aircraft, most to AA fire.

> Carrier experience (16,17 and 25 February): AA fire over TOKYO proved to be the most intense and accurate yet encountered. All types of fire were directed at the planes with the result that it was necessary to make all attacks at high speeds and with radical maneuvers, preventing deliberate attacks and complete observation of results. Two planes were definitely lost to this fire and considerable minor damage was received by others. —FLAK INTELLIGENCE MEMORANDUM, MAY 6, 1945

On August 15, 1945, the final antiaircraft action of the war took place. At 1316 hours, some seven hours after the Japanese surrender broadcast, a lone Yokosuka D4Y "Judy" was picked up on radar. Some 200 miles southeast of Tokyo, the USS *Heermann* (DD 532) was on radar picket station when it tracked the intruder. Ducking in and out of an overcast sky at 8,500 feet, the Judy began its diving attack 8 miles from the destroyer.

At a range of 8,000 yards the USS *Heermann* opened fire. A 5-inch VT burst exploded, knocking off the plane's wing or tail. Falling into a slow spin, the Judy swerved to the right and crashed into the sea.

Acknowledgments

I would like to thank my partner Janet, Mark Stille, Chris Goss, and Edward Westermann for their advice and assistance in completing this book.

BIBLIOGRAPHY

American Warplanes of World War II. London: Aerospace Publishing Ltd., 1995.

Atkinson, Rick. *An Army at Dawn*. New York: Henry Holt and Company, 2002.

Backus, R. J. *The Defense of Antwerp Against the V-1 Missile*. Fort Leavenworth, KS: Southern Colorado State College, 1965.

Bergerud, Eric M. *Fire in the Sky: The Air War in the South Pacific*. Cumnor Hill, Oxford, England: Basic Books, 2000.

Bowan, Martin W. *USAF Handbook 1939–1945*. Mechanicsburg, PA: Stackpole Books, 1997.

Copp, Terry, ed. *Montgomery's Scientists: Operational Research in Northwest Europe*. Waterloo, Canada: Wilfred Laurier University, 2000.

Cumming, Anthony J. *The Royal Navy and the Battle of Britain*. Annapolis, MD: Naval Institute Press, 2010.

Dildy, Douglas C. *Dunkirk 1940: Operation Dynamo*. Botley, Oxford, England: Osprey Publishing Ltd., 2010.

Dobinson, Colin. *AA Command: Britain's Anti-Aircraft Defences of the Second World War*. London: Methuen Publishing Ltd., 2001.

Doherty, Richard. *Wall of Steel: The History of the 9th Londonderry Heavy Anti-Aircraft Artillery*. Limavady, Northern Ireland: North West Books, 1988.

Donald, David, ed. *Warplanes of the Luftwaffe*. London: Aerospace Publishing Ltd., 1994.

Dunmore, Spencer, and William Carter. *Reap the Whirlwind: The Untold Story of 6 Group, Canada's Bomber Force of World War II*. Toronto: McClelland and Stewart Inc., 1991.

English, Allan D. *The Cream of the Crop*. Montreal: McGill-Queen's University Press, 1996.

Ethell, Jeffrey L., et al. *Great Book of World War II Airplanes*. Twelve Volumes. New York: Bonanza Books, 1984.

Franks, Norman L. R. *The Battle of the Airfields: 1st January 1945*. London: W. Kimber, 1982.

Freeman, Roger A. *B-17: Fortress at War*. New York: Charles Scribner's Sons, 1977.

Friedman, Norman. *Naval Anti-Aircraft Guns and Gunnery*. Annapolis, MD: Naval Institute Press, 2013.

Gooderson, Ian. *Air Power at the Battlefront: Allied Close Air Support in Europe, 1943–45*. Portland, OR: F. Cass, 1997.

Greenhouse, Brereton, Stephen J. Harris, William C. Johnston, and William G. P. Rawling. *The Crucible of War 1939–1945: The Official History of the Royal Canadian Air Force*. Volume III. Toronto: University of Toronto Press Inc. in cooperation with the Department of National Defence and the Canada Communications Group, Publishing, Supply Services of Canada, 1994.

Halliday, Hugh A. *Typhoon and Tempest: The Canadian Story*. Toronto: CANAV Books, 1992.

Hardesty, Von. *Red Phoenix: The Rise of Soviet Air Power 1914–1945*. Washington, DC: Smithsonian Institution, 1982.

Hess, William N. *'Down to Earth' Strafing Aces of the Eighth Air Force*. Botley, Oxford, England: Osprey Publishing, 2003.

Hogg, Ian V. *Allied Artillery of World War One*. Marlborough, Wiltshire, England: Crowood Press, 1998.

Hogg, Ian V. *Allied Artillery of World War Two*. Marlborough, Wiltshire, England: Crowood Press, 1998.

Hogg, Ian V. *Anti-Aircraft: A History of Air Defence*. Poulton House, London: Macdonald and Jane's Publishers Ltd., 1978.

Hogg, Ian V. *The Guns 1939–45*. New York: Ballantine Books Inc., 1970.

Irons, Roy. *Hitler's Terror Weapons: The Price of Vengeance*. London: Collins, 2002.

Jager, Herbert. *German Artillery of World War One*. London: The Crowood Press, 2001.

Jane's Fighting Aircraft of World War II. New Jersey: Crescent Books, 1994.

Jarrett, Philip, ed. *Aircraft of the Second World War*. London: Putnam Aeronautical Books, 1997.

Kaplan, Philip, and Jack Currie. *Round the Clock*. New York: Random House, 1993.

Kreis, John F. *Air Warfare and Air Base Defense 1914–1973*. Washington, DC: Office of Air Force History, United States Air Force, 1988.

Lake, Jon. *Halifax Squadrons of World War 2*. Botley, Oxford, England: Osprey Publishing Ltd., 1999.

Lee, Arthur Gould. *Open Cockpit: A Pilot of the Royal Flying Corps*. London: Grub Street, 2012.

Mackersey, Ian. *No Empty Chairs*. London: Weidenfeld & Nicolson, 2012.

Mahoney, Patrick, and Martin Middlebrook. *Battleship: The Loss of the Prince of Wales and Repulse*. London: Penguin Books, 1977.

March, Daniel J. *British Warplanes of World War II*. London: Aerospace Publishing Ltd., 1998.

Middlebrook, Martin, and Chris Everitt. *The Bomber Command War Diaries*. London: Penguin Books, 1990.

Murray, Williamson. *The Luftwaffe, 1933–45 Strategy for Defeat*. Washington, DC: Brassey's, 1989.

Nijboer, Donald. *Cockpit: An Illustrated History of World War II Aircraft Interiors*. Erin, Ontario, Canada: Boston Mills Press, 1998.

Nijboer, Donald. *Graphic War: The Secret Aviation Drawings and Illustrations of World War II*. Toronto, Canada: Firefly Books, 2005.

Norris, John. *88mm Flak18/36/37/41 & PaK 43, 1936–45*. Botley, Oxford, England: Osprey Publishing Ltd., 2002.

The Official World War II Guide to the Army Air Forces. New York: Bonanza Books, 1988.

O'Leary, Michael. *VIII Fighter Command at War: "Long Reach."* Botley, Oxford, England: Osprey Publishing Ltd., 2000.

Perkins, Paul. *The Lady*. Charlottesville, VA: Howell Press, Inc., 1997.

Price, Alfred. *Britain's Air Defences 1939–45*. Botley, Oxford, England: Osprey Publishing Ltd., 2004.

Price, Alfred. *The Last Year of the Luftwaffe: May 1944 to May 1945*. Motorbooks, 1991.

Price, Alfred. *The Luftwaffe Data Book*. Guilford, CT: Greenhill Books/Stackpole Books, 1997.

Price, Alfred. *Luftwaffe Handbook*. New York: Charles Scribner's Sons, 1977.

Pridham, C. H. B., Major. *Anti-Aircraft Defence Against Low Flying Enemy Aircraft*. London: Unwin Brothers Ltd., 1941.

Shores, Christopher, and Chris Thomas. *2nd Tactical Air Force*. Volumes I, II, III, IVL. Hersham, Surrey, England: Classic Publications, 2004, 2005, 2006, and 2008.

Smith, Carl. *Pearl Harbor: The Day of Infamy*. Botley, Oxford, England: Osprey Publishing Ltd., 2010.

Stille, Mark. *The Coral Sea 1942: The First Carrier Battle*. Botley, Oxford, England: Osprey Publishing Ltd., 2009.

Stille, Mark. *Midway 1942: Turning Point in the Pacific*. Botley, Oxford, England: Osprey Publishing Ltd., 2010.

Stille, Mark. *Santa Cruz 1942: Carrier Duel in the South Pacific*. Botley, Oxford, England: Osprey Publishing Ltd., 2012.

Stille, Mark. *US Navy Carrier Aircraft vs. Yamato-Class Battleships: Pacific Theater 1944–45*. Botley, Oxford, England: Osprey Publishing Ltd., 2015.

Stille, Mark. *US Navy Ships vs Kamikaze 1944–45*. Botley, Oxford, England: Osprey Publishing Ltd., 2016.

Weal, John. *Focke-Wulf Fw 190 Aces of the Russian Front*. Botley, Oxford, England: Osprey Publishing, 1995.

Welborn, Mary Catherine. *Over-All Effectiveness of US First Army Anti-Aircraft Guns Against Tactical Aircraft*. Washington, DC: The Johns Hopkins University Research Office, 1950.

Werrell, Kenneth P. *Archie, Flak, AAA and SAM: A Short Operational History of Ground-Based Air Defense*. Maxwell AFB, AL: Air University Press, 1988.

Westermann, Edward B. *Flak: German Anti-Aircraft Defenses, 1914–1945*. Lawrence: University Press of Kansas, 2001.

Zaloga, Steven J. *Defense of the Rhine 1944–45*. Botley, Oxford, England: Osprey Publishing Ltd., 2011.

Zaloga, Steven J. *Defense of the Third Reich*. Botley, Oxford, England: Osprey Publishing Ltd., 2012.

Zaloga, Steven J. *Operation Point Blank 1944*. Botley, Oxford, England: Osprey Publishing Ltd., 2011.

Reports and Histories

Antiaircraft Action Summary World War II October 1945. Headquarters of the Commander in Chief United States Fleet, Information Bulletin No. 29.

Anti-Aircraft Artillery Notes. Headquarters European Theater of Operations, Number 8, December 13, 1944.

Anti-Suicide Action Summary August 1945. COMINCH P-0011, United States Fleet Headquarters of the Commander in Chief Navy Dept., Washington, DC.

An Evaluation of Defense Measures Taken to Protect Heavy Bombers from Loss and Damage. Headquarters, Eighth Air Force Operational Analysis Section, November 1944.

Flak Facts: A Brief History of Flak and Flak Intelligence in the Ninth Air Force. APO 696, U.S. Army.

Flak Over Japan. Flak Intelligence Memorandum Number 6, CINPAC – CINCPOA Bulletin No. 127-45, May 30, 1945.

High Altitude Bombing Attacks on Flak Batteries. Fifteenth Air Force. U.S. Air Force Historical Research Agency, Maxwell AFB, AL.

The History of the 8th Canadian Light Anti-Aircraft Regiment.

The History of the Third Canadian Light Anti-Aircraft Regiment from 17 Aug. '40 to 7 May '45 World War II.

Light, Intense and Accurate. U.S. Eighth A.F. Strategic Fighters versus German Flak in the ETO, 1943–1945.

United States, Ninth Air Force, Flak Section. *Flak Facts: A Brief History of Flak and Flak Intelligence in the Ninth Air Force*, 1945.

United States Strategic Bombing Survey (Pacific). *The Allied Campaign Against Rabaul*. Naval Analysis Division, September 1, 1946.

Websites

www.ibiblio.org
www.jaegerplatoon.net
www.8thafhs.org
www.waroverholland.nl
www.history.navy.mil
maritime.org
aircrewremembered.com

Index